BOB YOUNG
AL STANKUS

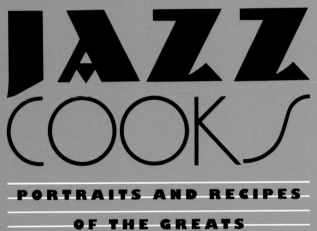

JAZZ COOKS

PORTRAITS AND RECIPES
OF THE GREATS

Photography by

DEBORAH FEINGOLD

STEWART
TABORI
& CHANG

NEW YORK

DEDICATIONS

To those jazz artists whose music has provided me with spiritual nourishment over the years and to my late mother, Margaret, my sister, Christine, and my wife, Jane, whose cooking has taught me that food can be so much more than sustenance.   —B. Y.

To stylish and tasteful improvisation and the people who practice it.   —A. J. S.

To Ray and Molly Brown.   —D. F.

AUTHORS' ACKNOWLEDGMENTS

For all their kind and generous help, the authors would like to express their heartfelt thanks to Brian Hotchkiss, Rob Hart, Jane Hart, Ann Campbell, Sarah Longacre, Jim Wageman, Jose Pouso, Rebecca Williams, Deborah Schneider, Terry Hoffer, Anne Dutlinger, Laura Sawyer, Lisa Ekhus, Gilmar Pinto, Walter Vittorino, Sue Auclair, Deborah Reinisch, Tisziji Muñoz, Steve Kuhn, Paul Weinstein, Monty Alexander, Daniel Humair, Barry Bransfield, Eliane Elias, Bill Cuccinello, Joshua Breakstone, Michael Fagien, Deborah Henson-Conant, Roy Nathanson, Carolyn Kelley, Hank Roberts, Datevik Hovanesian, Terri Hinte, and Ann LaCrosse.

PHOTOGRAPHER'S ACKNOWLEDGMENTS

The photographer gratefully acknowledges Scott Lee, Deborah Koncius, and Sarah Longacre; all the musicians who allowed themselves to be photographed and in return taught her about the world of improvisation; and Laura Sawyer, who with patience and perseverance managed everything.

Published in 1992 by Stewart, Tabori & Chang, Inc.
575 Broadway, New York, New York 10012

Library of Congress Cataloging-in-Publication Data
Young, Bob, 1951 –
Jazz cooks : portraits and recipes of the greats /
Bob Young, Al Stankus ; photography by Deborah Feingold
p. cm.
Includes index.
ISBN 1-55670-192-6
1. Cookery.   2. Jazz musicians—Miscellanea.
I. Stankus, Al.   II. Title.
TX714.Y68   1992
641.5—dc20   91-35854
*   CIP*

Distributed in the U.S. by Workman Publishing,
708 Broadway, New York, New York 10003
Distributed in Canada by Canadian Manda Group,
P.O. Box 920 Station U, Toronto, Ontario M8Z 5P9
Distributed in all other territories by
Little, Brown and Company, International Division,
34 Beacon Street, Boston, Massachusetts 02108

Printed in Japan
10 9 8 7 6 5 4 3 2 1

CONTENTS

Those smoky, late-night jazz moments that photographs romanticize so effectively—freezing the music in a mysterious black-and-white netherworld—are only part of the story of the life of a jazz artist. That became crystal clear during the long process of researching and writing *Jazz Cooks*. "The note is the main thing," saxophonist Joe Henderson pointed out, "but there's all that stuff that goes into the note that happens on the way to the bandstand." Like supporting a family and paying the rent, or the mortgage, or the tuition. And yes, like cooking dinner, or lunch, or breakfast.

Sheer survival is what motivated many players to learn to cook. They travel so often and expend so much energy practicing and performing, that they're unable to function—and earn a living—without maintaining good eating habits. But, like the rest of us, their choices are limited: locate good restaurants, hook up with someone willing to handle the cooking, or teach themselves to cook. A large number in the last category are included in *Jazz Cooks*.

Not every player in the book considers himself or herself a gourmet chef. A handful, in fact, feel proud when they don't overcook a hamburger. In those cases their wives, or grandfathers, or daughters pinch hit. In our search for those who knew their way around the kitchen, we contacted more than three hundred musicians and exhausted every lead from every source, especially those provided by our best source—the players themselves.

That said, we realize that we've probably omitted some fine cooks who deserve to be included. To those players we apologize. We had our share of disappointments and sadness, not least of which came when several jazz giants who had committed to the book, Stan Getz and Art Blakey among them, passed away before they were able to contribute. A few cooks of renown in jazz circles—such as Ella Fitzgerald and Johnny Griffin—simply declined the invitation to be in *Jazz Cooks*.

Given an often unsettled lifestyle, it is no small accomplishment that any jazz player finds the time and energy to cook well. While there is no "normal" day for a jazz musician, a fairly typical one might go something like this: check-in to a hotel in the afternoon, endure an hour-long sound check at the club at five o'clock, return to the hotel, eat, shower, return to the club and perform, hit the sack somewhere between one and four o'clock A.M., get up between eight and nine o'clock in order to catch a plane or drive either home or to the next gig. Mealtimes become precious. But, since these players spend so much of the year on the road, it's only natural that many of them throw themselves into domesticity when they're home. George Coleman tying on a chef's apron? You bet. Branford Marsalis offered another explanation for why there is no dearth of jazz artists who can cook. "There's a certain kind of independence you need in order to be a jazz musician," he said, "a certain kind of isolation and separation that's required to do the job well. You have to fend for yourself. If you can't, you're useless. Useless to the music, useless to society. Most jazz musicians are comfortable doing things themselves, like buying maps instead of asking directions. It carries over into every walk of life. It doesn't surprise me at all that a lot of jazz musicians can cook."

Jazz Cooks wouldn't have happened if my wife, Jane, a fine cook herself, hadn't suggested to me that jazz musicians probably held a treasure trove of interesting recipes and even richer stories. To do justice to the artists who contributed, *Jazz Cooks* had to be more than a cookbook. We've attempted, as Joe Henderson put it so well, to trace some of the "stuff that goes into the note that happens on the way to the bandstand," which means, of course, starting from the beginning of each player's life and then traveling in myriad directions. So we found out that Stanley Turrentine perfected dinners of rice and beans on hotel room hotplates in Georgia during the 1950s, because the restaurants wouldn't serve "coloreds"; and that Adam Makowicz wanted to play jazz so badly in a repressive Poland that he slept under the piano in a Kraków club and cleaned the floors in exchange for food. We discovered that Mercer Ellington's apartment is perpetually full of band members who can't get enough of his Soul Sole; and that Mark Egan articulately connects the dots between diet, spirituality, and improvisation.

Of course, *Jazz Cooks* wouldn't be complete without the music itself. Toward that end I received an assist from Al, a student of jazz as well as a gourmet cook, in a section we call Tasty Platters, our suggested guide to recordings to play along with the recipes. Since we made a point of including only releases that are currently available in the compact disc format, we reluctantly had to omit a number of great recordings on vinyl that are unfortunately out of print. Our selections are comprised of sessions that the player leads, albums on which he or she appear as sideperson, or simply recordings that we thought might be fun to accompany the dish. Be your own D. J. Take in Sun Ra's *Blue Delight* while eating Wynton Marsalis's gumbo or Paquito D'Rivera's inter-

pretation of "Tanga" during a second helping of Abbey Lincoln's fried porgy. It doesn't matter whose music you play with what. Add any of it to a meal—one from *Jazz Cooks* or from anywhere else—and it helps make things even finer.

So gather those ingredients, adjust that chef's hat, and turn on the stereo. I think you'll enjoy these culinary riffs.

—Bob Young

One of the questions most frequently asked of me as a writer is, "What are you working on?" For the past two years, *Jazz Cooks* has been my lead response, after which I'd hear something like, "I'll bet you're getting a lot of great Cajun and Creole dishes."

"Some," I'd always say.

Historically, New Orleans is widely regarded as the home of jazz, much in the same way Greece may be the home of wine or Springfield, Massachusetts, the home of basketball. They still make wine in Greece and play basketball in Springfield, but the products, and the best of them, have moved beyond their birthplace. So too with jazz.

For every Wynton and Branford Marsalis who grew up in New Orleans eating their mother's gumbo and fried catfish, there are scores of players from the heartland, steel towns, the Deep South of the United States, and even overseas, who fondly recall dishes like tamale pie, beef and beer, pasta fagiola, and *bacalao,* or cod, salad. After meeting with almost one hundred musicians and singers and chronicling what they had to say about food and music, I feel that *Jazz Cooks* has added a new dimension to the practitioners of what some rightfully call America's greatest gift to the world: jazz.

"Variations on a theme" is how saxophonist

Arthur Blythe described his life. It's also how you can see this book.

Just as there is no one kind of jazz or only one place where it is played, so these jazz artists don't eat just one kind of food. In *Jazz Cooks,* we pay homage alike to recipes culled from the musicians' pasts, such as Dizzy Gillespie's Salmon and Grits, born out of tougher times, and to contemporary dishes that reflect the players' culinary progressions, such as Sheila Jordan's Belgian Endive and Walnut Salad, which to the singer is part of her new way of looking at life.

This is a happy book, one that is full of life. The stories relate some scuffling and scrambling, stories told with humor and stories told seriously. Gourmets and gourmands have their say as do work-a-day cooks. On occasion, tales are recounted by veterans whose current strict diets are the payback for years of hard living. Hard feelings? Rarely.

Jazz Cooks mirrors jazz: Pig's Foot Souse, Bread Pudding, Zarzuela, Spaghetti with Peanut Sauce; bebop, Latin, vocalese, and free jazz. There's plenty to *dig* in these pages. The artists have provided the inspiration, now it's your turn to improvise.

—Al Stankus

REEDS

Turnip greens, peach cobbler, gospel music, and the blues all have important places in George Adams's earliest memories. It's boxing, though, that prompts one of the tenor saxophonist's most vivid recollections of his youth in Covington, Georgia.

"Two of my brothers had restaurants," he explains. "They weren't fancy. They were basically hamburger joints. What I remember about them, especially in the late forties, was that they would have Wednesday and Friday fight nights on television. Sugar Ray Robinson. Joe Louis. Kid Gaviland. Rocky Graziano. Ingemar Johansson. There were a lot of good boxers at that time. They would have all the kids in the neighborhood over because there were only a few televisions. That's when they made most of their money."

Covington turned out to be the ideal place for Adams to develop the brawny, soulful foundation that's still at the core of his improvising. He didn't have to travel far to absorb all kinds of live music. Atlanta was only a forty-minute car ride away, clubs in smaller towns even closer.

Born in 1940, Adams started studying piano early and eventually joined the high school band. "I brought a trumpet home," he recalls. "My mother and brother said, 'Why don't you get a saxophone? Louis Jordan and Earl Bostic, those guys are hot saxophonists. The trumpet, man, that's square.'" So Adams switched.

In the early fifties, his oldest brother returned from the army with a stack of Charlie Parker and Dizzy Gillespie records. Adams couldn't get enough. At fifteen he was hired for a steady gig at a club in Lithonia, a town not far from Atlanta. "I found myself playing piano for our little country church on Sunday morning and then playing at a nightclub on Sunday night," he says. "They brought in all these blues singers from the South Side of Chicago: Jimmy Reed, Muddy Waters, Howlin' Wolf, Willie Dixon. The club

TASTY PLATTERS

- George Adams, *Nightingale* (Blue Note)
- George Adams/Don Pullen, *A Song Everlasting* (Blue Note)
- Charles Mingus, *Epitaph* (Columbia)

owner felt that he had to cut his budget, so he hired me, and a buddy of mine to play drums, to augment the band."

Adams moved to Atlanta shortly thereafter, won a scholarship to Clark College, and began working with the likes of Sam Cooke and Hank Ballard and the Midnighters. He also found a steady engagement playing rhythm and blues at a spot called Hale's Supper Club. They were the kinds of jobs that compelled him to become adept at "walking the bar," where he'd climb onto the bar and step carefully between glasses and bottles, all the while blowing his horn. Half a decade in Cleveland followed. Through most of the years in Georgia and Ohio, he relied on the kindness of girlfriends or family for meals. When he moved to New York in 1968, he realized it was time to start cooking for himself.

"My mother always told us we'd better learn to cook because someday a woman might not want to cook for us," he laughs. "The woman might say, 'No, you do it yourself.' My mother taught us a few basic dishes, so I just went from there."

Adams took care of himself on stage, as well. He was eventually hired by Roy Haynes, Gil Evans, Art Blakey, and McCoy Tyner. In 1973 he landed a spot in the Charles Mingus band, a job he coveted. His years with the late bassist/composer taught him lessons that he still carries, especially when he's leading his own groups or working with the Mingus Dynasty Band.

"Mingus was masterful at getting his musical moods displayed by the musicians he had around him," Adams says. "He was very good at engineering certain types of responses. He didn't care what he had to do to do it. If he had to make you angry, he would do it. People say Mingus was violent. He could be when he wanted to be, but he had another side to him. He

Reunion Sweet Potato Pie

Far removed from his jet-travel diet is Reunion Sweet Potato Pie, a dessert that takes its name from the Adams family reunion, which used to take place each summer in Covington on the first Sunday in August.

"Everybody would pitch in and bring their own little something for the spread," Adams says. "This version of sweet potato pie is from Aunt Juanita, on my father's side. My father had five sisters, and they all could make it. But I remember Aunt Juanita. She was the oldest, and her house was the closest to the church where we held the reunion. We'd all congregate there first. My mother could make this pie too, but I figured it would be nice to remember Aunt Juanita."

Serves 6 to 8

- **3 large eggs**
- **1 cup sugar**
- **½ cup (1 stick) butter, softened**
- **2 cups (about 4 medium) mashed cooked sweet potatoes or yams**
- **1 tablespoon flour**
- **½ teaspoon nutmeg**
- **½ teaspoon cinnamon**
- **¼ teaspoon salt**
- **½ teaspoon each lemon extract, pineapple extract, and vanilla extract**
- **½ cup milk**
- **10-inch unbaked pie shell**

Preheat the oven to 400°F. In a large bowl, beat the eggs with the sugar and butter. Add the sweet potatoes (or yams) and mix thoroughly. Add the flour, nutmeg, cinnamon, salt, and lemon, pineapple, and vanilla extracts, and mix well. Stir in the milk. Turn into the pie shell and bake for ½ hour, or until a toothpick inserted into the filling comes out clean.

could be very, very meek as a lamb, but he didn't show that side to everybody. He stood up for his band and for his music, and I liked that about Mingus.

"I like honesty and integrity. I like the music to be something that's elevated to the point where it exceeds celebrity status, where the music is the celebrity, not the player. If I take care of the music, it will take care of me. That's the way I've always been doing it."

Adams may not be a prime-time star, but he has certainly attained celebrity status among his peers and fans. He has such a no-holds-barred approach to improvising that he sometimes seems to be trying to physically tame a runaway horn. That impression couldn't be further from the truth. Adams is always in complete control, whether he's roaring urgently on a stomping blues or laying into "Georgia on My Mind" with burly passion. More than a decade spent collaborating with the powerful pianist Don Pullen loosened any remaining restraint Adams may have had left in his playing. "When you feel like you have a musical ally," he says about Pullen, "you can reach as far as you want to reach." Adams is as comfortable honking and shrieking in jazz's avant-garde ionosphere as he is caressing a sentimental love song on tenor or flute.

The reedman enjoys a wide variety of food but eats pasta in particular when he's scheduled to fly to engagements in Europe or Japan. Like a marathon runner, Adams believes pasta keeps his energy level high. He'll eat the dish daily for as many as five days before a flight.

Soprano saxophonist Jane Ira Bloom is a firm believer in the link between playing jazz and cooking. The connection first hit home while she was attending Yale in the early 1970s. "I had a composition professor, baritone player David Mott, who always maintained that cooking and improvisation were very simpatico arts," Bloom recalls. "When I was studying and working in ensembles with him, he used to invite the whole group out for a huge, fifteen-course Szechwan dinner at his house. He applied his emotional and intellectual skills to food—all the intricacies and subtleties of taste—as strongly as he did to music. From that point on I thought, 'Hey, yeah. Improvising, cooking, eating, there's something similar going on.'"

While Bloom and her husband, actor Joe Grifasi, both pride themselves on their kitchen skills, it's the saxophonist's development as a talented player and composer that has earned her a large following. Whether utilizing her unconventional brand of electronics or a sleek but warm acoustic sound, Bloom nods to bop, soul, Latin rhythms, and free jazz to create a powerful and cohesive music that's rich in melody and spontaneity. Her dual gifts as composer and instrumentalist are bringing her closer and closer to the lofty heights attained by soprano saxophone giants Steve Lacy and Wayne Shorter.

Bloom's challenges reached new levels when she was commissioned by the National Aeronautics and Space Administration (NASA) to write a series of compositions based on the launch and landing of the space shuttle Discovery in 1989. The works premiered at the Kennedy Space Center and were performed subsequently at Carnegie Hall.

"It has affected me in all aspects of music," Bloom says about the NASA project. "I'm interested in different spatial and rhythmic relationships in the music. Thinking about weightless environments in space certainly helps."

Applying technology to movement and changes in sound has long captivated Bloom. She helped develop a device called a "velocity sensor," which is connected to foot pedals and to her soprano saxophone. It allows her to alter her sound, to form strings of notes like sonic vapor trails, for example. "My point of view is as a saxophone player and someone who has trained very hard and long in

Cut-Time Capellini

"Food has become more of a focus as I've gotten older and better at cooking," says Bloom. She credits her husband for the improvement.

"He's taught me to be an improvisational Italian cook," she points out. "We eat a lot of pasta. It's fast and easy, and I've also become more sophisticated about what kind of tastes you can apply to it."

Ease, speed, and sophistication are manifested in Bloom's Cut-Time Capellini. "I like to throw together a quick pasta dish like this when I'm in a hurry to get to a gig and want to carbo-load for some high-energy improvisation," she says.

"The secret to the sauce is fresh ingredients cooked in cut-time. But like all great solos, it all depends on how you choose to balance the differ-ent ingredients based on how you feel that day. I've made variations of this pasta with artichoke hearts, sun-dried tomatoes, and fresh tomatoes, and it's never tasted the same twice. This recipe can be looked at as the head of the tune, or the basis for your own pasta improv."

Serves 2

4 tablespoons pine nuts, lightly toasted
1/3 cup olive oil
2 large cloves garlic, finely minced
4 anchovy fillets
1/2 red, sweet pepper, cored and thinly sliced
1 small fennel bulb, thinly sliced
3/4 cup fresh parsley, chopped
3 tablespoons balsamic vinegar
Salt and pepper

3/4 pound capellini/thin spaghetti
Freshly grated Romano cheese

Toast pine nuts in 325°F oven for 5 minutes. Set aside. Heat the oil in a medium-sized frying pan over medium heat. Add garlic and anchovies; stir, breaking up anchovies and making sure the garlic doesn't burn. The anchovies will dissolve. Add the red pepper and fennel and sauté approximately 7 minutes, or until both soften. Stir in the pine nuts, 1/2 cup of the parsley, and the balsamic vinegar; cook for 3 minutes. Add salt and pepper to taste. Cook capellini according to package directions for al dente. Drain and place the capellini in a large serving dish; add the sauce and mix gently. Garnish with remaining 1/4 cup of parsley and freshly grated Romano cheese to taste.

the acoustic tradition, but also as someone who's fascinated and stimulated by the possibilities of electronic sounds," she says. "I'm still very much interested in the timbre, breath, and phrasing of a saxophone. I want the flow from my acoustic sound and electronic thoughts to be seamless. I'm interested in sounds that surprise my own ear."

Bloom grew up in the Boston suburb of Newton in a home filled with the music of the Gershwins, Richard Rodgers, and jazz artists like Ella Fitzgerald, Billie Holiday, Charlie Parker, and Duke Ellington. Her parents, former New Yorkers, had heard those jazz musicians in concert when they lived in the city. The jazz influence rubbed off on Bloom at an early age. Born in 1955, she was studying music and visiting Boston clubs like the Jazz Workshop by the late sixties. Booker Little, Eric Dolphy, and Ornette Coleman became important models. Significant in her

growth were trumpet player Leo Smith and trombonist George Lewis, both of whom she worked with later at Yale, where she received bachelor's and master's degrees in music. Smith and Lewis helped convince her that freedom of expression need not be limited to the traditional idioms. Bloom moved to New York after Yale and soon became involved in a multitude of projects, from composing for dance companies to writing pieces inspired by ice dancers Torvill and Dean.

Raised on hearty, home-cooked Jewish-American foods like brisket, kasha, and beef Stroganoff, Bloom didn't truly pay attention to international fare until her Yale years. "I really prefer ethnic cuisine to anything," she says. "Italian, Chinese, Indian. When I'm on the road and I'm looking for a place to eat, that's what I'll pick nine times out of ten. I stay out of American chain restaurants. I try to do what most musicians do: eat fresh vegetables

and a limited amount of meat. I also love to have something spicy before I play."

TASTY PLATTERS

- Jane Ira Bloom, *Mighty Lights* (Enja)
- Booker Little, *Booker Little 4 and Max Roach* (Blue Note)
- John Scofield, *Time on My Hands* (Blue Note)

Bloom praises Paris-based drummer Daniel Humair as a guide to the finest European restaurants. "Both Daniel and his wife are gourmet chefs, conversant with all the very famous chefs in France," Bloom says. "Whenever I play over there, he always makes sure that we have a four-star dinner. When we were going to Guy Savoy's, I remember him saying, 'You will feel like you are hearing Coltrane for the first time when you eat this food.'"

Predictable is a word rarely used to describe the day-to-day life of a jazz musician. Arthur Blythe's list of constants, however, may be a bit longer than most. The reason? He and his wife have three children under eight years of age. To his artistic obligations like practicing his alto saxophone and writing music, the reedman regularly adds trips to the playground and cooking family meals. "And sometimes I do the shopping, although it's not really my forte," he laughs. "But I am a parent, so I have to go out there and get it." Blythe is diffident about his kitchen abilities. "It's chuck-wagon style," he explains. "Nutritious, tasty, but no frills."

Blythe's playing is as meaty and straightforward as his cooking, but there is nothing about it that even hints at cattle-drive heavy-handedness. For the past two decades he has ranked among the saxophone's most original stylists, a player who moves deftly from one genre to the next and applies a sophistication to the alto that has helped expand its sonic limits. While he remains embarrassed by a record company boast during the late 1970s that put him a notch above even Charlie Parker in accomplishment, he has nonetheless gone on to forge an individual approach to the alto, which has met with such success that he was invited to join the

seminal World Saxophone Quartet. Few honors could be greater for a reed player.

Born in Los Angeles in 1940, Blythe was raised in San Diego with five siblings. His mother, a Texas native, did most of the cooking and also brought home many of the jazz and rhythm-and-blues records that sparked Blythe's early passion for the music. Albums by Duke Ellington, Louis Jordan, Earl Bostic, Tiny Bradshaw, and Ivory Joe Hunter were among them. At thirteen Blythe was playing alto sax in a blues band. It took him a while, however, to be pulled in completely by jazz. "I didn't want to be a jazz artist because the jazz

I was hearing in California was very uninspiring," he says. "As I got older, I found out about the connection between rhythm and blues and gospel and jazz and rock and roll. They're all members of the same family." When Blythe moved to Los Angeles at age nineteen, his commitment to jazz solidified. He spent much of the mid-1960s and 1970s refining his skills as a member of pianist/composer Horace Tapscott's band, the Pan-African People's Arkestra, and of the organization Tapscott founded, the Underground Musician's Artist's Association.

Even though Blythe was a seasoned veteran when he arrived in New York in 1974, work didn't just fall into his lap. When drummer Chico Hamilton offered him a spot in his band, Blythe was able to give up a job as security guard and cashier at a Manhattan porno theater, and he never looked back. Within a few years he had formed his own group, recorded a slew of successful albums for the Columbia label, and collaborated with groundbreaking peers like Lester Bowie and Jack DeJohnette. Blythe's ability to apply his soulful, bluesy improvising to both bebop and freer jazz material earned him accolades from colleagues and fans alike, allowing him to form not only standard ensembles, but bands that utilized instruments rarely heard from in modern jazz, such as the tuba and cello. Blythe's broad sound has been the ideal vehicle for his ideas. That his facility on all registers remains lyrical

and swinging, from raw, piercing highs to deep, honking bottoms, is one of his strongest assets.

"I'm basically influenced and inspired by the tradition and the roots of the music," he says. "All of what I do, whether it's inside or outside, I'm continually coming from someplace."

"I respond to the gift when it's given to me, when I can get into the mental or psychological head to receive the information about the music. It keeps me in check, keeps me humble. I'm a servant, not the master."

Blythe the cook generally turns out the same types of meals for his family that his mother prepared back in California: fish, chicken, ground beef, vegetables, and grains. He also tries to maintain a regular exercise and running regimen, although road trips and family obligations take their toll on the routine. "But the kids will keep you in shape," he laughs.

Tamale Pie

"Growing up, my mother used to make this tamale pie dish with cornmeal," Blythe recalls. "We ate what I've come to think of as 'Cal-Mex' food. Being in San Diego, right there on the border, it was almost impossible not to eat Mexican food, or a variation that was Mexican with some combination." This recipe substitutes tortillas for cornmeal—just another variation.

"I guess when I look at my life, variances are the things that keep me going," the saxophonist laughs. "My music and my food seem to be based on roots, focal points, and variances."

Serves 6

- 1 pound dried pinto beans
- Water
- 4 bay leaves
- 1 onion, chopped
- 2 cloves garlic, minced
- 2 teaspoons salt
- ½ teaspoon pepper
- 2 tablespoons vegetable oil
- ½ green bell pepper, diced
- 2 celery stalks, diced
- 1 to 1½ pounds ground turkey or beef, or a combination of both
- 2 small cans (12 ounces each) tomato sauce
- Salt and pepper
- 3 tablespoons cumin seeds
- 8 to 10 jumbo black olives, pitted
- 4 tablespoons honey or brown sugar
- 24 soft corn tortillas
- 1½ to 2 cups grated medium or sharp cheddar cheese

Sort through the beans, removing any debris, and soak them overnight in sufficient water to cover them. Drain, add fresh water to cover the beans, and add the bay leaves, onion, garlic, salt, and pepper. Bring to a slow boil over medium heat. Lower heat to simmer and cook uncovered (adding water as it evaporates) for 2 to 3 hours, or until the beans are tender.

In a deep pot, heat the oil over medium heat and add the green pepper and celery. Cook for 5 to 6 minutes or until the vegetables begin to soften. Add the meat, breaking it into small pieces with a fork. Stir the meat with the vegetables and cook until the meat loses its pink color. Add the tomato sauce, salt and pepper to taste, and cumin seeds. Stir, lower heat to medium-low, and cook for 3 minutes to incorporate the flavors. Add the olives (either whole or in pieces), honey (or brown sugar), and the beans. Cook over low heat for 10 minutes, stirring occasionally.

Preheat the oven to 350°F. Lightly grease a 10-by-14-by-2-inch baking pan. Spread a very light layer of the bean and meat mixture on the bottom of the pan. Then cover with a layer of tortillas. (You may have to cut some of them to fit the pan.) Continue to alternate layers of the meat and bean mixture with layers of tortillas until all of the tortillas are used. Finish with a layer of the meat and bean mixture on the top. Sprinkle the top with the cheese and bake for 50 minutes, or until the cheese bubbles.

Only Richie Cole could turn the title of a 1957 Jackie McLean and John Jenkins album, *Alto Madness,* into a way of life. Cole lives on Alto Acres overlooking the Russian River in northern California. His daughter is known as Alto Annie. Alta is the name of one of his dogs. He serves Alto Madness Chili, Alto Madness Spaghetti, and Alto Madness Soup. His band is called Alto Madness. And he blows the horn itself with so much imagination, technique, and just plain joy that he sounds like he's truly mad about the alto. Cole may have been inspired by McLean's and Jenkins's classic recording, but the fuel that keeps his career running on fast forward is a blend of humor, adrenalin, and no-holds-barred creativity that's uniquely his own.

He was exposed to the jazz world at a very young age. Born in Trenton, New Jersey, in 1948, Cole was an adopted single child. He did come into contact with his natural

TASTY PLATTERS

• Richie Cole, *New York Afternoon* (Muse)
• Richie Cole, *Popbop* (Milestone)
• Eddie Jefferson, *Godfather of Vocalese* (Muse)

father, however, who was the owner of two nightclubs in the city, one white, one black. "Some of my earliest memories are being pushed around in a stroller on top of one of the clubs in the summertime," he says. He's fiercely proud of his hometown state. "You can take the

boy out of Trenton, but you can't take Trenton out of the boy," he proclaims. "I'm Jersey all the way. I was glad to be born there."

While neither the food nor the music in the Cole household were particularly memorable, the alto player nonetheless educated himself in both areas. "I came from a middle-class white suburban family that just cooked the basics," he explains. "My father was a factory worker, my mother was a secretary. My mother had about five dishes, and it was those five over and over again. But I never complained because it was always cool. I just started cooking when I got out on my own."

Cole's musical schooling began before he left home. "I used to listen to jazz all night long, sneak it," he remembers. "I had my radio on real low upstairs when I was supposed to be sleeping." Charlie Parker was among the hornmen he heard those nights. On Sunday afternoons he'd sit outside Trenton's Fantasy Lounge and catch the live sounds of Cannonball Adderley, Oliver Nelson, and Sonny Stitt wafting out the door. He started formal music lessons at

ten, joined up with an accordion-led trio, and by fifteen was studying with Phil Woods. In 1969 he joined Buddy Rich's big band following a stint at the Berklee College of Music in Boston. After more than two years with the drummer and six months with Lionel Hampton, he set out on his own. Alto Madness was born.

Cole has carved out an offbeat corner of jazz all for himself. Hard swinging bebop is at the heart of it, while all around swirls just about every style imaginable. Polkas, country and western, and soul fit comfortably into the saxophonist's eclectic scheme of things. Only Cole would brag that he has recorded with both Art Pepper *and* Boots Randolph.

"I get bored doing the same things so I have a lot of different approaches, which has probably held me back over the years because people like consistency," Cole declares. "With me every song's going to be different. Maybe it confuses people, I don't know. But I don't care."

What will be consistent on every tune Cole plays—be it as a multi-instrumentalist with his Mega-Universal Saxophone Orchestra, with Alto Madness, or with the likes of Hank Crawford and Bobby "Wild Man" Enriquez—is a lustrous tone on ballads, stompers, and everything in between. It was during his tenure as a partner with vocalist Eddie Jefferson, an improvisatory genius, that Cole fully realized the possible uses to which to put that tone. He can cover "Danny Boy," "Salt Peanuts," and the "Theme from Star Trek" during one show and make them seem like the most natural, swinging combination of song choices in the world.

The alto player doesn't take himself too seriously in the kitchen. His wife, Ann, recommends his Alto Madness Milkshake—a shot of vodka in a regular chocolate milkshake—as among his finest creations. Otherwise, she jokes, "his cooking is essentially inedible. To test how bad his food is, we put it down and see if the dogs will eat it. Ninety percent of the time, they walk away."

Cole cites a meal he prepared on tour as a good gauge of his culinary prowess. "I made Alto Madness Spaghetti for these people in South Africa and everybody was laying around afterwards," he says. "It was like the Jim Jones massacre. I kind of snuck out."

Truth be known, Ann, who does most of the cooking, admits that her husband's a solid chef who has a penchant for adding oregano, basil, vinegar, olive oil, and salt and pepper to most of his dishes.

Jazzabells

"I have traveled around the world with him," says Ann, "and in Finland, he's got a phenomenal reputation for his spaghetti. In Hawaii, everyone wanted him to make spaghetti. Every time we go someplace, they ask, 'Are you going to make your spaghetti again?' I have a real sneaking suspicion it's never the same twice. Consistency isn't one of his strong points."

While Ann claims to be the more inventive of the two cooks in the Cole household, Jazzabells, a cracker spread, is Richie's creation. Pressed for its origins, Cole answers, "I'm unable to reveal the source without risking my life."

"It's great," Ann adds. "Put it in the refrigerator, it stays for months. It's great whenever people come over unexpectedly."

Serves "lots"

1 (18-ounce) jar pineapple preserves
1 (18-ounce) jar apple jelly
1 (3-ounce) jar prepared horseradish
1 (1¼-ounce) can dry mustard
1 tablespoon cracked black pepper
1 or more (8-ounce) packages
 cream cheese, softened
Crackers, preferably Wheat-thins

In a medium-sized bowl, mix together the pineapple preserves, apple jelly, horseradish, dry mustard, and black pepper. Refrigerate. Pour about 1½ cups of sauce over each 8-ounce package of cream cheese and blend. Serve with the crackers. Refrigerate the remaining sauce. "Whenever the boys stop by, you can create this spicy and unique appetizer," the saxophonist says. "Just add it to another package or two of cream cheese."

The address was the Sutherland Hotel in Chicago, the period was the mid-1950s, and the resident was tenor saxophonist George Coleman. The city was where he cut his teeth while becoming one of the most compelling improvisers on the horn. The hotel was where he experimented with cooking styles, a process that grew into a lifelong passion for good food.

"There were some lean days when I first got there," Coleman recalls. Onstage he was learning the ropes with established jazzmen like Gene Ammons and Johnny Griffin, while in his hotel kitchenette he was trying different ways to cook greens, beans, and chicken. He readily admits that some of his culinary feats weren't the stuff of legend. Kenny Dorham, the trumpeter with whom Coleman would work as a member of Max Roach's quartet, discovered that during one visit to the Sutherland.

"I remember cooking some corn bread for Kenny that was like a block of cement," Coleman laughs. "I forgot to put baking powder in it. It wasn't so good. Kenny said, 'Yeah, man, this soul bread is OK, but it's a little bit heavy.' And it was. But I finally figured out how to cook scratch corn bread."

Coleman today prides himself on the range of dishes that he's able to prepare. The worldwide touring schedule he embarked upon soon

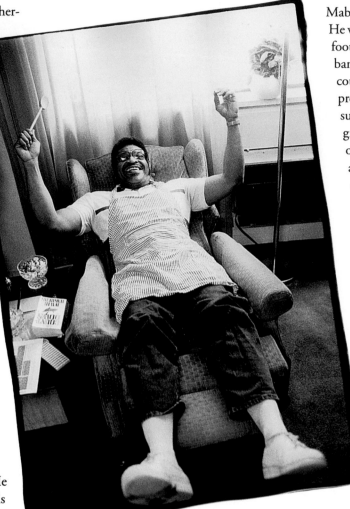

after he left Chicago, and that he maintained for decades, broadened his tastes immeasurably. Preparing escargot or clams with linguini now comes as naturally as the basic foods he was raised on in Memphis.

Coleman's father died when the saxophonist was very young, so his mother was both breadwinner and cook for him and his brother. "The food was very simple because of economics," he remembers. "We ate real Southern poor people's style—beans, fatback, that kind of stuff." Born in 1935, Coleman attended the same high school, Manassas, as future fellow jazz artists Harold

Mabern and Frank Strozier. He was actually torn between football and the high school band for a short time. "I could have probably been pretty good if I had pursued it," he says about his gridiron potential, "but I only went out for one year and then music overcame everything." He took up the alto saxophone in 1950 before concentrating on the tenor five years later. Memphis musical associations with the likes of Phineas Newborn, Jr., developed Coleman's confidence early, as did the job he landed with B. B. King's blues band when he was only seventeen.

Coleman's list of collaborators after Chicago reads like a jazz player's fantasy: Max Roach, Slide Hampton, Miles Davis, Lionel Hampton, Lee Morgan, Elvin Jones. He formed a quartet in 1972 and an octet in 1974 and has been recording and touring with various ensembles of his own ever since. His tenure with the Miles Davis Quartet during 1963 and 1964, when he appeared on such classic Davis recordings as "My Funny Valentine" and "Seven Steps to Heaven," proved to be a turning point in Coleman's stylistic approach to the music.

"Miles introduced a level of freeness in my playing. Before Miles, I was always very careful and precise. I always adhered strictly to the harmonic patterns of all the songs.

It started a metamorphosis in my playing where I felt I could obtain more depth."

The harmonic and melodic challenges that bebop poses remain the inspiration for much of Coleman's music and are at the core of the principles he teaches to his numerous students, including established stars like David Sanborn. The rugged, sinewy bravado with which he drives his uptempo material is in the tradition of "tough tenors" like Houston Person and Arnett Cobb. On hard boppers and even abstract modal flights, Coleman gives no quarter, often using a circular breathing technique to hammer home fluid, intense passages, thick with the blues feel he absorbed in Memphis.

Forceful as he can be, Coleman is also a subtle player with a rich lyrical streak, which makes sambas, funky gospel-ish blues, and lush ballads equally convincing.

"Basically my style hasn't changed that much," he says. "I like to play things that I don't know how I'm going to get out of.

"I hate when people start talking about bebop as old-fashioned. That doesn't mean you've got to play like Dexter Gordon or Wardell Gray. You can play your own thing and expand on it and modernize it, but don't stray from the true essence of the music."

Since his early twenties, Coleman has been keeping himself fit, and his attack powerful, by maintaining a regular regimen of weightlifting and exercise. He works out in the gym four days a week and walks from his apartment on Ninth Street in Manhattan to the Brooklyn Bridge the other three days. The reedman tends to stick to low-calorie food. When he's at home, he handles most of the cooking during the week, while his wife, Carol, takes over on weekends.

Penne Arrabiata

In step with her husband's weight-lifting routine, Carol Coleman has adapted a recipe for Penne Arrabiata, an Italian classic in which most of the calories are from carbohydrates.

"Carol's added more garlic and some fresh basil," says George of her tasty version. "You can't really make it without the fresh plum tomatoes. You could use canned tomatoes, but your best bet is to cook up a big batch of fresh tomatoes and freeze them. It's also a dish where you can improvise. Put in a little more of this, a little more of that. Cooking is like jazz. You have to improvise."

Not to be out-improvised, Carol notes that Italians don't use grated cheese on this dish. "But, George likes cheese and I don't," she says. "Also, if you add some capers and chopped black olives, this will make an excellent sauce for broiled fish."

Serves 4

¼ cup extra-virgin olive oil

Lots of minced garlic, to taste

3 to 4 dried red peppers (snip off fat end, then poke inside to get the seeds out), or a few shakes of red pepper flakes

12 to 20 ripe plum tomatoes, peeled, seeded, and chopped into ½-inch pieces

20 to 30 fresh basil leaves, either left whole or roughly chopped

Salt (needs a good bit to bring out flavor of tomatoes)

1 tablespoon to ¼ cup Italian tomato paste

1 pound penne, or other tube-shaped pasta

Half a medium-sized bunch curly parsley, chopped

In a large, noncorrosive skillet, over medium heat, warm the olive oil. Add the garlic and red peppers and sauté until the garlic is soft but not brown. Add the tomatoes, basil, and salt. Cook, stirring, for about 10 minutes. Sauce should be thick; if it's thin, which is usually due to the water content of the tomatoes, add between 1 tablespoon and ¼ cup of the tomato paste. Cook for another 10 to 15 minutes. Remove and discard the pepper pods. If time permits, let the sauce sit for a few hours before reheating to serve with the pasta.

Cook the penne according to the package directions. Slowly reheat the sauce over medium-low heat. Place the penne in a large serving bowl, and add almost all the chopped parsley. Add a few spoonfuls of the sauce to the penne, and stir to coat the pasta. Spoon the penne into four wide-rimmed bowls. Top each serving with a very generous dollop of sauce. Sprinkle extra parsley over the top.

Cuba is only ninety miles from the Florida coast, yet for Paquito D'Rivera and kindred spirits who yearn for a freedom that the nation will not grant, the island may as well be in another galaxy. That the creative flame there burns as brightly and steadily as it does is testament to the indomitable determination of natives like D'Rivera. What the reedman has accomplished, though, goes beyond that. Since he defected to the United States in 1980, his fire has become a blaze: He has joined the ranks of the finest clarinet and saxophone players in the world.

The sensibility D'Rivera brings to the bandstand is unmatched. He melds Cuban dance rhythms, Latin and South American folk music, classical music, and hard-charging bebop to create a sound that's singularly potent. If his music were a drink, it might be called a "Cool Tropical Roundhouse."

Born in Havana in 1948, D'Rivera remembers that the pre–Fidel Castro years were a time when concoctions of any kind were encouraged, whether on the concert stage, in the kitchen, or behind the bar. That ended when Castro took power in 1959. "When the Communists arrived, no food, no nothing," D'Rivera says. "Castro was like a wizard—he made everything disappear. The cooking hobby disappeared. Until '62 or '63, there wasn't anything. We got some food from the black market. Then you had to hide and eat. It was not fun."

His father, Tito, a classical saxophone player and representative of the Selmer Company, gave him a curved soprano saxophone when he was five. Between having musicians test instruments around the house and listening to recordings by Lionel Hampton, Harry James, and Benny Goodman on the hi-fi, young D'Rivera was exposed to an incredible amount of popular jazz. He picked up the fine points well enough to earn a performance on television at seven and an acceptance letter from the Havana Conservatory at twelve. By fourteen he was listening to Charlie Parker. And then he joined the army in 1965.

"Even in the army I kept listening to the music, but they didn't like it," D'Rivera remembers. "I was kind of an outrageous crazy mother. I organized a jazz band in the Communist army. Of course, we never played outside, but we rehearsed a lot."

D'Rivera joined his country's

TASTY PLATTERS

- Paquito D'Rivera, *Celebration* (Columbia)
- Paquito D'Rivera, *Manhattan Burn* (Columbia)
- Paquito D'Rivera/Arturo Sandoval, *Reunion* (Messidor)

most renowned band, Orquestra Cubana de Musica Moderna, in 1967. From it sprang Irakere, a group of eight of Orquestra Cubana's more restless and adventurous members. D'Rivera was one of the ringleaders. Their mix of rock, jazz, traditional Cuban, and classical styles, which they jokingly called "progressive socialist music," caught the attention of fans in the United States. One, Dizzy Gillespie, made it a point to seek out

D'Rivera in 1977, when he was in Cuba for a rare performance.

"I got home one night," D'Rivera recalls, "and on a paper bag was a message: 'Where have you been, conjo? I'm looking for you. Dizzy Gillespie.' I said, 'Dizzy Gillespie? What kind of joke is this?' Then I went to the store on the corner and they said, 'There was a very strange person here looking for you. He looked like a Martian. A black man with a trumpet and he was dressed very weird.' I asked, 'You mean a guy with big cheeks?' 'Yeah, yeah,' they said. 'A very strange person, looking for paper and pencil. We gave him a paper bag.'"

What attracted Gillespie then, and draws raves internationally now, is an alto sound that's sleek, brash, and fiery, and a liquid-toned clarinet that dances lightly through the thorniest chordal thickets. D'Rivera also plays flute and tenor and soprano saxophones, but he concentrates on alto sax and clarinet. He's one of the music's most versatile improvisers, tackling an incredible range of material, from boleros, Venezuelan waltzes, and Brazilian bossa novas to ecstatic, blistering bop and modern Argentine classical pieces. Strings, which can strangle even the best-intentioned jazz composers, are in capable hands with D'Rivera. On the classical side, he has shared the stage with conductor/composer David Amram. D'Rivera celebrated Mozart's two hundredth anniversary with a performance of his clarinet concerto.

"I am a Gemini and I get bored if I have to do the same thing," he says. "I like to do different things. That way I learn. I am an Ellingtonian person. I believe there is good and bad music only. Any positive energy or element I can add to my style, I go for it. I still learn from other people. I don't hesitate to put in any ingredients in my music that will make it richer."

Most of D'Rivera's family is now in the United States. His parents left Cuba before he did, and the Castro government finally let his son and his ex-wife leave in 1989 after the reed player waged an international publicity campaign for their freedom. D'Rivera now lives in Weehawken, New Jersey, with his wife, singer Brenda Feliciano, who handles the bulk of the cooking.

D'Rivera's eating habits have changed dramatically in recent years. "I was getting too fat," he says. "I decided to cut my diet in half." He has eliminated red meat and made seafood a staple. Despite the calories, however, he can't eliminate black beans and rice from his diet. He cooks them himself, but the version he prefers is his mother-in-law's. In fact, he thinks so highly of her rendition that he invited her to accompany him on a European tour in the late 1980s. She cooked the dish daily for him and for members of the band.

Paquito's Black Beans

"This is a recipe especially for those who really want flavor from their food," says D'Rivera. *"The key to bringing out its exquisite taste comes from allowing the required time for each stage."* Although it's a dish that has been on his table for many generations, D'Rivera notes, *"This particular recipe has probably never been written down before."*

This dish can be prepared in advance and refrigerated. The flavors join, and it becomes more delicious with the passing days. Serve with rice. Vegetarians can leave out the bacon for a delicious meal that will be slightly milder in flavor.

Serves 5 to 6 as a side dish

  1 pound black beans, washed and
     sorted through to remove debris

8 to 10 cups water
¼ pound bacon, cut into small pieces
3 medium onions, finely chopped
4 cloves garlic, minced
2 green bell peppers, halved
  and seeded
Salt and pepper

In a large pot, cover the beans with a generous amount of water and soak overnight. In the morning, drain and cover with fresh water. ("To make the beans even blacker, some may prefer not to change water," Paquito says. "I prefer to change it.") Cover the pot, and, over medium heat, cook until tender. This may take up to 2 hours. Occasionally check the water level and add more water if the beans appear dry. (*Note:* Be careful not to let the beans boil too rapidly, as the skins may pop.)

In a large frying pan, cook the bacon. When it throws off fat, add the onions and garlic. Lower the heat to medium and cook, stirring, until the vegetables are soft and the bacon reaches desired crispiness. Ladle 2 or 3 scoops of drained, cooked beans into the bacon mixture and mash with a potato masher. (This will release starch to thicken the dish.) After mashing, add the mashed mixture to the bean pot.

Spear the halved peppers with a long-handled fork and broil them over a gas flame, or place them under a broiler and roast them, turning frequently, until the skin is totally charred. Place the charred peppers in a paper bag. Close the bag and let the peppers sit for 15 minutes. Remove the peppers from the bag and peel away the skins. Chop the peppers and add them to the beans. Season with salt and pepper. Simmer the beans for at least one hour.

Few have been afforded the real-life educational opportunities that Ricky Ford had during his teens. From thirteen to eighteen, the tenor saxophonist traveled to Boylston Street clubs in downtown Boston to sit in with some of the greatest jazz musicians in the world, including Charles Mingus, Sonny Rollins, Rahsaan Roland Kirk, and Archie Shepp. So prodigious were his talents that several, including Mingus, asked young Ford to return again and again.

Back home on Devon Street in the city's Roxbury section, Ford was absorbing daily doses of another sort of lesson—the fine art of cooking. From the time he was born in 1954, he was surrounded by outstanding cooks. Not only were his mother and father comfortable in the kitchen, but so were his grandparents, who lived in an apartment in the same building. Although his grandfather Gordon was a chef at Boston's fabled Union Oyster House, the family, with roots in Barbados, specialized in Caribbean fare like fish-head stew and couscous, cornmeal-fried okra, and peas and rice.

Ford has the family touch around the stove, and onstage he has evolved into one of jazz's most consistently remarkable improvisers, composers, and theorists. The worlds of Boylston and Devon streets have intersected many times in subsequent years, but never more poignantly than during one of Ford's concert tours in Italy.

"I had dinner with the mayor of Messina, and he took us to a restaurant where the chef had all these gastronomy plaques on the wall," Ford recalls. "We had a twenty-course

dinner and the main course was fish with tomatoes and onions. I said, 'My grandfather used to make this!' The chef's eyebrows went up to the top of his head."

Ford's grandfather may have been the primary influence on his culinary life, but it was his grandmother and father who provided most of the musical inspiration. She was a guitarist and original member of the International Sweethearts of Rhythm. Ford's father stocked the house with recordings by Illinois Jacquet, Lester Young, Chu Berry, and Charlie Parker. He also took the young Ford to Boston clubs to meet musicians like Dizzy Gillespie and

Rahsaan Roland Kirk. Ford was soon so accomplished and comfortable with his abilities that he start hanging out on his own in venue like Paul's Mall, Wally's, and the Jazz Workshop, earning a reputation as a passionate young firebrand.

Intensity is a Ford trademark. He displayed it at the New England Conservatory and in subsequent stints with Mercer Ellington, Charles Mingus, and Abdullah Ibrahim. He's a stylist who would have fit right in during the vaunted tenor battles of the 1940s and 1950s, blowing riff after powerful riff in answer to another saxophonist's challenge. He can be as creamy

Bajan Codfish Cakes

In this recipe, Ford passes on a family heirloom that is as much a part of the Boston of his youth as the Bridgetown, Barbados, of his grandparents. In both of these former British colonies, salted cod was a staple trading commodity. Its continued popularity in both regions is an acknowledgment of both time-honored tradition and salted cod's unique flavor.

Serves 4

1 pound salted cod
1 large egg, beaten
1 cup flour
2 teaspoons baking soda
¼ cup diced green bell pepper
¼ cup diced onion
2 scallions, finely chopped
½ teaspoon pepper
½ teaspoon Old Bay Seasoning
   (optional)
Approximately 1 cup olive or
   canola oil

Soak the salted cod in water to cover overnight. Change the water a few times before you finally go to sleep. When ready to use, rinse the cod again and pat dry. Combine the egg, flour, baking soda, green pepper, onion, scallions, pepper, and Old Bay Seasoning (if using). Dice the fish into pieces smaller than bite-sized and add the fish to the flour-egg mixture. Shape the batter into 3-inch cakes. In a large skillet, warm ¾ cup of oil. Over medium-high to high heat, sauté the fish cakes, until golden brown on both sides, adding the remaining oil as necessary. Alternatively, preheat the oven to 400°F and bake the fish cakes on a lightly greased baking sheet, until both sides are brown. Or, roll the raw fish cakes in a beaten egg and then roll again in bread crumbs to form a light coat before frying. You may also add some bread crumbs to the fish and vegetable mixture, if desired.

and huge in tone as a Dexter Gordon and as dissonant and craggy in approach as an Archie Shepp.

Ford was paying homage to the jazz tradition long before it became fashionable to do so in the 1980s, but he has never been content to simply recreate an idiom. The depth, complexity, and range of his writing make Ford much more

TASTY PLATTERS

- Ricky Ford, *Hard Groovin'* (Muse)
- Ricky Ford, *Saxotic Stomp* (Muse)
- Ran Blake, *That Certain Feeling* (hat ART)

than a mere tenor blaster. His years as artist-in-residence at Brandeis University and his associations with strong conceptualists like Mingus and Ibrahim have led him to explore bebop, swing, South African music, and the blues with an ear toward taking those traditions in new directions, especially with his own ensembles. His material is charged with improvising opportunities that rarely fail to inspire his bandmates to greater heights.

When, at nineteen, he joined Mercer Ellington, Ford had little choice but to become acquainted with improvised meals on the road. Ellington's big band toured forty-eight weeks out of the year, so the saxophonist picked up a number of cooking skills he hadn't been taught on Devon Street.

"We had a giant Thanksgiving one year at the Croydon Hotel in Chicago that started us cooking on the road more," Ford says. "The

Texas contingent did most of the cooking: Anita Moore, the vocalist, Barry Lee Hall, Rocky White, James Spaulding. I'd never had dirty rice before. They had the pots. All we'd do was chip in money and go shopping."

After he joined Mingus, Ford's tastes became increasingly sophisticated, especially given the bassist's propensity for taking his band members out to eat. "He liked all good food," Ford says of Mingus.

Ford is an avid collector of cookbooks, picking them up in his travels around the world. He has become a connoisseur of ethnic cuisine, an interest shared by many of his peers. He recalls one particular tour of England with Ibrahim's band Ekaya during the late 1980s when the group ate in a different Indian restaurant every day. "I think the band set a record," he laughs. "I had a string of American Express bills for two weeks of eating in Indian restaurants."

The reasons, artistic and otherwise, why Donald Harrison is glad he was born and raised in New Orleans could fill a page. There's one near the top of the list, though, that couldn't be further away from life on the bandstand: fishing.

"When I was catching a lot of fish I forgot about the time," Harrison laughs. "I used to miss gigs because I was fishing."

The reedman nonetheless made it to more than enough gigs to build a foundation that served him well in subsequent years. Today, with sensibilities rooted in both the jazz tradition and his hometown's musical melange,

Harrison is one of the most thought-provoking young improvisers and composers on the scene.

When Harrison got a bicycle in his early teens, he'd ride to and from

City Park lake in New Orleans, often bringing home perch or largemouth bass for dinner. Lake

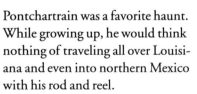

Pontchartrain was a favorite haunt. While growing up, he would think nothing of traveling all over Louisiana and even into northern Mexico with his rod and reel.

The only thing that's changed since Harrison has grown into an internationally acclaimed artist is that his fishing spots are now more far-flung. Tarpon off the South American coast, salmon in Canada,

and bluefish off Cape Cod have all been caught in Harrison's net. Now that he lives in New York he tries his luck deep-sea fishing off Long Island.

"I've been fishing all over the world, but Louisiana is still my favorite spot," Harrison says. "I really know the water, when's the best time, and when the fish are running."

Harrison was raised in a home rich in culinary and musical tradition. Born in 1960, he and his three sisters grew up on the northern Louisiana cooking of their mother, who regularly prepared dishes like jambalaya and gumbo. Their father, a New Orleans native, occasionally cooked breakfast. Young Harrison learned by watching. By fourteen he was given permission to use the stove himself.

His parents' musical tastes were catholic. "I feel quite fortunate because I had the opportunity to hear all kinds of music," he says. "I heard James Brown, Ravi Shankar, Charlie Parker, Bach, African music, the Beatles, Blind Lemon Jefferson. My parents just liked music." Harrison got his first horn in elementary school but didn't

Herreast's Eggplant Casserole

"Small as I am, you wouldn't think I'd like to taste so much food, but I really love the taste of food.

"I use a lot of rich things when I make sauces. I should gain a lot of weight, but I don't. I guess I have a high metabolism."

One of Harrison's favorites is this recipe, given to him by his mother, Herreast. A Cajun classic, it definitely qualifies as "rich."

Serves 8 as a side dish

**3 medium eggplants, peeled and
cut into ½-inch cubes**

**½ cup (1 stick) margarine or
butter, melted**

½ cup finely chopped onions

½ cup finely chopped bell pepper

½ cup finely chopped celery

¼ cup finely chopped parsley

2 cloves garlic, minced

3 tablespoons butter

1 pound shrimp, shelled and deveined

1 pound cooked ham, finely diced

1 cup seasoned bread crumbs

Salt and pepper

Preheat the oven to 375°F. In a large pot, bring enough water to cover the eggplant to a boil. Add the eggplant, cover the pot, and simmer, until the eggplant is tender, about 5 to 8 minutes. Drain. In a large skillet, warm 4 tablespoons of the melted margarine (or butter). Add the onion, bell pepper, celery, parsley, and garlic and sauté until the onions become transparent, about 3 to 5 minutes. In another skillet, heat the 3 tablespoons of butter. Add the shrimp and sauté until they turn pink, about 3 to 4 minutes. Remove the shrimp from the skillet and chop finely. To the skillet with the vegetables, add the eggplant, chopped shrimp, ham, ½ cup of bread crumbs, and salt and pepper. Mix thoroughly. Place this mixture in a greased casserole dish. Sprinkle the remaining ½ cup of bread crumbs on top of the casserole. Drizzle the remaining 4 tablespoons of melted margarine (or butter) over the bread crumbs. Bake for 20 minutes or until the bread crumbs are lightly browned.

---

really take his alto seriously until he was fourteen. He danced to, and eventually played in, brass bands at funerals and parades.

Harrison studied at the New Orleans Center for the Creative Arts under Kid Jordan and Ellis Marsalis, father of Wynton and Branford. Somewhere between working with rhythm-and-blues bands, playing jazz funerals, and studying, he heard Grover Washington's *Mr. Magic.* "And then I started to listen to Charlie Parker," he explains, "and

it was all over." He went to Southern University for a year and transferred to Berklee College of Music in Boston after that. Weekend work with the likes of Roy Haynes and Jack McDuff was a prelude to his 1982 enrollment in jazz's highest institution of learning, Art Blakey's Jazz Messengers. Much of Harrison's own bebop-based approach is Blakey-inspired.

"I try to learn as much as possible about the music that's passed," Harrison says. "Not just jazz,

everything. Play, like Art said, from your heart, from your life's experience. Play with musicians on the same wavelength so you can grow as a group. The main thing is to have your own sound as a group."

Harrison and trumpet player Terence Blanchard, a fellow New Orleans native, replaced Branford and Wynton Marsalis in Blakey's Messengers. With Blakey and later as co-leaders of their own ensemble, Harrison and Blanchard proved themselves to be musicians who used the jazz tradition not as an easy chair, but as a starting point for their own visions.

As a composer, and improviser on alto, soprano, tenor, and C-melody sax, Harrison owes no obvious allegiance to any one stylist. He is at his best when challenged by the often-thorny song structures he creates for himself. Using subtle, constantly changing rhythmic patterns and quirky meters, he makes sure that he and his soloists are prodded by grooves that vary and tempos that shift. Mix in the syncopated swagger of his New Orleans roots and its confluence of African, Indian, and Caribbean rhythms, and you've got a powerful core capable of supporting modality and lyricism side by side. Harrison's enormous technical and emotional range allows him to tell his stories in as many voices as he needs.

Not surprisingly, the saxophonist's search for freshness isn't limited to music and fishing spots. He's always looking for new stimulation for his palate as well. "I had a bad habit when I first started with Art Blakey of going into a restaurant and ordering five entrées just to taste them, to see what they were like," he laughs.

The message of the United States Army—"Be all that you can be"—isn't just a throwaway advertising slogan to Joe Henderson. He credits his two years spent in the service with crystallizing his attitude toward his life and, ultimately, with helping his development as a tenor saxophonist. Today he ranks as a titan.

"They've got this thing in the military that you've really got to

TASTY PLATTERS

• Joe Henderson, *Inner Urge* (Blue Note)
• Joe Henderson, *Page One* (Blue Note)
• Andrew Hill, *Point of Departure* (Blue Note)

challenge yourself," he says. "What I have, it was my sweat that got to that. It didn't fall out of the sky. Whatever accomplishments I may be enjoying now come from work that I did. I like to earn my own money and do my share of the work. I like to keep my floor swept and my bed neat. I like to shine my own shoes. There's something in just doing that for myself that I appreciate."

Henderson, born in 1937, the third youngest of fourteen brothers and sisters, quickly learned some poignant lessons about taking care of himself when he was seated at the family dinner table in Lima, Ohio. "You made sure you got your fair share, what you thought you needed to sustain yourself," he laughs. But it took him longer to appreciate the musical sustenance he received from his family.

"From the time I was six or seven years old I had seen my mother do nothing but dust off this keyboard that was in the front room of the house," he recounts. "It was like furniture. I had started playing the saxophone when I was nine. I would play the piano a little bit. When I was seventeen, I was in the front room playing the saxophone and my mother was preparing to dust off this magnificent old piano. All of a sudden she turned to me and said, 'Joe, tell me how this sounds.' And she went up to the

piano and played something and then played it again. I had no idea, although she would question me, 'Joe, who is that on the radio, Charlie Parker?' She got to the point where she could recognize Lester Young, Bud Powell, Oscar Peterson, Ella Fitzgerald. And she was not a young lady at that time."

Henderson's father, who worked in a steel foundry, also encouraged his son's budding talents. That, combined with the "Jazz at the Philharmonic" recordings of a brother, the rhythm-and-blues records of a sister, and the influence of two piano-playing neighbors, was the push the saxophonist needed. His enthusiasm for high school football and track eventually waned. "I just got more interested in music," he says.

He spent three years at Wayne University, later renamed Wayne State, before he was drafted into the army in 1960. "Some of the greatest things happened to me in the military," he recalls. "I met Horace Silver, Bud Powell, Kenny Clarke. I was with the Rolling Along Show. We worked for the Pentagon and traveled around the world wherever troops were stationed. We were morale boosters and that's as important as a Sidewinder missile."

When his hitch ended and he moved to New York, Henderson quickly established himself as a formidable sideman. Trumpeter Kenny Dorham hired him, as did Silver, Lee Morgan, and Herbie Hancock. He co-led a group with Freddie Hubbard and Louis Hayes called the Jazz Communicators, and became a regular on the Blue Note and Milestone labels. The last two decades Henderson has spent teaching, leading his own groups, and collaborating with the likes of Charlie Haden and Al Foster.

Henderson is inspired as much by Charlie Parker as by John Coltrane and Ornette Coleman. He's at his most compelling when his free flights travel within a bluesy, soulful bebop structure, a road he has explored more often in recent years. An aggressive stylist who's always powerfully rhythmical and swinging, he often builds his ideas by using extended, choppy bursts. The tension created by that

approach combined with a mastery of circular breathing and a muscular tone, which has grown gruffer with age, add up to an intense improvisational presence few tenor players can match. Henderson especially abhors repetition.

"The biggest sin I can commit is playing an idea more than once," he declares. "I'm trying to be as interesting and creative as I can."

Giving back what he has received is also high on the reedman's agenda. "I've become aware of planting some trees out here," he says. "Somebody planted trees so I could have nice shade from the sweltering heat of the day. I figure I'm supposed to do that now. I'm very much aware of giving something back. I've never been in this game for the money. I've been in it for some other reason and I'm not sure what that reason is, but I've enjoyed it. I'd like to try to

do my share in bringing some happy moments in a musical way to the audience."

His travels around the world have made Henderson a bit of a connoisseur of fine food. Two decades spent living in San Francisco, one of America's greatest culinary cities, has heightened his appreciation even more. A strict vegetarian for many years, Henderson now includes fish and chicken in his diet. "I'm a great seafood fan," he says. "For the last eight to ten years, I've gravitated toward the wonderful things that the sea will surrender." The saxophonist and his lady friend, Mariko Hopps, eat out often, with Hopps handling much of the cooking when they do stay home. Henderson does cook, and admits, "Aside from having a penchant for things musical, I think I'd be a great chef if I spent more time in the kitchen."

Joe Fu Yung

"I love many different types of seafood and vegetables," says Henderson. "We have an abundance of crab here in San Francisco and one of the things I like to do is combine crab with eggs in a dish I call Joe Fu Yung, a cross between an omelette and scrambled eggs. It's really very simple and something that's tasty without being pretentious."

Serves 2 to 3

1 cup cooked crabmeat, well picked over to remove any cartilage
4 eggs
2 tablespoons finely chopped scallions
⅛ teaspoon sea salt
¼ teaspoon freshly ground black pepper
3 tablespoons peanut oil

Flake the crabmeat with a fork and set aside. In a medium-sized bowl, beat the eggs until fluffy. Add the scallions, salt, and pepper. In a medium-sized skillet, over medium heat, warm half the peanut oil. Reduce the heat to low and add the crabmeat, cooking until the crabmeat becomes hot. Add the remaining oil, heat, and then add the egg mixture. Increase the heat to medium-high. With a fork draw the solidified egg to the center of the skillet, then tilt the skillet and let the uncooked egg run over the bottom of the pan. Keep repeating this process until most of the egg has set. Serve immediately.

"Sometimes I don't believe all that has happened to me," marvels Illinois Jacquet. "I'm one of the only ones who has been with Art Tatum, Earl Hines, Duke, Nat 'King' Cole, Oscar Peterson. That's the thrill, that I'm holding a torch."

No saxophonist has held it with more pride or distinction than the veteran tenor, alto, soprano, and bassoon player. Deep South–

being deprived of the real thing, the right stuff. And I'm trying to put out the right stuff."

Jacquet's "stuff" is indeed the genuine article. It's a potent, novel blend of the raucous, smouldering reed swagger he absorbed in his youth both listening to and playing in the territory bands that toured the South, and the

he has gone back to his Houston roots in his eating habits. "We grew up with vegetables," recalls Jacquet, who was born in 1922, the youngest of six children. "My mother used to grow all kinds in the big yard we had: tomatoes, corn, turnips, squash, radishes, zucchinis, snap beans. She knew a

born and big band–bred, Jacquet is one of the last of an illustrious line of powerful "Texas tenors" whose glory is to showcase the passion inherent in the best of the swing tradition.

"I want to continue to bring out the excitement of the big bands," he says. "Young people need to hear the music. They're not hearing it today and that hurts me. They're

tender ballad style he developed after years of working with the Ellingtons and Coles of the music business. His desire to explore every possibility of swing in both big band and small group settings has been unwavering.

Jacquet's nutritional approach, by comparison, has varied wildly, yet in an essential way it has come full circle. Now a staunch vegetarian after years of eating meat,

lot about the farm because she was Indian. Even in Depression days we didn't want for any food because we always had it in the yard. I didn't know anything about vegetarianism at the time, but we were eating it, so my mother must have known something was going on. She was a great cook. We all could cook. Learning how to cook for yourself was part of growing up. In case you got hungry and no one was there, you could get in the kitchen and whip up a few things."

The saxophonist's father, a mechanic on the Southern Pacific railroad, also ran a big band, which is where Jacquet got his first taste of onstage competition. When he was three or four years old, his dancing

abilities were put in the spotlight during the "battles" his father's orchestra would have with visiting territory bands. Later experiences as one of the Jacquet Brothers helped him land a seat playing alto in Milt Larkin's territory band. It was there that Jacquet developed his huge, bluesy tone and no-holds-barred approach to improvising. He had no choice: if he wanted to be heard above the band's roaring brass section, his blowing needed an exclamation point. His tack paid off when it came time to solo on the riff tune "Flying Home" with Lionel Hampton's band in 1942. Jacquet's rowdy tenor show-stopper, subsequently performed for many years, has become legendary in jazz lore and remains the saxophonist's timeless calling card.

"Flying Home," though, was only one moment in a career full of highlights accomplished in the company of the music's giants, Ben Webster to Cab Calloway, Ella Fitzgerald to Lester Young. Jacquet's current big band, put together in the mid-eighties, displays the exuberance

and flamboyance of its leader. His soulful horn—variously honking and squealing on up-tempo material and buttery-toned and touching on ballads—has laid the ground-work for several generations of rhythm and blues–influenced reed-men, from King Curtis to David Sanborn. The constant in Jacquet's sound is pure joy.

"Music has been the guiding light for my whole life," he says. "Without it I think I would have been some dumbbell sitting some-where. The importance of it is bigger than anybody. It's just a beautiful religion to be in. I don't see how I could be who I am if I didn't have music in me. With-out it I don't think life would be worth living."

A devotee of Gurumayi Chid-vilasananda, Jacquet meditates regularly in order to "get in tune with my mind and body and music." Diet, too, is extremely important to the saxophonist. Long gone are the days when Jacquet and his fellow big band members grabbed sandwiches for their bus rides. "Sometimes we had Christmas dinner coming out of the A & P," he remembers. "People were home having turkey and we'd be trying to get to that job somewhere on Christmas night. Bologna and bread when you're on the road."

In the early eighties Jacquet met his personal manager, Carol Scher-ick, a nutritionist who weaned him off meat and onto vegetables again. "I guess that's why I'm still here," he laughs. "I feel one-hundred per-cent better. It's good for your heart, for your bloodstream. It's too bad we wait so long to find out what's going on."

Veggie Roast

"You can make my Veggie Roast out of your favorite vegetables," says Jacquet. *"It doesn't have to be the way I fix it."*

Serves 6

Safflower, canola, or olive oil
4 to 5 peeled sweet potatoes or
  unpeeled white potatoes
10 to 12 small, fresh okra, left whole
1 to 2 carrots, peeled
½ to ¾ cup each of fresh, shelled
  sweet peas and snap beans
2 to 3 medium-sized tomatoes or
  ½ pint of cherry tomatoes
6 to 8 whole pearl onions, peeled
10 to 12 large, fresh mushrooms,
  preferably shiitake mushrooms
2 to 3 ears of corn, cut into pieces
2 to 3 pattypan squash
1 to 2 zucchinis
1 to 2 stalks of broccoli
1 to 2 red bell peppers
2 to 3 stalks of celery, with leaves
1 large leek, thinly sliced
Romaine lettuce, kale, or
  collard greens

Preheat the oven to 350° F. Grease the bottom of a large roasting pan with the oil. Wash all of the vegetables. Cut the vegetables as specified or as you wish. Lay the potatoes along the bottom of the pan and follow with the okra, carrots, sweet peas, snap beans, tomatoes, onions, and mushrooms. Fit in the remaining vegetables, except the celery, leek, and lettuce (or kale or collard greens). Top with the celery and sliced leek. Then sprinkle the whole with 2 to 3 tablespoons of oil and cover with the large leaves of lettuce (or kale or collard greens). Don't use any salt or pepper; the vegetables will give off enough flavor. Place a cover or aluminum foil over the pan. Cook for 1 hour, until the carrots and potatoes are tender.

first it's the salad
then the meat
then the vegetables . . .
      "WAIT"
bring all my food at one time on
    the same plate!

dixieland, be-bop, soul, rhythm &
    blues, cool school
swing, avant-garde, jazz, free
    jazz, rock, jazz-rock

WHAT KINDA MUSIC U PLAY?
     "GOOD KIND"

Aretha franklin & Sun Ra is the
    same folks,
Coltrane & the Dixie humming
    birds same folks
Miles & muddy waters same.
    there is no . . . there is no . . .
    LABELS DIVIDE! SEPARATE
    THE ORAL AND THE LITERARY

One music—diff feelings &
    experience, but same . . .
    the total
sound—mass sound—hear all
    the players as one

(from the poem "Separation"
by Oliver Lake)

"**W**e grew up eating everything at once on one plate," St. Louis native Oliver Lake says. "The salads, the vegetables, we ate everything at one time. Relating it to music, I'm not much into separating categories. If I want to express something, I just go ahead and do it."

That philosophy has pushed Lake into the middle of some of the most exciting collaborations of the past two decades. A founding member of the World Saxophone Quartet, arguably *the* trailblazing band of the late seventies and eighties, the alto player has thrust himself into a wide range of settings that subscribe completely to the sentiment of "Separation": his reggae/funk/fusion band Jump Up, his own jazz group, and duets with similarly adventurous players like Leroy Jenkins and Joseph Bowie.

Born in 1942, Lake was initiated early into a world where food and music intersected. His mother, Alvia, owned a restaurant with her four sisters in midtown St. Louis named, appropriately, the Five Sisters Restaurant. "There was a lot of music on the jukebox, a lot of the blues tunes—Lightning Hopkins, Muddy Waters, Lowell Fulsom," Lake remembers. "I ate in there every day. I must have been ten years old when it started. I used to mop up and take out trash to earn a little money when I was a kid. It was a soul food restaurant, barbecue and all that. One of the hot items was a twenty-five-cent pig ear sandwich. That was the hot thing on weekends. They sold hundreds of pounds of pig ears."

When Lake was in his late teens he became an Orthodox Muslim. "I got out of the soul food zone," he says. "I stopped eating pork. It started to be kind of strange around my family because it was a big staple. They just didn't understand because everybody ate pork and I came home talking about Islam. I'm not Muslim now, but I still don't eat pork."

Besides the blues on the restaurant jukebox, Lake was exposed at an early age to several other kinds of music that would affect his own sound later. His mother played spirituals at home on the hi-fi and sang them in the church choir. And at fifteen, when he joined the drum and bugle corps as a cymbal player

Pumpkin Fritters

Lake's Pumpkin Fritters is one of those dishes whose sum is derived from a whole lot of parts.

Here, fritters, those deep-fried delectables known to almost every food culture, are given a northern feel with pumpkin, and a southern twist with sugar, vanilla, and raisins, ingredients that frequently go into sweet potato pie. Depending upon your mood, these fritters can serve as a nice nibble with cocktails, a side dish with roast chicken or fried fish, or a dessert.

Serves 4

1 cup grated raw pumpkin
1 large egg
1 cup flour
1/2 cup sugar
1 teaspoon vanilla
Dash of salt
Handful of raisins (optional)
Vegetable oil for deep frying
Brown sugar (optional)

In a large bowl, combine the pumpkin, egg, flour, sugar, vanilla, and salt. Blend in the raisins (if using). Form the batter into approximately 20 loosely packed 1- to 1¼-inch balls. In a large skillet, heat 1 inch of oil to approximately 350° to 375°F. Drop the fritters into the oil, being careful not to crowd, and brown well on all sides. Drain the fritters on paper towels and, if desired, sprinkle with brown sugar.

Note: If you use canned pumpkin, the dish will take on a completely different character, lacking in the crunchy texture that comes from the tendrils of fresh pumpkin.

and bass drummer, Lake's musical horizon truly began to widen.

"A lot of musicians in the drum and bugle corps were into jazz—older guys, eighteen or nineteen. They turned me on to the music. Sonny Rollins, Paul Desmond, Charlie Parker, 'Trane, Miles. I went to jam sessions and hung around with them. I had a little tape recorder and taped all the sessions.

TASTY PLATTERS

- **Oliver Lake and Jump Up,** *Compilation* **(Gramavision)**
- **World Saxophone Quartet,** *Metamorphosis* **(Elektra/ Nonesuch)**
- **World Saxophone Quartet,** *Dances and Ballads* **(Elektra/ Nonesuch)**

Eventually I said, 'Hey, let me get a horn and sit in with you guys.'"

Lake chose the alto and at nineteen, encouraged by friends such as schoolmate/trumpeter Lester Bowie, began working with local rhythm-and-blues bands that accompanied singers such as Rufus Thomas and Solomon Burke on their Midwest regional tours. In 1968, Lake became one of the founders of the St. Louis–based Black Artists' Group (BAG), a collective of approximately fifty musicians, dancers, poets, and actors, modeled loosely after the Association for the Advancement of Creative Musicians in Chicago. Lake was a quick study, but when he lived in Paris from 1972 to 1974 with an ensemble of BAG players, he experienced very different worlds—both musical and culinary.

"I scrounged," Lake laughs, recalling his first few months in the City of Light. "We had some rough times because nobody really knew who we were. In terms of eating, it was a different situation getting into French cuisine. It was a surprise going into a restaurant and seeing raw meat with a raw egg in the middle of it. Being from the Midwest, I'd never seen anyone eating steak tartare."

Lake would have many opportunities to acquaint himself with international fare in subsequent years. His music has garnered acclaim worldwide. By combining virtuosity, a respect for the past, and a relentless need to be fresh,

the World Saxophone Quartet, in particular, has pioneered an approach that captures the jazz tradition's spirit of risk taking. Lake has been a leader in making sure that the music maintains wit, volatility, and subtle beauty, whether in the band's almost anarchic, freewheeling improvisations or their graceful harmonies. His horn playing has always exhibited powerful elements of both.

Even though the saxophonist doesn't eat pork, he still prides himself on his barbecuing skills, grilling fish, poultry, and vegetables at the Montclair, New Jersey, home he shares with his wife, Marion, and their two children.

The widened horizon that young veteran Branford Marsalis has experienced touring with British pop star Sting hasn't been limited to the stage or recording studio. It extends even to minutiae about the relative physical fitness of rock and jazz musicians, a subject near and dear to the heart of the health-conscious saxophonist.

"Rock-and-roll guys are actually in better shape than jazz guys nowadays," says Marsalis, a phenomenon he believes can be attributed to the less-destructive lifestyles many of today's rock musicians lead. "The money was a joke to the rock-and-roll guys we grew up with," he continues. "They believed in the anarchy that they talked about and they lived like wild boys. Now, for the most part, the wildness is calculated."

Despite the tenor and soprano player's jocular, free-spirited persona, you won't find him partaking in any on- or offstage wildness, either. Taking his young son, Reese, to Shea Stadium to see the Mets is his idea of a good time. But you will find him working hard to keep up his health and fitness. "The amount of concentration required to play what I play takes a toll on your body," Marsalis points out. "There's a lot of mental and physical stress. When you're not in good physical shape, the stress messes with you much more."

Besides a workout routine, the reedman pays close attention to his diet. But it wasn't always that way.

Born in 1960 and raised in New Orleans in the now legendary musical family, Marsalis loved the city's culinary traditions—in retrospect maybe a bit too much. He agrees wholeheartedly with the

Favorite Catfish Recipe

While his mother, Delores, remembers Branford as being "a little fussy" as a youngster, today he craves strong flavors, such as those found in this catfish dish. The saxophonist's recipe calls for sprinkling each fillet with dill and letting it sit overnight. The assertive herb penetrates the flesh and imparts a pleasant, almost grassy flavor to the fish.

Serves 4

4 catfish fillets, approximately 5 ounces each
Salt and pepper
Approximately 1½ tablespoons dried dillweed
Approximately ¾ cup yellow cornmeal
2 eggs
Peanut oil

Wash and dry the fillets. Sprinkle lightly with the salt, pepper, and dillweed. Cover loosely with waxed paper and refrigerate overnight, or for as long as 1 day. When ready to cook the fillets, place the cornmeal in a paper bag and, in a small bowl, beat the eggs. Dip each fillet in the egg, then place it in the paper bag and shake, until the fillet is coated with cornmeal. In a skillet or deep-fryer, heat up enough oil to cover the fish. Fry the fillets until golden and crisp all over. Drain on paper towels and serve with Tabasco sauce and corn bread.

observation of his mother, Delores, that the Crescent City considers food a celebration: "That's the thing that separates New Orleans from every other city in America," he says. "New Orleans is more like

Europe. When people eat, they sit down and eat. What the food represents to society is more than just the need to fill your stomach." But those same tasty meals that his mother prepared for the family— Branford, trumpeter Wynton, their four other brothers, and father, Ellis—didn't hold up nutritionally once Marsalis relocated north in the early eighties.

"My diet changed for the better when I moved to New York," he says. "I was eatin' like a damn fool back in New Orleans. I'd eat everything. Ham hocks. Hot sausage. Pork chops. Big, thick steaks. Eggs. Crawfish. Shrimp creole. Mirlitons. Red beans and rice. Stuffed bell peppers. Shrimp po' boy sandwiches. Alligator soup. Lobster bisque, high in creamy content. Fried this, fried that. Lots of red meat, lots of pork."

In New York, Marsalis cut way back on fried foods, eliminated pork, and incorporated more fresh vegetables into his diet. The passing years have altered his nutritional needs further. "My metabolism's slower so I don't have to eat as much," he says. "I don't have as much meat on my bones, either. In high school I weighed 185 and I wasn't fat. I'm down to 170 now. I have this routine of five hundred abdominal exercises a day. I watch what I eat. I take vitamins. I'm going to bulk up again so I'm starting to lift weights. I need to get to 180, 185, but muscle, not flab."

There's plenty of muscle in Marsalis's music nowadays. His development into one of his generation's most distinctive and significant voices has come about because he has consistently sought out the next level of challenge. He switched from playing in rhythm-and-blues bands to jazz groups in his late teens, hooked up for brief stints with Lionel Hampton and Clark Terry, joined brother Wynton on the front line of Art Blakey's Jazz Messengers, became an integral part of Wynton's own ensemble for several years during the 1980s, and began his association with vocalist Sting in 1985. He's "Mr. Versatile," working as convincingly with Tina Turner, Dizzy Gillespie, and Public Enemy as on classical recordings or soundtracks for *Do the Right Thing* and *Mo' Better Blues.* He took his acting opportunities in the films *Throw Mama from the Train* and *School*

monic conceptions of mid-sixties Miles Davis and Wayne Shorter into a zone of abstract expressionism that's closer to John Coltrane's middle- and late-sixties modal explorations. Lyricism still remains high on the Marsalis agenda, propelled by a rich, fat, Ben Webster tone that shimmers with warmth. The reedman's own compositions flow as cleanly as his improvisations, and with a longtime supporting cast that includes pianist Kenny Kirkland, drummer Jeff Watts, and bassist Robert Hurst, he is developing a true ensemble sound that's slowly becoming as recognizable as some of the music's classic sounds of the past. He's already one of contemporary jazz's most influential hornmen and sees no reason not to continue making strides.

TASTY PLATTERS

• Branford Marsalis, *Crazy People Music* (Columbia)
• Branford Marsalis, *The Beautyful Ones Are Not Yet Born* (Columbia)
• Ed Thigpen, *Young Men and Olds* (Timeless)

Daze with a similar seriousness of purpose. "I want to be good at everything I do," he says.

In spite of the pop and movie exposure, Marsalis's jazz pedigree has provided him with perspective on his accomplishments. "I don't

think that I'm some big hotshot," he says. "No musician is ever larger than the music. Never has been and never will be. The music never pats you on the back when you're finished and tells you you've done a great job. The art of it is so much bigger and better than any of us that it's humbling at the same time."

Possibly because it is so humbling, Marsalis has thrown himself into the fray with a vengeance, becoming consistently bolder and more intense stylistically, especially since the late eighties. He has progressed beyond bebop and the har-

"With jazz musicians the logic is the thing that excites me, how they come to develop and what they develop," he explains. "The only limit one can have in music is your own imagination."

Marsalis shares the cooking with his wife, Teresa, in their Westchester County home, where the menu usually includes plenty of fish and vegetables.

"Halfhearted" will never be a word used to describe James Moody's approach to life. The reedman has made a career of throwing himself fully into every venture and making the moment count, onstage and off. He wouldn't be among the world's elite flute, alto, and tenor players if he hadn't.

His nutritional commitment is similarly unequivocal. He subscribes to the tenets found in the books *Fasting Can Save Your Life*, by Herbert Shelton, and *Where There Is Light*, by Paramahansa Yogananda, so much so that he carries them with him on the road. "Let's face it: all the food that people eat now is for the birds," Moody says. "Sugar and salt and white flour and white rice are poisons because they're all dead foods. Dead in that they have no nutritional value. They do nothing but deplete your body of whatever good is in it.

"Live food will keep you alive. Dead food will kill you. People are killing themselves with hamburgers, hot dogs, nachos. I was guilty of it too, because every once in a while I'd hit one of those things. But I've made up my mind to leave that stuff alone. Now I eat fresh fruit, fresh vegetables, brown rice, stir-fry with spinach, zucchini, mushrooms. All fresh."

Moody's diet today is a far cry from the food his mother cooked for him and his brother and sister. Born in Savannah, Georgia, in 1925, he was raised in Newark, New Jersey. "The main dishes were a pot of rice and a pot of beans," he recalls. "Navy beans. Lima beans. Black-eyed peas. On Sunday we'd have fried chicken and vegetables. We didn't have much meat because we didn't have the money. Now that I look back on it, we were better off for it."

The reedman's mother was a jazz fan who played records by the likes of Chick Webb, Jimmie Lunceford, and Maxine Sullivan. Moody absorbed it all. He set aside Saturday afternoons to listen to "The Make-Believe Ballroom," a radio show that featured big band jazz. As soon as he was old enough, he started frequenting Newark's Adams Theater. One show in particular left a lasting impression: the Count Basie Orchestra with tenor stars Don Byas and Buddy Tate. When his uncle Louis gave him a secondhand silver alto sax, he finally had a horn of his own. Jimmy Dorsey, Georgie Auld, Coleman Hawkins, and Lester Young became role models. "Then I heard Charlie Parker and Diz'," he remembers, "and I said, 'That's it.'"

Dizzy Gillespie would remain a thread connecting much of Moody's life. After a three-year stint in the air force, it was the trumpet legend who hired him; Moody's sixteen-bar tenor solo on "Emanon" with Gillespie's big band helped establish his reputa-

---

Vegetable Stir-Fry with Brown Rice

There are no "dead foods" in James and Linda Moody's Stir-Fry with Brown Rice. "Anytime you eat right," opines Moody, "it helps everything. Of course it helps your music because your brain and body work better. You're healthier."

Serves 2

3 cups water
1 cup brown rice, washed and drained
6 tablespoons sesame oil
1 tablespoon finely chopped garlic
Few drops of Braggs amino acid liquid (available in health food stores) or soy sauce

3 cloves garlic, finely chopped
3 scallions, chopped
1 bunch broccoli, florets only
1 zucchini, cut into ovals or cut into strips
10 mushrooms, thinly sliced
½ green bell pepper, cut into strips
½ red bell pepper, cut into strips
2 tablespoons cornstarch dissolved in a mixture of 1 cup chicken broth and 3 tablespoons Braggs amino acid liquid or soy sauce
5 leaves bok choy (Chinese cabbage), cut into 1-inch pieces

To prepare the rice, in a medium-sized saucepan, over high heat, combine the water, rice, 2 tablespoons of the sesame oil, 1 tablespoon garlic, and the drops of amino acid liquid (or soy sauce) and bring to a boil, stirring continuously. Reduce to a simmer, stir once, and cook, uncovered, until all of the liquid is absorbed, about 1½ hours. To stir-fry the vegetables, just before the rice is cooked, in a large skillet or a wok, over medium-high heat, warm the remaining oil. Add garlic and scallions and sauté for 15 seconds. Add the broccoli, zucchini, mushrooms, the bell peppers, and cornstarch mixture and cook, stirring, for 30 seconds. Add the bok choy and stir-fry for about 30 seconds, until leaves wilt; other vegetables will and should be al dente.

tion as a nimble-footed, hearty-toned player. He moved to Paris in 1949 to be with Uncle Louis, stayed several years, and returned to the States only after hearing that one of his songs, "I'm in the Mood for Love," had become a hit in America. Moody had recorded the ballad in Stockholm using a borrowed alto. Vocalist Eddie Jefferson subsequently put lyrics to it and retitled it "Moody's Mood for Love." When singer King Pleasure recorded it, the tune climbed the jazz and rhythm-and-blues charts. It has been the reedman's calling card ever since, a song he never fails to make sound fresh.

Back in the United States Moody began playing with a succession of vocalists, from Jefferson to Dinah Washington. He overcame an alcohol problem in the late fifties and rejoined Gillespie in 1963, this time for seven years.

Several aspects of the trumpeter's character have influenced Moody, not the least of which is Gillespie's musical depth. "His rhythm rubbed off, and his concept musically, the way he goes from one chord to another," Moody says. "What's important is how you get from one chord to the next chord to the next chord."

Moody himself seems to do it effortlessly. He's one of jazz's smoothest and most lyrical phrase-makers, capable of shifting into flinty, high-end explosions without jarring the swing in his songs. Oblique though his harmonies may at times be, his ideas are glued together with a passion and deep blues feel that never falter. He occasionally sings too, in a raspy voice that's as soulful as his instrumentals. Moody has elevated the flute from a jazz vehicle that's too often cloyingly sweet to one that's supple and emotionally powerful.

He's also one of jazz's most jocular showmen, another Gillespie-inspired trait. Moody is loose and witty onstage, tossing out offbeat, comic monologues between songs that belie the serious artistry that's to follow. He's a jazzman whose exuberant personality matches his playing perfectly.

A sense of humor surely helped him get through 6½ years in the pit at the Las Vegas Hilton, where he performed with everyone from Liberace to Elvis. His return to the jazz world in 1977 was greeted with celebration, as have been his recordings and appearances since then, with his own groups and configurations like Gillespie's United Nations Big Band.

In 1989, Moody moved to San Diego from Jersey City to marry Linda Petersen. Dizzy, naturally, was his best man. Since then one of the saxophonist's major adjust-

ments has been in his eating habits. He went on a twenty-one-day water-only fast in 1990, during a European tour with Gillespie's band, and is steadfast in maintaining a healthy diet.

"It makes me mad because grown people have been getting the wool pulled over their eyes about what they eat," he says. "Go to a supermarket and the smallest section is the produce. That's the only place people should be getting food from. Everything else is death."

London in the mid-1960s was the epicenter of the musical quake generated by the Beatles and the Rolling Stones, yet as with every cultural upheaval, its effects were felt more by some than by others. Saxophonist Ralph Moore was among those English natives who found themselves listening to the likes of Earl Bostic's "Temptation" and Erroll Garner's "Misty" as often as "Under My Thumb."

Moore's London-born mother was a professional tap dancer, his father an American air force officer.

Born in 1956, Moore was an only child raised in his early years by his mother, who introduced him to many of her friends in the entertainment world and exposed him to the jazz of Bostic, Garner, Louis Armstrong, Johnny Hodges, and others. "She was instrumental in getting me into the music," Moore points out. "She had me dancing for a minute, but once I started hanging out with the guys, that wasn't cool anymore. But whenever there was anything on the TV that had to do with music and show business, my mother

always had me front and center in front of the set. That was who she was, so that's who I became."

His mother bought him a trumpet at twelve and a tenor saxophone at thirteen. He soon realized, however, that playing weekend gigs in London pubs with his teacher might be as far as he could go in that city's relatively sluggish jazz scene, so when he turned fifteen he moved to Santa Monica, California, to join his father. Moore had little trouble adapting to the United States, quickly discovering that the sky was the limit musically. He hooked up with several Latin rock bands and a pair of junior college jazz ensembles and played everything from high school proms to weekend gigs in clubs up and down coastal Highway 101.

TASTY PLATTERS

- Ralph Moore, *Images* (Landmark)
- Ralph Moore, *Furthermore* (Landmark)
- J. J. Johnson, *Quintergy* (Antilles)

Unlike the music and the weather, the California diet took a bit of getting used to, an adjustment made smoother by the fact that Moore's father was just as fine a cook as his mother. Fresh produce became king, while wintertime British specialties like stews fell by the wayside. Moore also acquired a taste for barbecue during trips to Dot's Barbecue, his uncle Ray's restaurant in Los Angeles. All of this prepared the saxophonist for the further dietary fluctuations he would go through over the next several years. When he moved to Boston in 1975 to attend Berklee College of Music, he became a vegetarian. Soon after that, when he went on the road with pianist Horace Silver, he started eating meat again.

Moore's playing, meanwhile, continued on a steady, maturing path. Four years with Silver and stints with Roy Haynes, Dizzy Gillespie, J. J. Johnson, and Freddie Hubbard established him as a seasoned improviser steeped in hard bop, adept at ensemble interplay, and bursting with the adventurism of hero John Coltrane. His tenor sound moves between the classic, huge, oaken power of a Hank Mobley and the more silvery, slicing attack of a Joe Henderson. Moore's confidence comes out most clearly in his pacing: he rarely rushes an idea, sounding relaxed and unhurried on even the most frenetic boppers. On originals or underexposed bop-based gems, the saxophonist is intent on sounding different from anybody before him.

"I'm trying to play from my heart and not feel pressured," he says. "I don't feel that I should have to prove anything. That's not to say that I'm not trying to grow. I just want to be able to touch some people, make a decent living, play with some good players, keep learning, and play from my heart.

"I really want to create my own personal sound and perspective. If you have an individual style, there's no pressure to prove something or live up to something. You don't have to live up to somebody else's standards. Music is very trendy now, and in a lot of situations they want you

to sound like this or like that. If I can develop a sound and enough people like what I do, then I'm under no pressure to compete with people other than by being myself.

"I love Sonny Rollins and 'Trane, Hank Mobley and the whole forties, fifties, and sixties thing. That's what I came out of. I'm not ashamed of that at all. I'm one of the younger players out here, so no matter how much influence I have from 'Trane or others, I'm not going to be like

that. I'm going to be what I am. If you can just relax and be yourself, then you'll stay fresh. I don't have to prove that I'm fresh and young, and I don't have to be ashamed of the roots. I figure you can stretch only as far as your roots are buried."

Moore's touring and recording schedule doesn't leave much time for meal preparation, a job usually handled by his wife, Cheryl, who fits it in between her own career and her role as Moore's manager.

Bad Mama Jama Chile

While vegetarianism generally rules the Moore kitchen—with herbs straight out of their Brooklyn back-yard garden enhancing meals in the summer—the reedman decided to honor his family with Bad Mama Jama Chile. "This was passed down from my paternal grandmother who was from Texas," says Moore. "My father and uncle have been responsible for keeping it alive in the family. It was part of the menu at Dot's Barbecue."

A true original, this chile, unlike most Texas versions, uses beans. And possibly unlike any other chile recipe on record, the Bad Mama Jama rendition also calls for cactus and brewed coffee.

Serves 6 to 8

3 tablespoons olive oil
I clove garlic, minced
I green bell pepper, chopped
I medium onion, chopped
2 pounds lean ground beef
2 tablespoons chili powder
I tablespoon crushed red pepper
I teaspoon salt
½ teaspoon black pepper
I (15-ounce) can whole tomatoes
I cup water
I (2-ounce) can cactus (nopales), chopped (optional; available in Hispanic grocery stores or specialty food markets)
¼ cup brewed coffee
4 (15-ounce) cans pink or pinto beans

In a large skillet, over medium heat, warm the olive oil. Add the garlic and sauté, until soft. Add the green pepper and onion and sauté, until they just soften. Add the ground beef and brown, stirring often. Stir in the chili powder, crushed red pepper, salt and black pepper, adjusting the heat to avoid scorching the mixture. Stir in the tomatoes with their juice, breaking up the tomatoes as you add them. Stir in the water. Simmer over medium heat, uncovered, for ½ hour. Add the cactus (if using). Stir in the coffee. Reduce the heat to low and simmer another ½ hour. Remove the skillet from the heat and carefully pour the mixture into a large pot. Drain and add the beans and simmer over low heat, uncovered for 15 minutes. Remove from the heat, and allow the chile to sit for about ½ hour before serving. "BAD, BAD, BAD," says Moore.

With Chopin preludes, Brazilian pop star Roberto Carlos, and the Beatles sharing equal time on the turntable, it seemed natural that matzo balls, feijoada, and black beans would coexist on the stove in the São Paulo household where Ivo Perelman grew up. Born in 1961 of a Polish father and Russian mother who had settled in Brazil as children, the tenor saxophonist had little choice but to appreciate the world's cultural diversity at a young age. Traditional Jewish and Brazilian meals were the fare, a potpourri of international sounds, the music.

Perelman carries with him a similar desire to cross-pollinate his jazz. No South American reedman since Gato Barbieri mixes a flare for sweet melodies with fierce, American-influenced free blowing as powerfully as Perelman does. "I'd like to get the essence of black American jazz and the essence of Brazilian music and meld them," he says.

Unlike some musical fusions, there's nothing watered down about Perelman's union of these two distinct cultures. A disciple of the spiritually explosive jazz of John Coltrane, on occasion he even visits the late saxophonist's grave on Long Island to pay homage. Perelman's passion for carving out a jazz career for himself was so strong that he moved from Brazil to New York because he felt the music was not taken seriously enough in his native country. "Gilberto Gil and those people are wonderful, wonderful composers and singers," Perelman says. "But the instrumental tradition is not respected there. The instrumental is always in the background."

His mother, a pianist and music teacher, made sure that Perelman and his older sister were well versed in the classical repertoire. He was playing music by Bach and Brazilian composer Heitor Villa-Lobos by nine and at various times tried his hand at the violin, cello, trombone, and piano. He even took up the clarinet as a member of the São Paulo Dixieland Band before settling on tenor sax. By sixteen, Perelman had moved from progressive rock to heavy doses of Dexter Gordon, Sonny Rollins, Coltrane, and Brazilian alto saxophonist Victor Assis Brazil. "I would buy whatever I could put my hands on," he recalls. "It's hard to find jazz records in Brazil. You have to go to obscure places and really shop around."

TASTY PLATTERS
- Ivo Perelman, *Ivo* (K2B2)
- John Coltrane, *Ballads* (MCA/Impulse!)
- Tom Ze, *The Best of Tom Ze* (Luaka Bop/Warner Bros.)

In 1981 Perelman moved north to Boston. He attended Berklee College of Music briefly before heading on to Montreal and then Italy, where he played with Brazilian electric guitarist Irio de Paulo. America soon beckoned again, but not before Perelman, a devotee of the macrobiotic diet when he had arrived in Italy, was converted to the magnificently varied tastes of Italian cuisine. "I used to go to a club in Milano where the owner, right before and after you play, would treat you to a delicious dinner with wine and the whole works. You

would eat like a pig. It was such a heavy meal that I couldn't even play. It wasn't funny back then.

"When I left Brazil I was into natural, macrobiotic food, and I've been trying to keep that ever since. I eat a little white meat and fish, and I'll have a beer once in a while, but I'm very conscious of health food. If you start eating industrial food, I feel you really become more aggressive. You become greedy and always unsatisfied. You put your body out of balance. Eating light, you live lighter. If I'm more in balance with myself, I can reach deeper into myself and express myself in more satisfying, consistent, and meaningful ways."

Perelman's jazz indeed sounds like it emanates from deep in his soul. In the company of artists like Fred Hopkins, Flora Purim, and Mino Cinelu, he comes off as genuine whether he's splattering atonal ideas on a fragmented chordal canvas or waxing lyrical on a beautiful Brazilian children's song. When he was in Los Angeles for a time, he discovered that he didn't have much choice about his music. "I tried to be a commercial musician, but I wasn't successful," he says. "I don't have the attitude. I was called for a studio gig and it took me hours to play an eight-bar intro to a pop ballad in C, whereas any sax player would have done it in thirty minutes. From that day on I learned that it was definitely not my thing. The music I'm playing is the only thing I know how to play."

Perelman's macrobiotic diet includes soups like miso, brown rice with lentils, azuki beans, fish, salads, and fruits, but he often ventures from his Manhattan home to try a new restaurant.

Pato No Tucupi—
Amazonian Duck

Much as his background epitomizes the polyglot landscape of contemporary Brazil, Perelman's recipe for Pato No Tucupi, liberally translated to Amazonian Duck, is also a hybrid, created from a number of cultures.

Passed down in the family, Pato No Tucupi is at once Old World and New World, an Eastern European casserole swimming in tropical herbs. Although its original form calls for jambu, a herb indigenous to Brazil that is almost impossible to find in America, Perelman has devised an alternative, using cream of sorrel soup and spinach to approximate jambu's bitter, deep taste.

Serves 6

VINHA D'ALHO MARINADE
Juice of 1 lemon
¹/₂ cup red wine vinegar
¹/₂ cup olive oil
1 medium onion, finely chopped
1 to 2 cloves garlic, minced
¹/₄ cup finely chopped parsley
¹/₄ cup finely chopped cilantro
Salt and pepper

3 (4¹/₂- to 5¹/₂-pound) ducks,
  cut into quarters

TUCUPI
2 bunches jambu leaves and
  about 1 cup cassava root flour, or
  1 (12-ounce) can cream of sorrel
  soup and approximately 2 cups
  finely chopped spinach
4 to 5 tablespoons heavy cream

To prepare the marinade, in a large nonreactive bowl, combine the lemon juice, vinegar, olive oil, onion, garlic, parsley, cilantro, salt, and pepper. Add the duck quarters, turning to coat all sides. Cover and marinate in the refrigerator overnight.

To prepare the tucupi, cut off the stems from the jambu leaves and boil the leaves in 2 quarts of salted water, until the leaves are wilted, about 5 minutes. Remove the leaves from the water and set aside, reserving the water. Slowly add the cassava root flour to the water, stirring constantly, until the mixture reaches a paste-like consistency. (If you cannot find jambu in a tropical market or specialty store, combine the cream of sorrel soup with the spinach and just enough of the heavy cream to make a thick paste.)

When ready to cook, preheat the oven to 450°F. Remove the duck quarters from the marinade, slit the skin, and roast for 20 minutes, placing a pan under the duck to catch grease that will seep from the skin. Place the duck quarters in a casserole dish; add 2¹/₂

cups of water. (If using tucupi made with spinach, add two-thirds of the tucupi instead of the water.) Place the uncovered casserole in the oven and lower the oven temperature to 350°F. Cook for approximately 40 minutes, or until the duck is cooked through and tender. Add the tucupi made with jambu leaves during the last 10 minutes of cooking. (If using the tucupi made with spinach, every 15 minutes or so, add about 1 cup of the remaining tucupi until it is all used up or the duck is cooked through and tender, approximately 40 minutes.)

"This is one of those dishes where my mother and now my girlfriend don't measure, or even time the cooking," Perelman says. "It's done by look and taste. Just keep opening the oven, look at it, and take a small taste."

"I was just a blue-collar eater with blue-collar tastes," tenor saxophonist Houston Person admits about his dietary habits before he married his late wife, Doris. "She was wonderful. She would try everything, make me more worldly."

His twenty-seven years with Doris and his decades as an international performer have sensitized the reedman's palate well beyond anything he might have imagined when he was growing up in Florence, South Carolina.

Person's musical skills have acquired a similar fine edge. There was a time earlier in his career when Person's soulful, mountainous sound was considered by some

TASTY PLATTERS

- Houston Person, *The Talk of the Town* (Muse)
- Houston Person, *Why Not!* (Muse)
- Houston Person/Ron Carter, *Something in Common* (Muse)

a one-dimensional throwback to the rhythm-and-blues honkers, a style denigrated by some jazz purists as being as blue-collar as his youthful eating habits. The criticism was sadly misplaced. Without sacrificing an ounce of feeling, the saxophonist has become a master of melodic nuance, infusing bebop and the blues with an originality that keeps them vital and stirring.

"I like anything that swings," Person maintains. "I try to keep it simple and play things that an audience will relate to. I want a good sound, nice melodies, and

Catfish Stew

"This is an old recipe from my father," says Person. "It's one of the fish stews he used to make."

Houston Person, Sr., is modest indeed about his Catfish Stew. "It's just a simple, homemade thing," he says. "Nothing fancy."

Serves 4

Large piece of pork fatback
I large green bell pepper, chopped
I large onion, chopped
I large (29-ounce) can of
   tomato sauce
½ cup tomato juice
Hot sauce
Salt and pepper
Finely chopped hot peppers
1½ pounds catfish fillets, deboned
   and cut into bite-sized chunks

In a large pot, cook the fatback with the green pepper and onion, until the fatback is crisp and the peppers and onions begin to soften. Lower the heat and add the tomato sauce and the tomato juice. Season with the hot sauce, salt, pepper, and hot peppers. Cook under a slow simmer for about 10 minutes, stirring to thoroughly mix. Increase to a steady simmer, then add the catfish. It only takes about 5 minutes for the catfish to cook if the sauce is hot. Remove the fatback, and serve the stew over rice.

clarity. That's what I mean by keeping it simple."

Uncomplicated also describes Person's upbringing. Born in 1934, the saxophonist, along with his brother, Charles, was primarily preoccupied in his youth with sports. It was no great surprise, though, when football and basketball gave

way to music after Person graduated from Wilson High School. "My father sang in the choir and my mother played piano," he says. "I was in the church and school choirs. We had a wide range of music in the house. We had to listen to the "Metropolitan Opera Hour" every Saturday—that was required. On Sunday we'd be in church singing. Florence was a small town. But we had a nice bebop band and a lot of gospel quartets and good radio out of Charleston. I had a nice childhood. No clubs, just the annual dance and prom. Just a small town."

There was also plenty of fresh fish on the Person dinner table, although the saxophonist rarely had anything to do with putting it there. "I hate fishing," he laughs. "I just want to eat it. We grew up near Myrtle Beach, about sixty miles away. We had rivers and lakes. Real outdoors. My mother did most of the cooking. She was a wonderful cook. My father took the fish duty. He's a great cook."

Person gained admittance to the school band at South Carolina State College and joined the air force from there. During his three years in the service, much of it based in Germany, he developed as a player both in the air force band and on informal weekend gigs with the likes of Cedar Walton and Eddie Harris, army band members who were stationed nearby. Upon his return to the States, he went to the Hartt College of Music in Hartford for three years, then joined Johnny "Hammond" Smith's band for a two-year stint. In the late sixties he set out on his own and began a series of high-level collaborations that continue to this day, including one with vocalist Etta Jones that spans more than two decades.

Person's goal, keeping it simple, is far easier said than done. The fact that his probing, funky strolls seem as effortless as a Magic Johnson between-the-legs pass is testament to his talents as an improviser and student of the jazz tradition.

His inspiration for lyrical invention includes tenor behemoths like Coleman Hawkins, Earl Bostic, and Gene Ammons, but the stout, opulent sound that he puts out is all his own. In recent years he has found an additional way to impart his wisdom and experience—as a record producer.

Since his wife passed away, the tenor player, who lives in Newark, New Jersey, has been treated regularly to the cooking of his daughters. "I've been eating too well," he laughs. "I have to start losing weight. And I play Scrabble, Chinese checkers, canasta, all sit-down games. I'm going to take up golf."

FLIP · PHILLIPS

Even though he has been a Floridian since 1957, Flip Phillips's palate still seems to reside in Brooklyn—the Italian section circa 1930 near the old Brooklyn Paramount Theater. At least once a week, Phillips, born Joseph Edward Filipelli in 1915, treats himself to the *pasta fagiola* that his mother prepared for him as a small boy.

Her cooking would ultimately affect his life in more ways than she could have imagined. When he played at New York restaurant clubs in the 1930s, he often declined the meals offered to him after the gig and instead headed back to Mrs. Filipelli's kitchen. Her culinary prowess later inspired him to put together his own creations on the road as a member of Woody Herman's first Herd and the "Jazz at the Philharmonic" touring troupe.

"I worked in Schneider's Lobster House in Brooklyn in 1934," he recalls. "It had the band and a dining room. It was a good restaurant. But I did most of my eating at home. I couldn't beat that. The best food was at the house.

"The first band I ever traveled with was Woody Herman's. I never really wanted to go out of town at that time. After that, with the 'Jazz at the Philharmonic,' we went all over the world. Then I had to eat in restaurants. But sometimes I used to get an efficiency that had a kitchen and I would cook for myself—which was better than all the restaurants. A lot of guys used to come by, Bill Harris, Cole-

TASTY PLATTERS

- **Flip Phillips, *A Real Swinger*** (Concord Jazz)
- **Flip Phillips/Scott Hamilton, *A Sound Investment*** (Concord Jazz)
- **Woody Herman, *The Thundering Herds, 1945–1947*** (Columbia Jazz Masterpieces)

man Hawkins. They'd rather eat at my place than go to restaurants. I'd cook macaroni, *pasta fagiola*, peppers and sausages, and steak.

"Cooking is like playing music.

You put the right changes in your solo, it sounds good. You put the right changes in your cooking, put the right ingredients in, it comes out good."

Phillips has been putting the right changes into both arts for years. He starred in Herman's Herd from 1944 to 1946 and later brought down houses for eleven years in "Jazz at the Philharmonic" tenor battles with fellow sax powerhouses like Illinois Jacquet. His rendition of "Perdido" was a command performance at most shows. Phillips also plays bass clarinet, but it's his tenor sax playing that best defines his jaunty approach to the music. His warm-toned, swaggering tenor on burners or ballads captured the excitement of swing for an entire generation in the forties and fifties. Hearing him live or on a recording now, it's easy to imagine his onstage peers exhorting him to "blow, baby, blow" during one of his patented furious solos. That combination of stomp and creamy smoothness has prompted Scott Hamilton, a much younger saxophonist with a love for the swing tradition, to perform and record with Phillips in recent years. Phillips recalls the first time he heard an eighteen-year-old Hamilton at the old Sandy's Jazz Revival, a club north of Boston.

"The night before that there was another tenor man there," he remembers. "I wanted to choke him. He was screeching all over the place. The next night I heard Scotty. When he came off the stand I just grabbed him and hugged him! I said, 'That's the way to play the tenor.' You can only play so many notes. Young fellas coming up are playing different horns. They're sounding like cats and dogs. The way the tenor should sound is the way we play it, not getting funny howls out of it. Tenor's a beautiful instrument."

Phillips's philosophy about playing is the same now as it was nearly sixty years ago, when he was working hard to get the dinner crowd excited at Schneider's:

"If you wanna make a dollar, you gotta make the people holler." While he still gigs occasionally with players like Hamilton and pianist Dave McKenna, these days Phillips is mostly content to enjoy the laid-back Florida life. "I just take the jobs that make me comfortable," he says. "Otherwise I'll play golf."

Pasta Fagiola

"Once a week," says Phillips, "I have Pasta Fagiola. Maybe a couple of times a week. My wife makes it, too. I showed her."

Serves 2

- 2 tablespoons olive oil
- 1 medium onion, chopped
- 2 cloves garlic, chopped
- 1 small (12-ounce) can tomato sauce
- 2 (19-ounce) cans cannellini beans
- ½ teaspoon each salt, black pepper, and red pepper
- ¼ teaspoon each oregano, basil, and parsley flakes
- 1 tablespoon grated Parmesan cheese
- 8 ounces elbow macaroni

In a medium-sized skillet, over medium heat, warm the olive oil. Add the onion and garlic and sauté, until soft. Add the tomato sauce and cannellini beans. Stir in 2 cans of water measured in one of the bean cans. Add the salt, black and red peppers, oregano, basil, parsley flakes, and Parmesan and simmer while preparing and cooking the macaroni. Prepare the macaroni according to the package directions for al dente. Drain and add the macaroni to the bean mixture. Simmer for 5 minutes, stir well, and serve.

COURTNEY · PINE

For British saxophonist Courtney Pine, celebrating his parents' West Indian roots spills over from the stage into the kitchen. Not only does his jazz embrace the free-spirited feel of the reggae, ska, and calypso that he heard on the stereo when he was growing up, his cooking now leans toward the Caribbean meals he rejected at a younger age in favor of fish and chips and burgers.

"At the age of ten I learned how to pretend to vomit," he recalls about his ploy to avoid the dishes he grew up with. "What we ate was pea soup on Saturday, really thick with yams and green bananas, and on Sunday rice and pigeon peas with chicken. For quite a while I wasn't eating home food. Then, when I left school at sixteen or seventeen, I got involved with reggae bands, and the food I ate then seemed to be much more me." That fare turned out to be fairly close to the meals that he'd found so awful a few years earlier. Even-tually, he developed a taste for Jamaican cooking. "The food is very starch-based and filling," he points out. "And for me as a player, it's strengthening."

Pine's mother and father met in England after moving separately from their native Jamaica in the late 1950s, a time when the British government offered civil service jobs as an incentive for would-be émigrés. Besides the recipes for West Indian dishes, his parents also brought along a love of their native music.

For young Pine, this led to his taking up the recorder at eight and the clarinet at thirteen. He listened especially intently to the instrumental, sax-laced B sides of the Skatalites, Bob Marley, Peter Tosh,

and Desmond Dekker singles his parents would play, and particularly to the work of Jamaican saxophonist Tommy McCook. This was, in fact, his first exposure to jazz.

Pine dropped out of London's Kingsbury High School to travel with reggae and funk bands and eventually found himself drifting toward jazz. "It happened by chance," he says. "At fourteen or fifteen, I saw a program on TV with Grover Washington, Jr., and the announcer said, 'This is jazz fusion.' I wanted to know more about the music so I went to a record library but couldn't find any records by anybody that I knew. So I just picked out the ones with the best album covers. One of them was Sonny Rollins's *Way Out West* and I started from there."

That cover—of Rollins sporting a gun belt, a Stetson, and a tenor under his arm—and the music inside made an impression on Pine that's still evident in his own music. Traces of the earthquaking grit of Rollins as well as the soaring ethereal modality of John Coltrane lie

within the intense sonic torrents and turbulent rhythms that Pine often unleashes on tenor and even more stirringly these days, on soprano. His playing on both his own originals and songs like "Giant Steps" and "Take the Coltrane" is unapologetically derivative, an approach that has left him open to charges of slavish imitation. Yet the combination of Pine's raw virtuosic urgency and subtle West Indian–rooted rhythmic colorations adds up to an artist who is slowly but steadily shaping an individual concept of jazz.

Pine is England's most acclaimed player since Joe Harriott, George Shearing, and Marian McPartland, but unlike the latter two piano greats, who emigrated to the United States, Pine has stayed home and is making a musical and personal commitment to England. He formed the Abibi Jazz Arts, an organization dedicated to promoting black music and culture, from which sprang the Jazz Warriors, a big band of which Pine is also a member. "I'm trying to make my music out of my heritage," he explains. "I play jazz because it's the only music that can embrace all the different elements in music without taking from it."

When he has the time, Pine relaxes by swimming, playing a few games of badminton, or toying with his computer. But due to the demands put on him as a British jazz star, he finds that time can be tight. "I was asking people, 'When are they going to invent a pill that you can take so you don't have to waste time sitting down and eating?'" The saxophonist never found that pill and discovered instead that he actually enjoys

Banana Fritters

It's from Jamaica—specifically, from Pine's sister—that we get his recipe for Banana Fritters, a very versatile dish. "It can be a breakfast food served with eggs, or at dinner, a great side dish to anything Caribbean."

Serves 6 as a side dish

1½ cups all-purpose flour
½ cup self-rising flour
Few pinches of cinnamon (optional)
Two pinches freshly ground black pepper
Pinch of salt
2 large yellow bananas
Vegetable oil

On a large piece of waxed paper or a plate, combine the all-purpose and self-rising flours, cinnamon (if using), pepper, and salt. Cut the bananas lengthwise into thin strips (the thinner the better) and coat the banana strips with the flour mixture. In a skillet (preferably cast iron) large enough to hold the banana strips without crowding, heat up enough oil to reach about ¼ inch up the sides of the skillet. When the oil is hot, but not smoking, add the bananas and fry until the bottom side is golden brown, then flip and cook on other side until golden brown. Drain on paper towels and serve, or keep warm in the oven for no more than 15 minutes.

cooking. He has even taken to handling most of the meals at the home he shares with his fiancée, June Guishard. "She's a psychologist, so she comes home from work kind of late," Pine says. "I'm usually home practicing, so I'll just have something waiting for her when she comes in."

If you've ever heard the world's greatest living tenor saxophonist, Sonny Rollins, tear off one of his monumental, indefatigable solos, it comes as no surprise that he's extremely circumspect about how he treats his body. In no other player is the link between physical and musical power as complete as it is in Rollins. His inspiration emanates from his heart, mind, and soul, but the robust, thunder-deep Rollins sound flows from a sheer physicality that the saxophonist keeps honed through diet, meditation, and exercise.

Rollins is able to maintain the balance between a demanding performance schedule and a regular regimen that keeps him fit by spending as much time as possible at the ten-acre farm he shares with his wife/manager, Lucille, in the Hudson Valley north of Woodstock, New York. His daily routine includes practicing in his studio for several hours, riding a stationary

bicycle, yoga, and keeping to a diet that's light on salt and red meat and heavy on fish, poultry, fresh fruits, and vegetables. After years of lifting weights, he now works out only occasionally with dumbbells.

As whole as Rollins's personal and musical life is today, the road he has traveled to make it that way has been long and twisting.

Born in 1930 in Harlem, Theodore Walter Rollins was the youngest of three children. Both his older brother and sister took to music

early; Rollins himself loved baseball and illustration. He earned the nickname Newk by being an avid fan of Brooklyn Dodger pitcher

TASTY PLATTERS
- **Sonny Rollins, *Tenor Madness* (Fantasy/OJC)**
- **Sonny Rollins, *G-Man* (Milestone)**
- ***The Best of Sonny Rollins* (Blue Note)**

Don Newcombe. Since his parents came from the Virgin Islands, the meals his mother cooked were Caribbean-based. "I didn't like a lot of the food," Rollins recalls. "I didn't like rice, which my family ate a lot of. I didn't eat what everybody else ate. I loved spinach and white potatoes mashed together. My mother really had to cook special for me."

When his older siblings were in classes, the preschool Rollins spent a great deal of time at home with his grandmother and uncle. These circumstances turned out to be

propitious, as it was through his relatives that he was exposed early on to disparate musical influences.

"I heard a lot of gospel music," he recalls. "My grandmother used to take me to Mother Horn's church, a very popular spiritual church. My uncle used to go with a girl from Georgia who would play all these Deep South blues records for me. My mother would take me to Caribbean dances. And, of course, growing up in Harlem, that was *the* place during that period of time. So I had a beautiful education."

Rollins also became enamored of the rhythm and blues of Louis Jordan and his Tympany Five. The bandleader often performed at a club right across from Rollins's school, PS 89 on 135th Street and Lenox Avenue. That the neighborhood was populated by future jazzmen like Jackie McLean, Art Taylor, and Kenny Drew didn't hurt his education one bit either. At night Rollins would even linger in front of the apartment house of one of his heroes, Coleman Hawkins, until the tenor saxophonist returned from gigs. Although he didn't take up the horn until he was seventeen, Rollins was soon good enough to rehearse with Thelonious Monk after classes at Benjamin Franklin High School. By 1950 he had recorded with Bud Powell, Fats Navarro, and J. J. Johnson.

Then came the first of a number

Lucille and Sonny's Vegetable Stew

"I've been eating like this for a long time, since the 1960s I would say," says Rollins. *"I'm into a regimen of good eating and a good practice of yoga and all that stuff."*

At their farm, Lucille handles most of the cooking. *"I don't really cook anything, except when I'm in the city by myself and have to cook something,"* the saxophonist admits.

Says Lucille: *"He eats mostly vegetables with maybe some chicken breast or fish. We're not 'normal people' in that we don't really sit down and eat meals. You could say I make a lot of vegetable stew."*

Makes a big pot

5 to 6 carrots, cut into bite-sized
   pieces
3 potatoes, cut into bite-sized pieces
2 to 3 bell peppers, sliced

2 to 3 summer squash or zucchini,
   trimmed and cut diagonally
   into ovals
2 leeks, washed well and trimmed
Seasonings such as oregano, thyme,
   and basil (but no salt)
1 whole chicken breast, or 1 pound
   thick cod fillet (optional)
Vegetable stock or water

Preheat the oven to 300°F. In an oven-proof pot large enough to hold everything, combine all of the vegetables along with the seasonings. Add the chicken, or fish (if using). Put in about 2 to 3 cups vegetable stock (or water) so that the stew doesn't stick. Cover and cook for about 1½ hours. Check the level of liquid every once in a while, adding more stock (or water) if the stew looks too dry. **"When it's done, turn the oven off, and when you want it, you can have it,"** the saxophonist's wife says.

---

of disappearances and resurfacings. Rollins battled a drug problem for several years in the early 1950s. When he finally licked it in 1955, he moved to Chicago briefly.

"I had to go through a period of really getting myself back together in order to come back on the music scene and be strong enough to face all the temptations," he says. "During that period I actually lived on tomato juice. I used to get cases of it. I was living at the YMCA and I ate there at times, but there was a lot of tomato juice."

Rollins did come back strong. He spent nearly two years with the seminal Max Roach/Clifford Brown Quintet, returned to New York, and turned out some of his most timeless recordings, like *Worktime, Saxophone Colossus,* and

Freedom Suite. By 1959, however, he again needed to take stock of his life and music. He spent much of a two-year sabbatical practicing alone at night on the pedestrian level of the Williamsburg Bridge between Manhattan and Brooklyn. He recorded his classic album *The Bridge* in 1961.

Another fertile period followed, highlighted by work with Ornette Coleman and alumni Don Cherry and Billy Higgins and the soundtrack recording for *Alfie.* He also began to get into Eastern philosophy and macrobiotic eating. "It all came together," he says. "Proper eating and proper behavior, proper exercise and proper living."

In 1967 he dropped out of sight again, this time putting down his horn completely, traveling to Japan

and India, and studying hatha-yoga, Zen Buddhism, and Vedanta. By the time he was back on the music scene full-time, in the early 1970s, he had only added to his legend and potency.

Rollins is one of jazz's deepest, most exhilarating, and most emotional improvisers. No one comes close to him rhythmically. He infuses bebop, calypso, romantic ballads, the blues, show tunes, and free blowing with conviction and authority. His bold, propulsive forays are breathtaking in their range and might, employing modal harmonies and slightly bent, swing-based melodies with equal command. When he sets off on a lengthy solo, as he does often in concert, he takes the listener on a chorus-after-chorus ride that might start from the delicate, then barrel into the incendiary, and land on a billowing cushion. It's impossible to know where Rollins will take you, but there's never a question that it was worth the trip.

"I just try to improve my work and keep up," he says. "I don't want to go back. My work changes according to the music I hear, the people I meet, life. I'm still searching to make myself better, so that sort of consumes my whole effort. I'm still searching for the perfect way of expressing myself."

Rollins eats cheese, plenty of fruit, like papaya, mangoes, and apples, and up to a loaf a day of wheat bread made with organically grown grains but without butter, eggs, or honey. "The direct line between my diet and my music I can't draw, but I know it makes me feel better about myself and enables me to be reasonably healthy," he says. "So at least indirectly it helps my music."

The résumé of baritone saxophonist Gary Smulyan takes an interesting detour from 1985 to 1987. Nestled between stints with Woody Herman, Mel Lewis, and the Philip Morris Superband sit these lines:

EDUCATION: The New York Restaurant School
EXPERIENCE: Café Evergreen, Pearl River, New York.

Smulyan, a bebop-influenced stylist whose buffed, sonorous sound becomes more distinctive with each passing year, essentially dropped out of the music scene to devote himself full-time to cooking in a French restaurant. It was an

TASTY PLATTERS

• The Mel Lewis Sextet, *The Lost Art* (Music Masters)
• The Mel Lewis Jazz Orchestra, *To You— A Tribute to Mel Lewis* (Music Masters)
• Pepper Adams, *Mean What You Say* (Fantasy/OJC)

experience that helped him gain an important perspective on the direction he wanted his life to take.

"The whole idea behind it was just to augment music with cooking so I could eliminate some of the dumb gigs I was playing—weddings, bar mitzvahs. Not high-quality music at all. I figured I would do something that was pretty creative. And cooking is very artistic. But eventually it just took over. To really succeed as a restaurateur or a chef, you have to

have as much devotion as a musician, if not more. I was working cold station, *garde-manger*. I was doing the salads and desserts, but also working the line, doing sauté and broil work. I would help out when the sous-chef wasn't available. I was working long hours, and I got very far away from my horn and playing. I wasn't practicing. I wasn't

writing. I wasn't really doing much of anything.

"Actually, it was the best thing I could have done because it gave me a fresh philosophy and a new appreciation of what being an artist is. As an artist you're really forced to create your own work and you

have to do a lot more inner evolving than you would otherwise. I gained a whole new appreciation of that, and I think my playing really got stronger as a result. My commitment to music certainly did."

Smulyan's cooking is now confined to preparing meals for the family, a job he shares with his wife. Judging from an increasingly full musical plate, he made the right decision choosing the Village Vanguard over the Café Evergreen. Besides performing and recording work, Smulyan maintains a busy teaching schedule; he has conducted clinics in locales as far-flung as Moscow, Cairo, and Manila.

Born in 1956 and raised in the town of Wantagh on Long Island, Smulyan was absorbed only in rock and roll until just before junior high school. And then he heard Fats Waller on the radio. "It just threw me for a loop," he recalls. "I never heard anything like that in my life. I tried to explore it as much as I could. At that time Ed Beach had a great jazz show on WRVR radio, and I would listen to it every night. My parents were amazing. When I started to be interested in becoming a jazz musician, they would take me to clubs so I could sit in. And support hasn't stopped. They're wonderful."

Smulyan got a chance to join Lee Konitz, Jimmy Knepper, and Chet

Baker in the jazz clubs near his home and by 1978 was confident enough of his abilities to drop out of school and switch from alto to baritone to fill a seat in Woody Herman's big band, a job he kept for two years. A long-running Monday night gig with drummer Mel Lewis at the Village Vanguard followed, as did more work with Konitz. Lewis remains an especially important influence on Smulyan's approach to music.

"Mel was the most honest person I ever met in my life," he says. "He was very strong in his convictions, and that's a pretty honorable way to live your life. And he was very open musically. He was always growing musically, never happy to stay where he was."

Smulyan strives to master another Lewis trait, individuality. "I'm trying to get my personality into my playing, to have a recognizable and distinguishable voice. It's not easy, but it's certainly the pinnacle you can reach. I'm trying to be as honest as I can through my music and, hopefully, touch people through that honesty."

Although his baritone playing has been deeply affected by the gruff, deep-bottomed sound of Pepper Adams, Smulyan stands apart as an improviser who is establishing a unique style of his own. On his baritone sax—and bass clarinet too—he fluidly adapts to lightning changes within the bop, Latin, and free jazz idioms, all the while maintaining a firm, flowing, swinging core. In critics' and fans' polls, he is recognized as one of his instrument's surest-handed and most inventive artists. His current inclusion in the Mingus Big Band attests even further to his talents.

Zarzuela de Mariscos—Catalonian Fish Stew

Consistent with his culinary background, Smulyan's kitchen simplicity is imaginative, with heavy emphasis on fresh fish, vegetables, and pasta. The last two form the basis of Zarzuela de Mariscos, the classic Iberian fish stew that Smulyan discovered in 1985.

"I was touring Europe with Mel Lewis and we were in Barcelona," he says. "Everything was delicious. I found Catalonian food to be really amazing. One night I ate this wonderful dish in a Barcelona restaurant, and the chef was generous enough to share his recipe with me." Serve with crusty slices of bread rubbed with garlic, and a dry white wine.

Serves 4 to 6

¼ cup olive oil, preferably Spanish
2 red or yellow bell peppers, chopped
2 medium-sized yellow onions, finely chopped
4 cloves garlic, minced
⅓ pound Serrano ham or prosciutto, chopped
1 cup dry white wine
2 pounds tomatoes, peeled, seeded, and chopped
½ cup almonds, blanched, skinned, and ground with either a mortar and pestle or in a blender or food processor
2 bay leaves
1 teaspoon saffron threads
Salt and pepper

Approximately 2½ cups water
Juice of 1 lemon
12 littleneck clams, scrubbed
12 mussels, scrubbed and debearded
1 (1½ pound) lobster, split, cleaned, and cut into bite-sized chunks
1 pound medium shrimp, shelled and deveined
½ pound bay scallops or halved sea scallops
Minced parsley

In a cast-iron kettle or large casserole fit with a tight-fitting lid, over medium heat, warm the olive oil. Add the peppers and sauté for 3 minutes, or until they begin to soften. Add the onions and garlic. Sauté the mixture until all of the components are soft but not brown. Add the ham (or prosciutto) and cook for 2 more minutes. Add the wine, bring to a boil, lower to a simmer, and cook until the wine is reduced by half. Add the tomatoes, ground almonds, bay leaves, saffron, salt, and pepper. Return to a boil, reduce the heat to a simmer, and cook until the liquid is reduced in half. Add the water slowly, stopping when the thickness reaches the consistency of clam chowder. Add the lemon juice and stir vigorously. Add the clams and mussels, cover, and cook for 3 to 5 minutes, until the shells begin to open, discarding any mussels or clams that do not open. Add the lobster, shrimp, and scallops and cook for another 3 to 5 minutes, until the lobster is cooked through. Discard the bay leaves. Garnish with the parsley, and serve.

Saxophonist John Stubble-field is truly a product of his environment. His brawny tenor playing drips with the swaggering southern soul made famous by Mississippi-born Lester Young and "Texas tenors" Arnett Cobb and Buddy Tate. The Arkansas native can improvise on a hard-driving, structured blues as convincingly as on a jagged free-blowing jam. He's equally comfort-able playing with a bebopper like Nat Adderley or within the more ethereal ensemble magic conjured up by Abdullah Ibrahim.

Southern soul food prepared by his mother was the staple of the Stubblefield household, when he was growing up in Little Rock. While the saxophonist has since cut back on much of the heft and most of the meat from that diet, his Arkansian palate holds sway as he proclaims, "I'm a connoisseur of the best ribs in the world."

After studying piano for four years, playing in the school band, and absorbing the church music that his parents exposed him to, Stubblefield landed his first profes-sional gig at fifteen. "I grew up in show business on Ninth Street in Little Rock," says Stubblefield, who was born in 1945. "Ninth Street was to Little Rock what Fifty-second Street was to New York. Duke Ellington's band, Count Basie's, Andy Kirk and the Clouds of Joy, and all the territory bands played Ninth Street. When I started there, they still had groups like B. B. King and Bobby "Blue" Bland. I was in the house band at the Flamingo Club, the largest club in Little Rock. I played with Hank Crawford, Jackie Wilson. There were at least ten clubs on Ninth Street. The Eldorado, Jim's Place, Chez Paris. I was current there till about 1963."

The first recording Stubblefield ever appeared on was with a rhythm-and-blues group named York Wilborn and the Thrillers on Stax Records in 1962. He went on to tour with soul singer O. V. Wright for several years and worked with Junior Parker, Solomon Burke, and Ike and Tina Turner. He was also deep into jazz at an early age, pick-ing up tips from fellow Little Rock native Pharoah Sanders, then a clarinetist, and later from tenor saxophonist Don Byas, who mar-ried into a family that was close to Stubblefield. During this entire period, of course, he was partaking of his favorite cuisine.

Sweet Potato Pie

Tapping into the archives of the Soul Food Hall of Fame, Stubblefield goes back to his pre-lowfat days with his mother's rendition of Sweet Potato Pie. Unlike the more usual version that calls for one cup of evaporated milk and only a half cup of sugar, Mrs. Stubblefield opts for a sweeter filling that uses a half cup of sweetened condensed milk and one cup of sugar.

Serves 8 to 10

- 1/2 cup (1 stick) butter, softened
- 1 cup sugar
- 2 large eggs
- 1 tablespoon vanilla
- 1 teaspoon nutmeg
- 1 teaspoon cinnamon
- 1/2 teaspoon salt
- 4 to 5 large yams, peeled, boiled, and mashed (to yield 2 cups mashed yams)
- 1/2 cup sweetened condensed milk
- 10-inch pre-baked flaky pie crust, chilled

Preheat the oven to 350°F. In a large bowl, cream together the butter and sugar, then add the eggs and mix well. Blend in the vanilla, nutmeg, cinnamon, and salt. Add the mashed yams and milk and mix well. Lightly prick the pie shell, then pour the pie filling into it. Bake for 30 to 40 minutes, until a knife inserted into the middle of the pie comes out clean.

"I was eating a whole lot of soul food," he recalls. "We'd get off work and go get some. The soul food joints on Ninth Street, oh yeah, they were something. Ribs and sweet potatoes and greens, that kind of stuff. But I never ate a chitterling. I don't even know what a chitterling tastes like."

Stubblefield moved to Chicago in 1966 and stayed until 1971, playing with the progressive musical lights of the Association for the Advancement of Creative Musicians and honing skills that would earn him a spot in Charles Mingus's band after he moved to New York in the early seventies. He also hooked up with pianist Mary Lou Williams around this time, a collaboration that had nutritional ramifications as well as musical. "I would go to Mary Lou Williams's home and she would cook greens for me," he says. "We would share recipes for cooking greens. For weight reasons I tried to become a vegetarian. I had to discard steaks and ribs around that time."

The meatless diet lasted until 1976, when he started touring with trumpet player and cornetist Nat Adderley, brother of saxophonist Cannonball and a native Floridian. Adderley loved dishes like barbecued alligator. "There was a lady in San Francisco who would always cook for Nat's and Cannonball's bands," Stubblefield recalls. "We had all kinds of food, health food, soul food, gourmet. She would *cook* for the band! Once I broke Cannonball's record for the number of courses eaten. He was always good for three and once he had four. I downed five courses in one day. And I was really thin."

New York has been home for Stubblefield since 1978. He has led and accompanied many of modern jazz's finest improvisers: McCoy Tyner, Freddie Hubbard, Hamiet Bluiett, Mulgrew Miller, and George Russell. "The reason for my eclectic approach has been because I started playing all types of music all at one time," he explains. "It has taken years to find my voice because so many great

TASTY PLATTERS

- John Stubblefield, *Bushman Song* (Enja)
- Louis Hayes, *The Crawl* (Candid)
- Ben Webster/Don Byas, *Ben Webster Meets Don Byas* (Verve/MPS)

people have influenced me. That's what I'm doing now, playing my voice and my spirit by using the training and experience I've had in all walks of American music."

Stubblefield is consistent in his diet now. Although he'll treat himself to an occasional plate of ribs, he basically eats lightly. Sushi is a particular favorite. "At my age I have to eat very light, to stay in my clothes, to keep my body a certain way, and to be strong enough to breathe as I breathe when I play—I do a lot of circular breathing. I have to watch out for food that's high in cholesterol."

Experiences as eye-opening as the ones Stanley Turrentine absorbed as a teenager during the early 1950s fade from memory very slowly. Even subsequent decades of success for the Pittsburgh-born tenor saxophonist have done little to dull the intensity of his ear-liest tours of the South with Lowell Fulsom and Ray Charles.

"When I first went on the road we couldn't stay in hotels," Turrentine recalls. "And we had to order from the back of the restaurant. We didn't have a menu. We didn't have a selection. They'd say, 'If you want something to eat, this is it.' And we paid for it.

"Racism and segregation were everywhere. A lot of times our lives were in jeopardy because we wanted to play music. We used to play in tobacco warehouses and they would have a rope separating the floors. They'd have whites dancing on one side and blacks dancing on the other side. I'm sixteen, seventeen years old and I'm looking at this crazy stuff.

I'd never run into anything quite so bizarre as this racism. Sometimes we'd go through a town where there was nothing to eat, and we had to get on a bandstand and play like we had a seven-course meal.

"Even at that, there was a camaraderie that we had then. It was a necessity for us to survive. Basically the music always came first. Everybody just helped one another."

Turrentine grew up in an environment where lending a hand was second nature, especially when it came to music. Born in 1934 and raised in the Pittsburgh ghetto, as a child he heard both gospel music and jazz. His grandmother exposed him to gospel at her Baptist church. Many nights he fell asleep hearing the music from the church right next to his house. His mother was a pianist. His father played saxophone and clarinet with the Savoy Sultans. His older brother Tommy, Jr., was a trumpeter. "After dinner, our form of entertainment was to sit around and listen to the big bands on the radio," he remembers. "Basie. Tommy Dorsey. And we'd discuss who was playing what."

Home was on La Place Street, later made famous to the jazz public as the title of a Turrentine album. The neighborhood was filled with friends who wanted to hear the latest jazz as badly as the reedman did. "We'd exchange records because we didn't have any money to go to concerts," he says. "If we did go, we'd usually sneak in. But it was a really nice atmosphere growing up. I felt a lot of love."

Baked Chicken

Turrentine's hot-plate days are a memory, in more ways than one. "I'm on a diet, man," he explains. "I can't eat any greasy foods, salt, and all that stuff. Barbecue, greens, and chitterlings, I know I can't eat that."

Judith is his dietary warden. "She's a great cook," he says. "She usually travels with me. This dish fits with the diet, just vegetable oil. And it's baked. Judith stays on top of my diet. Of course, I sneak out and put a little salt on some things."

Serves 4

One whole (4- to 4½-pound) chicken, quartered
Thyme, garlic powder, lemon pepper, and paprika

½ cup vegetable oil
Approximately ¾ cup Wish-Bone bottled Italian dressing

Preheat the oven to 325°F. Clean the chicken thoroughly and dry with paper towels. Season the chicken with the thyme, garlic powder, lemon pepper, and paprika, and place in a roasting pan. Pour the vegetable oil and dressing over the chicken, turning each piece to coat evenly on all sides. (Use enough dressing to cover the bottom of the roasting pan as well.) Cook the chicken, skin-side up, until the skin is browned, about 30 minutes, then turn the pieces and continue to cook for an additional 30 minutes, or until the other side is well browned.

Pittsburgh was alive with jazz clubs and concerts during that era. The city's Musician's Club was *the* spot for local and visiting players, like Charlie Parker and Illinois Jacquet, to hang out and jam.

"The secretary of the union, an alto player by the name of Leroy

Brown, used to sneak me in as long as I didn't make any noise," Turrentine recollects. "I was fourteen, fifteen. They served barbecue and their chile was great. My first time there I saw Art Tatum. It was just amazing. I'll never forget it. There was an old upright piano at the club and I saw him reach on top of it for a beer while he was playing. I said, 'How many hands does this man have?'"

The myriad musics in Turrentine's life remain an integral part of his playing: the gospel from childhood, the blues from Fulsom, loose-limbed rhythm and blues from Earl Bostic's band, complex bebop from Max Roach, soulful funk from the eleven years spent with organist and former wife Shirley Scott. Whether on joy-ful stompers or the likes of "Mood Indigo," Turrentine's big tenor sound is jaunty, laced with rhythmic grooves, and steeped in the blues. But especially during the seventies and eighties, he was criticized by some as a musician too ready to adopt the latest style, be it soul, funk, or fusion. Accessible, big-selling albums like *Sugar* and *Pieces of Dreams* broadened his appeal immensely, yet invited brickbats from purists at the same time. The saxophonist remains unapologetic about his choices.

"The only thing I try to do is play," he says. "I try to keep an open mind. I've been accused of selling out, but if I did I'd like to know how much they paid me. If I have a song or an idea and feel comfortable with it, I play it. I like to play a lot of things.

"Who is to say what is jazz? The music is too ambiguous.

I like to just say, 'Hey, man, you're playing music.' Hopefully you're playing something that can make somebody smile, cry, tap their feet, whatever they want to do."

In 1989, Turrentine lapsed into a twenty-eight-hour coma diagnosed as pulmonary edema brought on by the combination of being overtired, going off his diet, and not taking his high blood pressure pills. He recovered and was back on the road in a few weeks, but the experience changed his outlook on life dramatically.

"Today I try to live a day at a time and do something in that day that's positive," he says. "It's not that self-interest that I used to have. Healing in the hospital made me think about a lot of things in life that I no longer take for granted."

Although his wife, Judith, does most of the cooking at home, Turrentine is completely comfortable in the kitchen. He learned to cook with the bare essentials on hotel room hotplates while he was with Earl Bostic's band in the fifties. "If you had the opportunity to cook, you cooked, because you really didn't have enough money to go out and eat," he says. "A lot of guys used to get navy beans and ham, throw all that stuff together, make some corn bread and boom, that filled us up. I had all kinds of special ways to cook."

Time can offer perspective, especially when it comes to re-examining the anxieties of youth. For Sadao Watanabe, the passing years have dismissed one early concern and provided enlightenment about another.

When after high school the reedman arrived in Tokyo from his hometown of Utsunomiya, ninety miles north, he had two primary worries: developing as a jazz musician and losing his hair. Musically, he pushed himself hard to become the artist that he is today, celebrated in Japan and internationally renowned. But if he'd known as a teenager what he knows now about the reasons for his hair loss, he likely would have made a few dietary adjustments, relaxed, and put the additional energy into

TASTY PLATTERS

- Sadao Watanabe, *Parker's Mood* (Elektra)
- Sadao Watanabe, *Round Trip* (Vanguard)
- Charlie Parker, *Bird: The Complete Charlie Parker on Verve* (Verve)

music. For it seems that a poor diet was at least one of the reasons Watanabe was losing his hair.

"When I first went to Tokyo I had little money," he recounts. "I rented a small room and started to cook. Next door was a student. We ate just boiled rice, cucumber, and miso, and sometimes cans of corned beef.

"My hair started falling out. I worried about that very much. People said it was good to brush your

hair, that it would grow back, so I brushed and I bought some hair tonic and it just kept falling out. Every morning I saw so many hairs on the pillow, I was scared. My father was a completely bald man. I thought I was going to have a completely bald head when I was twenty-three or twenty-four."

Watanabe eventually discovered that a combination of factors, including poor eating habits and moving away from home, accounted for his hair loss, but that realization—and the solution—came only after he got married. "My diet changed and then the hair grew back," he laughs. "I still have some left."

It also helped that by his midtwenties Watanabe had honed his skills enough to have graduated from playing rhythm and blues in Tokyo clubs and on local United States military bases to becoming a fixture in pianist Toshiko Akiyoshi's bebop quartet.

Born in 1933, one of five children, Watanabe was raised under circumstances uniquely favorable to his chosen profession. Not only was music an extremely important part

of family life, post–World War II was an incredibly fertile period for jazz in Japan, especially with United States Armed Forces Radio pumping out many of the newest sounds being created in America.

Watanabe's father, an electrician by trade, played the *biwa,* a traditional, four-stringed Japanese instrument. When a fifteen-year-old Watanabe requested a clarinet after seeing Bing Crosby play one in the movie *Birth of the Blues,* his father didn't fight it. He bought one for his son. By the time he joined Akiyoshi, Watanabe had switched to alto, and his career picked up speed from there. He took over leadership of the pianist's ensemble for several years, and in 1962 moved to the United States to study at Berklee College of Music. His musical experiences in Boston were invaluable. His culinary memories are another story.

"I was living at 395 Marlborough Street in Boston and had a classmate who was excited that I made curry," he recalls. "I had made it pretty well. I was lucky. So he told me he had invited his saxophone teacher, Joe Viola, and Mike Gibbs, the arranger, for dinner and said, 'Sadao, you must make curry like you made.' So I tried. But I thought that if you put in lots of curry powder it made it better. I put in so much that nobody would eat it. So Joe took us to a restaurant."

The reedman had much better luck on the bandstand, touring with Gary McFarland and Chico Hamilton before returning to Japan in 1966. He has been a legend in his homeland, and a hitmaker internationally, ever since.

Incorporating influences from

Soba with Mushrooms

"When I return home to Japan after being on the road," says Watanabe, *"one of the first things I always eat is soba noodles."*

Here, soba, or buckwheat noodles, are topped with mushrooms cooked in a mix of soy sauce, sake, and dashi tsuyu, a stock made from kelp and dried fish.

Serves 4

1 pound assorted mushrooms, such as shiitakes, oyster mushrooms, white mushrooms, and chanterelles

2 tablespoons butter

1 tablespoon oil

²/₃ cup dashi tsuyu (see *Note*)

3 tablespoons sake

2 tablespoons soy sauce

1 ½ pounds soba noodles (see *Note*)

Handful of enoki mushrooms, for garnish

3 tablespoons minced parsley, for garnish

Wash and dry all of the mushrooms except the enoki, then cut them into bite-sized pieces. In a large skillet, melt the butter and oil. Add the cut-up mushrooms and sauté for 2 minutes. Add the dashi tsuyu, sake, and soy sauce. Reduce the heat to a simmer, cover the pan, and cook for 15 to 20 minutes, until the mushrooms are soft and filled with flavors from the sake, soy, and dashi tsuyu. In the meantime, cook the soba according to the package directions. Drain the noodles and place in a serving bowl. Pour the warm mushroom sauce over the noodles and stir until the noodles are well coated. Cut the stems off the enoki mushrooms and sprinkle the caps over the noodles. Sprinkle with parsley and serve at once.

Note: Bottles of dashi tsuyu and soba noodles and are sold in Asian markets. Soba noodles may also be found in health food stores.

Brazil, the Caribbean, and Africa, and expanding his scope from bebop to pop-ish jazz fusion, Watanabe has applied his sleek, rounded, fluid sound on alto and sopranino to a wide range of styles: funk; hard bop; light, lyrical jazz rock; and, on rare occasions, even free jazz abstractions. The bright, catchy melodies he writes aren't always the meatiest improvisational vehicles, but they do grab listeners; among his more than sixty recordings, crossover albums like *Elis* and *Fill Up the Night* have been best-sellers. Still, Watanabe has shown in recent years that he remains a bebopper deep down. *Parker's Mood,* his straight-ahead tribute to Charlie Parker, is one of his strongest efforts.

"I try to write songs that are as simple as possible," he says. "I try to be natural, honest, and be myself. I never try something that's not natural. To me that would be a lie."

Both Watanabe's visage and music are very familiar in Japan, what with snatches of his tunes accompanying commercials and the reedman's face appearing in print and television ads for everything from jeans to soft drinks. Many others know him from his weekly radio show, "My Dear Life," and from his efforts with the Japanese concert series "Bravas Club." These days he prefers to tour less overseas and to concentrate on his golf game, his family, and eating well. When he's not enjoying the meals prepared by his daughter, Mako, and wife, Mikko, he searches for restaurants that range in scope from those serving traditional French cuisine to the noodle shops that seem to be found on every Japanese street corner.

If you've grown up on Mom *and* Dad's cooking at home, perfected your culinary imagination on a hotplate in Brooklyn, and then eaten the best cuisine France has to offer for more than five years, you're probably going to feel mighty comfortable around the kitchen. Phil Woods, one of jazz's finest alto saxophonists, is so much at ease there that he does most of the cooking in the Delaware Water Gap household he shares with his wife, Jill Goodwin. His philosophy about food has more than a little to do with his willingness to handle the cooking: "You have to eat, so enjoy it. To me, the greatest part of the day is eating."

Woods started paying attention to cooking back when he was growing up in Springfield, Massachusetts, in the thirties and forties. "Mom did most of the cooking, but Dad was actually a better cook," he says. "He was famous for his antipastos and French-fried bread. Dad loved to cook, and I guess I take after him."

In 1947, at age nineteen, Woods moved to New York City to study at the Juilliard School with some hometown connections intact. His first roommates in Brooklyn were a pair of his Springfield buddies, guitarist Sal Salvador and piano player Al Sera. Besides sharing musical war stories, they made sure that Woods got enough to eat.

"I learned a lot about cooking from those cats," Woods recalls. "Sal's dad owned a real Italian delicatessen in Springfield and he used to send down care packages—

salami, rice and beans, stuff like that. I started right off on a couple of hotplates to do single dishes. It was a way of surviving. I couldn't afford to eat out. It was a matter of expediency."

Juilliard studies took up most of Woods's days until he graduated in 1952, but many of his nights were spent in Fifty-second Street clubs listening to bebop wonders like Bud Powell and Charlie Parker. It wasn't long before he was out trying to break into the business himself. Fortunately for both Woods and his appetite, there were a few places in town where he could satisfy both needs.

"In the old days there were a lot of joints in Brooklyn," he says. "I remember one in particular, Tony's, on Flatbush Avenue. If you came in for the Monday-night jam session,

at the end of the night Tony would make a huge pot of pasta. Everybody was invited to have some wine and pasta. If you did enough joints to go jammin', you could always find a free meal. At home, I'd cook or my wife would cook. They were pretty lean times, but we made it pretty good."

Woods started putting in regular stints with players like Charlie Barnet, Buddy Rich, and Quincy Jones, and he soon began making a musical impact of his own that's still felt today. He never looked back after being named "new star on alto" in *Downbeat* magazine in 1956, developing into much more than "a child of Charlie Parker," as he was dubbed more than once during his early years.

On alto and clarinet he has proven himself to be a poet of melody. His rapid bop phrases and sweet balladic lines are delivered

TASTY PLATTERS
- Phil Woods, *Here's to My Lady* (Chesky)
- Phil Woods, *Real Life* (Chesky)
- Benny Carter/Phil Woods, *My Man Benny, My Man Phil* (Music Masters)

with equal precision in a tone that's smooth and liquid. Woods's horn has been heard on discs by pop stars like Paul Simon and Steely Dan while his own records have earned him a wall full of Grammys and other awards. A hard-driving bopper through and through, Woods has established himself as more than a stunning improviser. He's one of jazz's great bandleaders, even keeping cohesive working units together for more than a dozen years; his quintet of trumpeter Tom Harrell, drummer Bill Goodwin, bassist Steve Gilmore, and pianist Hal Galper was long one of the music's most creative ensembles.

Woods ran one of his most powerful bands, the European Rhythm Machine, when he lived in France from 1968 to 1973. He also honed his culinary tastes there. "I really got into food when I lived in France," he says. "It wasn't the cooking as much as the appreciation of it." Woods is even more partial, however, to the food of one of France's neighbors. "Italy is still the best," he declares. "They were eating *gastronomie fantastique* when the French were still painting themselves blue and calling themselves David. I just love touring Italy for that reason."

Woods is on the road at least half the year, but when he's home he puts together meals like casseroles and rib dinners. His Barbecue Sauce DuBois is the result of many years of experimentation.

"Cooking is like improvising," he says. "There are only so many ingredients and you try to make something up. The great chefs, the imaginative chefs, are the ones who come up with those wonderful combinations. I think music is like a good meal, man. You try to touch somebody's heart and their innards, try to stir up something, make 'em feel something. I think the same rules apply to music. When I play I try to touch something, your heart or any part of your body that's operating at the time."

Barbecue Sauce DuBois

"There was this rooming house back in Philly," says Woods, "summer of '56, remember it well. Man, there was this lady who cooked meals for the guys in the band—two dollars a day—great stuff.

"Philly, D.C., New York, Baltimore, these are the places where you'd get great ribs and chicken in the summertime. In a big pit, usually at a busy corner, there'd be some guy just slow-cooking slabs of ribs and chickens."

It's from these memories that Woods has come up with Barbecue Sauce DuBois, titled for his family's original French-Canadian name. In describing the barbecue sauce, Woods reminds us, "This is urban-black barbecue sauce. Not that fiery Tex-Mex stuff, but what I call 'big city tame,' with just a little touch of sweetness."

"The butter and wine go real well with chicken. I really love the way butter smooths things out and imparts a flavor. Five years of living in France," laughs Woods, "taught me that you can't get enough butter." Don't sauce your meat or chicken until the last minute on the grill: "The corn syrup will make this sauce burn," he warns.

This recipe will make about four cups of barbecue sauce. Well-sealed, it can keep for ten days in the refrigerator.

"Serves one big band, three quintets, or me and Bill Potts."

1 medium onion
1 stalk celery
1 red bell pepper
3 shallots
3 cloves garlic
3 tablespoons virgin olive oil
1 cup white wine (see *Note*)
½ cup lemon juice
¼ cup Worcestershire sauce
¼ cup wine vinegar
¼ cup light corn syrup
1 tablespoon balsamic vinegar
1 cup chili sauce
½ cup brown sugar
¼ cup brown mustard
1 teaspoon salt
½ teaspoon paprika
½ teaspoon white pepper
½ cup (1 stick) butter, cut into chunks (see *Note*)
Hot sauce

Finely chop the onion, celery, red pepper, shallots, and garlic, and in a medium-large skillet, sauté in the olive oil, until soft. In a large saucepan, stir together all of the remaining ingredients, except for the butter and hot sauce. Add the sautéed vegetable mixture to the sauce and slowly bring to a boil, stirring frequently. Reduce the heat to a simmer and cook, uncovered, for at least ½ hour, or up to 2 hours, stirring occasionally. During the last 5 minutes of cooking, add the butter and hot sauce.

Note: If the sauce is going to be used with ribs, leave out the white wine and butter.

BRASS

Like a classic solo phrase that's embedded as a pleasant memory, the spirit and influence of Cannonball Adderley permeate his brother Nat. Julian "Cannonball" Adderley, a major alto saxophone voice for more than two decades and proclaimed by some "the new Bird," died in 1975, but his soulful, exultant hard bop lives on in the music of Nat Adderley.

The cornetist, a cornerstone of the Cannonball Adderley Quintet for sixteen years, is far from a nostalgia act, however. He's an original himself, a composer of jazz standards like "Jive Samba," "Work Song," and "Hummin'," and a stylist who uses offbeat colors and textures, wit, and a bluesy edge on trumpet, flügelhorn, and cornet to keep the music relevant. "I haven't gotten away from the basics: swing hard and try to get the same kind of blend that Cannon and I got," he explains.

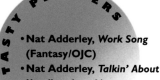

TASTY PLATTERS

- **Nat Adderley, *Work Song* (Fantasy/OJC)**
- **Nat Adderley, *Talkin' About You* (Landmark)**
- ***The Best of Cannonball Adderley: The Capitol Years* (Blue Note)**

Born in Tampa, Florida, in 1931, three years after his brother, Adderley was raised in Tallahassee. His father wore a number of hats over the years—hotel bellman, Pullman porter, post office worker, drugstore manager, health inspector for the city. He was also a semiprofessional cornetist. Adderley's mother taught

school in various rural districts and was the family cook. Being from Georgia, she prepared the basic array of soul food dishes. "Everything was very tasty and very 'cholesterolly,'" Adderley remembers.

Neither Nat nor Cannonball was particularly heavy in his early years although things started to change when the alto saxophonist was about fourteen. "Cannonball was painfully thin until one summer he went to work in a dairy delivering milk," Adderley recalls. "You could eat all the ice cream and drink all

the chocolate milk you wanted. Cannonball gained about fifty pounds and grew about three inches." Among his peers, his eating became nearly as legendary as his playing. "He was a trencherman," Adderley laughs. "That was his word for being a big eater."

Florida A and M, the black college in Tallahassee which had a high school as well, was a major influence on the brothers in both the music and sports arenas. Nat played tennis and basketball; Cannonball, football—for one practice. "Of course Cannonball was a lineman. A tenor player we grew up with was an end and they were next to each other. When the guy next to them got his hand stepped on, they both looked at each other and said, 'Unh-unh,' and immediately returned their uniforms."

The jazz that was always playing in their house inspired the Adderley brothers to pick up instruments early. They formed a group called the Royal Swingsters and soon became good enough to get admitted into the A and M band. Nat joined in the seventh grade and stayed until he finished college in 1951. They played in the school's first Marching 100 Rattlers' Band, the group famous for high-stepping 180 times a minute.

The brothers' lives continued to intersect once they left home. Nat and several friends followed Cannonball into the army in Fort Knox, Kentucky. "We paid our own way to Kentucky so we could join the band that Cannon was in because he told us we wouldn't have to go to Korea," Adderley explains. "And we didn't. He had pull. We had a marvelous time for two years." Except for the food. "To southern boys accustomed to eating rice it was difficult to adjust to eating potatoes," he says.

Their musical careers began in earnest after the army. Nat landed spots in Lionel Hampton's band, worked briefly with his brother, then hooked up with J. J. Johnson and Woody Herman. Cannonball matured in Miles Davis's vaunted late-sixties group with John Coltrane. In 1959 the brothers came together in the Cannonball Adderley Quintet, and they formed the core of the band until Cannonball's stroke in 1975. While the 1967 hit "Mercy, Mercy, Mercy" was their best-known song, the group left a legacy of funky, jubilant bop that Nat keeps fresh.

Besides teaming on and off with stars like Joe Henderson, Woody Shaw, and Cedar Walton, Adderley has made certain that his own bands, featuring veterans like Jimmy Cobb and up-and-comers like Vincent Herring, pack a wallop. "Sometimes we all seem to get that evangelical quality that Cannonball and I used to get," he enthuses.

When the brothers first moved to New York, the saxophonist taught Nat's wife, Ann, how to prepare many of the West Indian dishes he had learned when he was a high school music director in Fort Lauderdale.

West Indian Souse

"Fort Lauderdale in those days had a big West Indian population, mostly from Barbados," Adderley explains. "They'd cook up this spicy souse that really took a long time to make. But this West Indian souse wasn't the same as the souse that came from North Carolina. This one's more like a soup that you eat over rice. I'd say it's a West Indian version of gumbo. I know it's a high cholesterol dish and that the doctor has put me on a low cholesterol diet, but just talking about it gets me hungry." Souse is served cold in the South. West Indians eat it hot.

Enough for a big party

- 10 fresh pig's feet, quartered
- 5 pounds pig ears, trimmed of fat and cut into small pieces
- 5 pounds pig tails, trimmed of fat and cut into at least three pieces per tail
- 1 bunch celery, diced
- 3 large onions, chopped
- 1 green bell pepper, seeded and chopped
- 7 limes, juiced, or 1 cup bottled lime juice
- 3 hot chile peppers, such as Scotch Bonnets, chopped
- 1/2 cup hot sauce (Tabasco), preferably Matouks from Trinidad
- 1 teaspoon red pepper flakes
- Salt and pepper
- 2 cucumbers, peeled and diced

Place the meat in a large pot filled with water and bring the water to a boil. Reduce the heat to a simmer and cover. Every 5 minutes or so, using a slotted spoon, skim off the fat that rises to the top of the water. After 1 hour, drain the water, add an equal amount of fresh water, and return to a boil. Reduce the heat and simmer for another 30 minutes, again skimming the fat that rises to the top of the water. Drain. (By this time most of the loose fat should be gone.) Add the celery, onions, and green pepper, and fill the pot with fresh water. Cover and bring the mixture to a boil. Remove the cover and reduce the heat to a simmer. After 1 hour, stir in the lime juice, chile peppers, bottled hot sauce, red pepper flakes, salt, and pepper. Cook for 2 more hours over low heat. Add the cucumber during the last 5 minutes. Drain and serve the pork and vegetable mix over rice.

Louis Armstrong would have loved the buoyant soul of Ray Anderson's music. Five decades and nearly as many stylistic evolutions separate the two, yet the trombonist/composer has an ingredient in common with "Pops" that's as valuable now as it was in the great trumpeter's heyday: a spirited need to explore that prods him to investigate every imaginable concept and sound. And like Armstrong, he never sacrifices substance for musical gimmickry or fashion.

The trombonist has been making the right moves for years, if his popularity in jazz polls is any indication. Given that he works in a range of eclectic settings that frequently produce deeply challenging music, that's no mean feat. While Anderson performs most often now with rhythmically and harmonically freewheeling musicians like Gerry Hemingway, Anthony Davis, and Mark Helias, the simmering

TASTY PLATTERS

• Ray Anderson, *What Because* (Gramavision)
• Ray Anderson, *Blues Bred in the Bone* (Gramavision)
• Les Miserables Brass Band, *Manic Traditions* (Northeastern)

funk and salsa from his past still surface regularly. It's impossible to fit Anderson's creations into a neat little box, which is the way he prefers it. He uses myriad jazz traditions as his starting points and, like Armstrong, values depth and possibility.

"For me, playing music is very much a voyage of self-expression," he explains. "To discover who you are and express that, you wind up struggling with and expressing things that are really universal to people. The fundamental fuel for the music is the emotional reality that you're in, and those basic emotions are shared all over the world. Everybody feels fear and love and anger and pain and joy and passion and desire. The impetus comes from that, so it's a process of telling the truth about who you are and what you're feeling. Otherwise, the music is an act as opposed to a really authentic thing."

Anderson, who was born in 1952, got his first taste of the expressive power of music from the records his parents played in their home on Chicago's South Side. Both professors, his mother at Chicago State University, his father at the Chicago Theological Seminary, they listened to everything from popular music to Dixieland. "The only place I had heard the trombone was on those Dixieland records," Anderson recalls. "Those cats sliding around sounded like fun, so I went for that." He began tackling the instrument in the fourth grade.

Drummer Barry Altschul and, later, avant-garde reedman Anthony Braxton gave Anderson his first major jazz work. His career evolved from there, running the gamut from the jazz-funk of the Slickaphonics to Charlie Haden's Liberation Music Orchestra to Bass Drum Bone, his trio with Hemingway and Helias.

Scrambled Tofu

From a recipe found in a health-food cookbook, Anderson's Scrambled Tofu has evolved over the past ten years from the precisely detailed directions of the original recipe to one reliant on the trombonist's senses.

"I found it difficult to figure the amounts of the various ingredients," says Anderson. "I make it by sight and smell without measurements." (As further proof of his extemporaneous technique, Anderson includes several variations.) "Like the music, this is a recipe in which the art of the improviser can shine," he says.

Even though the finished product bears a strong resemblance to scrambled eggs, Anderson and family always eat it for dinner, not breakfast. "With a salad or green vegetable and brown rice, it makes a very simple, but satisfying, quick and easily prepared meal," he says.

Despite his ability to "whomp it up in about twenty-five minutes," Anderson issues a warning to those unfamiliar with the nature of tofu. "The only thing at all tricky is squeezing the tofu," he explains. "If you squeeze it too much, the other ingredients won't mix in well and it will be dry on your plate. If you leave it too wet, the dish will have an unsatisfying soup-like consistency. It's better to take too much water because you can always add some water to the pan if you see that it's really too dry."

Serves 4

2 pounds firm tofu

2 tablespoons vegetable oil, preferably canola or safflower

I medium onion, plus any combination of the following vegetables:

I cup sliced mushrooms

I large green bell pepper, seeded and chopped

3 stalks celery, chopped

½ pound spinach, chopped

I teaspoon turmeric

2 tablespoons tamari (a soy-based sauce sold in health food stores)

½ teaspoon cayenne pepper, or to taste

Any combination of the following cheeses:

1½ cups sharp cheddar cheese, grated

½ cup smoked gouda and I cup cheddar

½ cup Jarlsberg or Swiss and I cup cheddar

I cup chopped parsley

Place the tofu in the middle of a clean linen or cotton kitchen towel. Gather the four corners of the towel in one hand and use your other hand to twist the tofu, squeezing out most of the water.

In a large skillet, over medium-high heat, warm the oil. Add the vegetables you've decided to use and cook until soft. Add the tofu, chopping it up and then spreading it out with your spatula. Sprinkle the turmeric evenly over the mixture, then add the tamari and cayenne, stirring constantly. Continuing to stir, add the cheese. When the mixture is a nice yellow color, add the parsley (if it is not yellow enough, add more turmeric). Stir and serve it up!

Besides a respect for swing and the blues, the constants for Anderson in every setting are a burnished tone, a virtuoso control over an instrument that's not particularly jazz-friendly, and an ability to conjure up a range of moods that goes far beyond funeral sadness and circuslike goofiness, clichés too often associated with trombone. Anderson manages to make the instrument sound funny, otherworldly, or just plain odd, and still maintain its integrity. What could be taken as sonic trickery is really a jaunty and masterful way of taking the music in new directions. Anderson even sings on occasion, which he does with a wit and grit similar to his trombone playing.

He and his brother and sister were reared on "real standard American fare." His mother, who had been a home economics major in school, was highly aware of good nutritional habits. "She was very much into having the four food groups on the table," he remembers. "We ate really well."

Today, Anderson is main cook for his wife, Jackie Raven, and their young son and daughter. A diabetic, he sticks to high-protein, low-carbohydrate meals that veer toward the organic. "I'm horrified by what the American food practices are, particularly regarding meat. So I'm very much into getting organic stuff whenever I can. It's just a matter of trying to make it work with the diabetic requirements, which is a bit tricky. I'd be happy with a whole bunch of brown rice and vegetables with a little cheese on it, but diabetically it won't work. It sends me off into stuff like scrambled tofu."

"usic and baseball, those are my two hobbies," declares Mario Bauzá. "My brother was a professional player and my father was a manager for the old Havana Sugar Kings. I love baseball: morning, afternoon, and night. Every time the Mets lose, I'm sick. Nothing is more exciting than baseball."

Nothing, that is, except the

Afro-Cuban jazz that Bauzá almost single-handedly created during the 1940s and 1950s, an invention that has made him a seminal figure in both the jazz and Latin music worlds. The Cuban-born composer/arranger/saxophonist/ trumpeter ingeniously fused that country's complex polyrhythms with advanced jazz harmonies. The result: an infectious, percusive sound that has packed dance floors for decades and thrilled careful listeners with its exuberance, depth, and sheer locomotive power.

"The most important thing was

to present to the people how two cultures could work together," he says. "I was able to marry these two things."

Bauzá's background made him the ideal candidate to come up with this visionary synthesis. Born in Havana in 1911 into a family of six children, Bauzá was raised by a

grandmother who encouraged his budding musical talents. By five he was enrolled at the Havana Philharmonic Symphony Orchestra. His formal studies, though, were only part of his education. Cuba during the 1920s and 1930s was a vibrant cultural center, filled not only with a vital folk heritage but with sophisticated society bands that held sway throughout the country, and especially in ballrooms in the capital. Bauzá started playing in Havana nightclubs like the Casino and the El Tokyo when he was seventeen.

"It was a country of elegant people," he recalls. "Havana was the Paris of the Americas. All the Euro-

pean aristocrats met in Havana. We don't know what we lost."

Bauzá moved to New York City in 1930, but not before he had prepared himself artistically—and gastronomically—for life in the United States. His grandmother long before had laid the culinary groundwork. "She said, 'Mario, you are learning to be a musician and you can travel all over the world,'" he remembers. "'Cuban types of food you aren't going to find in any other place, so you might as well be prepared to eat any way you want.' So she had books for different countries and when I got married, I told my wife to do the same thing. So anywhere I go, I've got no problem."

Bauzá quickly got work at a high level in the States, becoming the lead trumpeter and orchestral director for Chick Webb's swing band in a few short years. His five years with the drummer were notable not

TASTY PLATTERS
- Dizzy Gillespie y Machito, *Afro-Cuban Jazz Moods* (Fantasy/OJC)
- Machito, *1983 Grammy Award Winner* (MCA/Impulse!)
- Machito and His Afro-Cuban Salseros, *Mucho Macho* (Pablo)

only for the recording of Webb's classic "Stompin' at the Savoy," but for his role in helping to discover a young lady about sixteen years old named Ella Fitzgerald.

In 1938 Bauzá joined Cab Calloway's orchestra and convinced the bandleader to hire the man he calls "his son," Dizzy Gillespie. Schooled

Rabo Encendido—Oxtails on Fire

Cuba's early reputation as "the pearl of the Antilles" was well-founded: It was larger in size, blessed with more foodstuffs, and part of the international scene well before the other Latin American islands. Spanish cuisine, and a smattering of European and Asian dishes, found their way into the indigenous products of the island.

Bauzá's wife, Lourdes, a native of the Dominican Republic, has added Cuban fare to a personal culinary roster that includes Dominican and French dishes that she learned while in medical school in France. Rabo encendido—*oxtails on fire—is one specialty that's indicative of the tasty fare for which Cuba is renowned. "It's a traditional Cuban dish," she says, "and one of Mario's favorites." Recommended side dishes include black bean soup, rice, and fried sweet plantains.*

Serves 4

2 pounds oxtails
Salt and pepper
Garlic powder
2 large onions, chopped
2 green bell peppers, seeded and
    chopped
6 cloves garlic, mashed

2 teaspoons fresh oregano, crushed,
    or 1 teaspoon dried
3 cups dry red wine, preferably
    Burgundy
2 tablespoons red wine vinegar
½ cup olive oil

Cut the oxtails into small serving-size knots and place them in a large bowl. Sprinkle them with the salt, pepper, and garlic powder. Add the onions, green peppers, garlic, and oregano, and toss to combine. Add half of the wine and all of the vinegar and stir well. Cover the oxtails and vegetables and allow them to marinate for a few hours, if desired.

In a large pan fit with a cover, over medium-high heat, warm the olive oil. Remove the oxtails from the wine marinade, reserving the marinade, and add the oxtails to the hot oil. Sauté for 3 to 4 minutes, until the oxtails are just browned. Reduce the heat to low and add the reserved marinade. Bring the marinade to a simmer, cover, and cook for 1 hour, occasionally skimming off any fat that rises to the top. When the meat is tender and the wine turns a golden brown, add the remaining 1½ cups wine. Over low heat, and uncovered, cook for an additional 25 to 30 minutes.

---

by Bauzá, the trumpeter would eventually play nearly as important a role in establishing Afro-Cuban jazz as Bauzá himself.

Two years later Bauzá hooked up with his brother-in-law, one of Cuba's most renowned bandleaders, singer Frank "Machito" Grillo, to form Machito's Afro-Cubans. With Bauzá as lead trumpet and musical director, Machito gathered a group of Americans, Cubans, and Puerto Ricans who wrestled with, and ultimately found, a common ground for the structures inherent in each native music: jazz's thorny chord changes and the two-bar pattern with a two-three or three-two syncopated beat, known as the *clave,* that forms the foundation of most Latin music. With the hits "Tanga," and later "Mambo Inn,"

under their belts, the Afro-Cubans, with young players like *timbalero* Tito Puente on board, consistently laid down a new sound that fused smooth horn voicings with Latin music's more jagged vocalizing.

"In the beginning the musicians didn't like the idea, but little by little they began to learn," Bauzá says. "Now it's a whole 'nother music to play. It worked perfectly."

The music's influence spread from there, inserting itself into bebop through Dizzy Gillespie and even Charlie Parker. It was the primary fuel for the forties and fifties mambo mania and ultimately laid the groundwork for what is known today as salsa. But as far as Bauzá is concerned, those contributions are just the beginning. "I think Afro-Cuban jazz is the music of tomorrow," he states.

Before he followed his brother-in-law to the United States, Machito was a restaurant owner as well as a bandleader in Cuba. "He was a hell of a cook," Bauzá says. "He used to make a hell of a paella. He never let anyone else cook. He'd say, 'The people here don't know how to cook, man. The food don't taste like nothing.'"

Machito's sister Graciela, a vocalist who was an integral part of the Afro-Cubans from the mid-1940s to the mid-1970s, when she and Bauzá left to form their own big band, cooks every day for Bauzá. She and Bauzá's wife, Lourdes, share the culinary chores since he isn't much on meal preparation himself. Good food, arranging and composing, baseball, and dancing help keep him young. Especially dancing. Every Sunday he and Lourdes take to the floor at a New York club. The music? Afro-Cuban, of course.

When he left his hometown of New Orleans for Rutgers University in his late teens, Terence Blanchard had no illusions that he would dazzle anyone with his culinary prowess. With his music, maybe. With his cooking, no. Even so, having grown up in a household where the meals often reflected the spice and variety of New Orleans's food traditions, the young trumpeter had developed a passion for authenticity. He remembers that after moving north, he was taken aback on at least one occasion by a less-than-authentic interpretation of a native New Orleans dish.

"It was when I was playing with Lionel Hampton's band," he recounts. "The singer, who used to call me 'Nelson,' for 'Baby Face Nelson,' was from Texas and one day said, 'Nelson, I know you haven't had a home-cooked meal, living down there at Rutgers, so you come up to my house and I'll cook you some red beans!' My mouth was watering for red beans, with maybe some French bread on the side. I laughed when I saw what she had—black beans! I just looked at that and thought, 'Well, she tried.' "

It was later, after he had established a reputation as an improviser and composer with a fresh vision and voice, that Blanchard became comfortable with cooking. "I'm one of those cooks who'll figure out a way to make something taste good. I can't cook from a recipe book. That doesn't make sense to me. It's kind of like playing jazz. You've got the fundamentals, but after a while it's up to you."

Blanchard had his musical fundamentals down pat before he ventured from New Orleans. Born in 1962, he grew up hearing the likes of Verdi's *Rigoletto* and Handel's *Messiah*. His father, an insurance man by profession, was a student of opera who sang in a New Orleans group called the Harlem Harmony Kings during the early 1930s. Classical piano and then trumpet lessons led naturally to Blanchard's enrollment at the rigorous New Orleans Center for the Creative Arts. All the while he was expanding his musical breadth. There were few better places to do it than his hometown. "I got a chance to hear how people like Teddy Riley and Danny Barker were dealing with the tradition," he points out. "At the time I had no idea how rich that tradition was."

Blanchard didn't have to wait long to apply his talents. In 1982 he took over Wynton Marsalis's seat in Art Blakey's Jazz Messengers. His friend and fellow New Orleans native Donald Harrison replaced saxophonist Branford Marsalis. It was the beginning of a valuable four-year education for the trumpeter and, concurrently, a fruitful artistic relationship with Harrison. He and Harrison co-led one of the most acclaimed post-bop bands of the eighties.

Listening to Blanchard build a solo is like watching a master archi-

---

Wilhelmina Blanchard's Bread Pudding

"I like foods with texture," says Blanchard. "And my mother's bread pudding isn't soft like most other bread puddings. She'd cook it until the top had a toasted look to it. And when you took a bite, every spoonful seemed to have some raisins in it."

Says the trumpeter's mother, Wilhelmina Blanchard: "This was always one of his favorites, even way back when Terence was a fussy eater."

Serves 6 to 8

3 large eggs
½ cup (1 stick) butter, softened at
  room temperature
1 cup sugar
3¾ cups Pet evaporated milk
2 teaspoons vanilla extract, or
  to taste
¾ teaspoon nutmeg
¾ teaspoon cinnamon
1½ cups seedless raisins
½ medium- to large-sized apple,
  peeled, seeded, cored, and
  sliced thin
4 cups of stale (about two days old)
  French bread broken into small,
  bite-sized pieces

In a large bowl, beat the eggs until frothy. Cream together the butter and sugar and add to the beaten eggs along with the evaporated milk, vanilla, nutmeg, and cinnamon. Stir in the raisins and then fold in the bread. Let the mixture soak for 30 to 45 minutes. While it's soaking, preheat the oven to 350°F. Check the sweetness and taste of the soaking liquid and add more sugar, vanilla, nutmeg, or cinnamon if desired. During the last 10 minutes of soaking, add the sliced apple and mix gently. When soaking time is over, add the bread and liquid to a buttered or greased deep-dish (1½- to 2-quart) casserole. Set the casserole into a pan of hot water and bake for 1 to 1½ hours, or until the top is crusty brown.

hired the trumpeter to handle various composing and arranging assignments on films such as *Mo' Better Blues, Jungle Fever,* and his treatment of the life of Malcolm X. And if you thought actor Denzel Washington played a mean horn in *Mo' Better Blues,* think again. That was Blanchard's improvising coming out of the trumpet. Typically, Blanchard's attitude toward the movie business is the same as toward his music: "You want to do something that's worth something, that will stand the test of time."

While the trumpeter readily acknowledges that he owes several debts to drummer Blakey, there is one that he would have gladly done without. "I had a big problem with Art," he remembers, "because that's when I started gaining weight. The band had a habit of eating after the gig. You'd finish at 1 A.M., go out to

TASTY PLATTERS
- *Terence Blanchard* (Columbia)
- *Terence Blanchard/Donald Harrison, Crystal Stair* (Columbia)
- *Ralph Peterson, Volition* (Blue Note)

tect at work. Whether on ballads, boppers, or modal pieces, there's a clean-lined logic to his caramel-toned horn playing, which is both exigent and emotional. He shines just as brightly on his own compositions, which at their best are rich, multi-layered dramas. He is especially proud of absorbing some of Blakey's compositional pointers.

"Art said, 'Look, man, the easiest thing in the world to do is to write something that nobody can play,'" Blanchard recalls. "He'd say that what makes jazz interesting is when you have simple melodies that become complex because of your usage, how you shift the rhythms around, how you put the rhythms

on top of things. That's one thing that has always stuck with me.

"I always try to be consistent in dealing with my own emotions in terms of how I feel about what it is I'm doing. Sometimes people get so caught up in being inventive and different that they take the heart out of what they do just for the sake of being different. They think that that will spawn some new creativity. I don't think that's necessarily the case. Innovation comes from being yourself, having a passion for what you're doing, honestly loving it, and putting it out there for the listener to enjoy. If you're sincere, the people will enjoy it."

Filmmaker Spike Lee is one Blanchard fan who agrees. He has

eat, and then hit the bed. That's the wrong thing to do."

In subsequent years, Blanchard has tried to eat healthily and keep up a running regimen. He admits, though, that it's not always easy. "Sometimes when you're on the road, you don't really have enough energy to go through all this exercise stuff. You're still a musician and that takes priority over everything."

Long before "world music" became a stylistic buzzword in the recording industry, Don Cherry was living it. The multi-instrumentalist is a veritable walking atlas of global sounds, driven to explore by the same inquisitive musical spirit that led him to become part of Ornette Coleman's stunning free jazz experiments in the late fifties and early sixties.

"I don't think that it's my music and I don't think there's any new music," Cherry says. "Everything is coming from a source that to me is like a river that continues. The spiritual side and the dancing side of music have always been the essence of what it's all about."

The connections Cherry makes transcend music. His studies of Hinduism and Sanskrit, raga singing, and flamenco guitar in India, the Far East, Africa, and Europe are tied firmly to every aspect of his life, including nutrition.

Cherry's eating habits have indeed undergone a number of transformations over the years, most of them a far cry from the food of his roots, a melting-pot combination of African, Native American, and Mexican. He was born in 1936 in Oklahoma City

TASTY PLATTERS

- **Don Cherry, *Multi Kulti* (A&M)**
- **Old and New Dreams, *A Tribute to Blackwell* (Black Saint)**
- **Ornette Coleman, *The Shape of Jazz to Come* (Atlantic)**

and raised in the Watts section of Los Angeles. "We came to Los Angeles from Oklahoma in 1940 by Route 66," Cherry explains. "You know the song? That was us."

His father's mother, a Choctaw Indian, took her means of earning a living with her when the family relocated west. "She made Choctaw beer," Cherry recalls. "That's the way she survived. It was made in a barrel with all kinds of fruits. Apricots, peaches, everything. It came out like a brown beer. I remember when I was young these old guys would come with their little brown sacks with their jar inside. The law was that it was not illegal as long as it was not in a barrel. I would dig a hole in the garage where she would be distilling and attach a rope to a rock underneath the barrel so if you pulled the rope the barrel would fall over and the beer would spill into the hole. The hole was lined with canvas and old raincoats. After the police left you could always get the beer back."

Before he was born, that same grandmother had also played piano in a silent movie house. Both sides

Sweet Potato Salad

While his tastebuds may have circled the world, Cherry's contribution comes from New Smyrna Beach, Florida. "I was at this barbecue down there while I was teaching and giving a workshop at the Atlantic Center of the Arts in Daytona Beach," he recalls. "And we had lamb, corn bread, and this incredible sweet potato salad."

Cherry liked the salad so much that he not only duplicated it in his kitchen, he set the ingredients to a rap, "Rappin' Recipe," which is included on his Homeboy *album on the Barclay label.*

Serves 4 to 6

- **6 medium-sized sweet potatoes**
- **Approximately ¼ cup mayonnaise**
- **Approximately ⅛ cup plain yogurt**
- **¼ teaspoon coriander (optional)**
- **4 ribs young celery, chopped**
- **½ cup walnuts, chopped into small pieces**
- **1 cup chopped apple (If the skin is tender and sweet, leave it on; if not, peel the apple)**
- **1 carrot, grated (optional)**
- **3 tablespoons fresh lemon juice**
- **2 tablespoons light brown sugar (if for some reason you substitute yams for sweet potatoes, use less sugar)**
- **1 bunch scallions, chopped, for garnish (optional)**

In a large saucepan, boil the sweet potatoes until al dente, about 25 to 35 minutes (do not continuously puncture with a fork to test). Drain, cool, peel, cut into bite-sized chunks, and place in a large bowl. In a small bowl, blend the mayonnaise, yogurt, and coriander (if using). Add the mayonnaise mixture, celery, walnuts, apple, carrot (if using), lemon juice, and brown sugar to the sweet potatoes. Mix gently but thoroughly. Add more of the mayonnaise-yogurt mixture, if necessary. Cover and refrigerate for at least 3 hours. Serve at a temperature that's slightly cooler than room temperature. Garnish with the scallions, if desired. "It's great with all kinds of home-cooked meals, at picnics, and at barbecues," Cherry says.

of the family were musical. Singing in the Baptist church on Sundays was a command performance. His father, who was a bartender before getting into the furniture business, played the trumpet. All of which made it natural for Cherry to seek out the likes of Billy Eckstine, Charlie Parker, and Billie Holiday when they came to town. In high school he immersed himself in bebop, supported his musical ventures by delivering prescriptions for Schwab's drugstore in Hollywood, and subsequently formed his first group, the Jazz Messiahs. By seventeen he was playing cornet and pocket trumpet with Ornette Coleman. He stayed with the saxophonist for several years and a slew of recordings, associating himself forever with Coleman's revolutionary breakthroughs that freed improvisers from bebop's set chordal patterns. That experience, and later collaborations with Sonny Rollins, Albert Ayler, and Gato Barbieri, opened Cherry's eyes to a literal world of musical possibilities. In the 1960s he set out on a global search that would last more than two decades.

A number of those years in the late sixties found him traveling throughout Europe by camper with his wife, Moki, stepdaughter Neneh, who has gone on to become a pop star, and son Eagle-Eye, now an actor. After he settled in a renovated schoolhouse in Moki's native Sweden in 1970, his diet became macrobiotic.

In the various traditions of music Cherry has been involved with in the past twenty years, he has dug deeply into disparate cultures, yet maintained a solid link with his bebop and free jazz roots. "I'm striving for balance," he explains. "In Brazil they say *Balanceo,* which is translated as 'it swings.'" Cherry uses eclecticism to reach his goal. He has formed a Coleman alumni band and a world music group called Codona, played with rockers like Lou Reed, and explored the synthesis of reggae, African music, and various folk sounds with the ensemble Multi Kulti.

Whether he's using cornet, pocket trumpet, melodica, keyboards, percussion, or the *doussn' gouni,* a hunter's stringed instrument from Mali, there's a dancing jaunt to much of what Cherry plays, be it shuffles, funkish jazz fusion, or ethnic sounds. His cornet and pocket trumpet have a sturdy, but never huge, tone that bends between the tart and the lyrical. Compactness, rhythmic drive, lots of colors, and, most of all, surprises are part and parcel of Cherry's composing and improvising. He's a cultural wanderer with an agenda: unearth beauty wherever he finds it and shape it to fit his personal vision.

Gregory Davis reached a crossroads during the mid-1980s. The success of the Dirty Dozen Brass Band, of which he was a member, forced him to decide between giving it a go as a full-time musician or continuing to support his family with the steady income of a teacher supplemented by moonlighting as an insurance salesman. He chose the former.

"It got to be too many gigs for me to get up in the morning and do," the New Orleans–based trumpet player explains. "Teaching music didn't work because I also had to commit to the football games and parades. Every night that there was a football game there was also a gig. Then I tried to dedicate myself to teaching history and mathematics. But I couldn't do it right so I gave it up. I continued to sell insurance, but it got to be a problem servicing the clients. I had an office overlooking the Mississippi River and I was making decent money, but I couldn't commit to it like a salesman needs to do."

Davis never expected to have to choose between careers when he first helped form the band in 1977. "At that time it was just something to do," he says. "I didn't think it was going to be anything, but within the first six to eight months, we were doing two or three gigs a week. By the time 1980 rolled around, we were working six nights a week, sometimes two or three gigs a day."

The Dirty Dozen's fortunes changed even more dramatically after the rest of the band gave up their day jobs to devote themselves fully to the music. It was obvious that they had made the right choices when they went from being an ensemble popular primarily around New Orleans to a group in demand around the world.

Their sound is unique. The blend of traditional New Orleans marching band music, rhythm and blues, funk, bebop, free jazz, and Afro-Caribbean rhythms keeps winning fans. Pop stars like Elvis Costello, who collaborated with them on an album, and David Byrne, are among their biggest admirers. Now on the road at least eight months a year, the band is redefining the traditional New Orleans brass band style. They have made the combination of sousaphone, two saxes, two trum-

Macaroni and Cheese with Shrimp

A fan of New Orleans's abundant seafood crop—"Trout, red fish, catfish, we love them all," he proclaims—Davis fittingly contributes a recipe that combines shrimp with a soul food staple rooted in the Mississippi of his grandmother: macaroni and cheese.

Serves 6

MACARONI AND CHEESE

I pound elbow macaroni

½ cup (1 stick) butter, melted

Salt and pepper

¾ pound sharp cheddar cheese, grated

2 to 3 cups milk or half-and-half

SHRIMP MIXTURE

½ cup (1 stick) butter

I small onion, finely chopped

I small bunch scallions, whites and about ½ inch of the green, finely chopped

I small red or green bell pepper, finely chopped (optional)

2 cloves garlic, finely chopped

6 to 8 mushrooms, thinly sliced

Few dashes of cayenne pepper

¼ cup dry white wine

1½ pounds shrimp, shelled and deveined

2 cups light cream

¼ pound sharp cheddar cheese, grated

Heat the oven to 325°F. Follow the package directions for cooking the macaroni and cook until almost done, about 80 percent of the time recommended. Drain well, place in a very large baking dish, and toss with the butter. Season with the salt and pepper. Add the cheese, mixing it well. Pour in enough milk (or half-and-half) to almost cover the macaroni. Bake for 35 minutes. Remove from the oven and stir well.

Meanwhile, to prepare the shrimp while the macaroni and cheese is baking, in a skillet large enough to hold all the shrimp, over medium-high heat, melt the butter. Add the onion, scallions, bell pepper (if using), garlic, and mushrooms and sauté for 4 minutes, until the vegetables begin to soften. Stir in the cayenne and cook for 1 minute longer. Stir in the wine. Add the shrimp and toss well, adding more butter or oil if the pan seems dry. Cook the shrimp for about 3 minutes, until they just turn pink. Turn off the heat. In a large bowl, combine the shrimp mixture, cream, and cheddar cheese. Add the shrimp mixture to the macaroni and cheese. Season with additional salt, pepper, and cayenne, if desired. Return the casserole to the oven and cook for 20 to 30 minutes, until the cheese is thoroughly melted. Cool for about 2 to 3 minutes before serving.

pets, trombone, bass, and snare drum one of the most exhilarating and danceable in jazz. Their tumbling syncopations, brawny riffs, and offbeat musical wit honor everyone from Thelonious Monk to King Oliver to Professor Longhair. No one but the Dirty Dozen Brass Band could turn a medley of "The Star Spangled Banner," "Reveille," and the "Flintstones' Theme" into a Crescent City *tour de force.*

"We try to play what is good music to us," Davis says. "We don't pigeonhole or categorize ourselves. We're basically a gumbo."

Born in 1957, Davis learned about food—and gumbo—long before he ever picked up an instrument. He spent much of his youth living with a dozen family members in his grandmother's large home in New Orleans's Sixth Ward. "The best cook in my family was my grandmother," he points out. "She was from Mississippi. I don't know if I'd call her cooking New Orleans–type cooking, but it has the same flavor and spices as New Orleans. She never used a recipe for anything."

Davis's mother and grandmother inspired him in the kitchen at an early age. "I was in the second or third grade and I tried to fry some eggs," he recalls. "That was a big disappointment. I did not put any butter or grease in the skillet and the eggs just stuck to the pan and burned up. Then I asked a couple of questions of my mother to get it right. From that point on I was interested in cooking.

"My mother and father were divorced when I was real young so she would always be at work in the evening. I got tired of waiting for her to come home so I started learning more and more about how to cook. The first big meal I cooked was fried chicken, salad, macaroni and cheese, and vegetables. I was ten or eleven."

By the time he was twelve, Davis was toying with the baritone sax his brother had brought home from summer camp. His inspiration was the blues and rhythm and blues of Ray Charles and James Brown he heard constantly around the house. The following year he enrolled in music class, settled on cornet because French horn was too cumbersome to carry on the school bus, and set his mind to mastering it.

"I was a homebody," Davis says. "I used to read and study and do my homework, so I spent a lot of time practicing. I was not into sports as much as my brother was. By the time I was thirteen, I was doing nightclub gigs with rhythm-and-blues bands. I worked with Jean Knight, Johnny Adams. To me it was weekend money. I would try never to miss school, but there was always somewhere to play. We weren't very poor, but we weren't very rich either, so this was a way for me to buy clothes, bicycles, do whatever I wanted to do. By thirteen I didn't need to

receive an allowance anymore or ask my parents to buy me clothing. I would make fifty, sixty bucks on weekends."

During high school, Davis switched to trumpet and bought every Freddie Hubbard, Miles

Davis, and Dizzy Gillespie record he could. The gigs kept coming, through college at Loyola University of New Orleans right on up to the period when he started playing clubs like the Dirty Dozen and the Glass House.

"We did not set out to be different," Davis says. "We started out being a traditional brass band. Once we realized we weren't going to get those types of gigs, we started rehearsing other types of music. We play a little bit of everything and by doing that we're doing what we want to play, not necessarily what people tell us we should be playing."

When he's not touring, Davis can usually be found at home in the late afternoon preparing dinner for his wife, Gerlina, and their three children. "I'm not the type who waits until somebody does it," he points out. "When I'm home," he says with a chuckle, "I think the children prefer that I cook."

Several lifetimes' worth of inspiration, a thick, glorious book of music, and a level of artistic accomplishment that rivals the Picassos and Gershwins: these are the incredible gifts bestowed upon Mercer Ellington by his father, Edward Kennedy "Duke" Ellington. A lesser man might have crumbled under the weight of blessings as rich and charged as these. Instead, by wisely choosing to build on his father's tradition, Ellington has thrived. Nearly two decades after its leader's death, the Duke Ellington Orchestra, with his son at the helm, is still one of the busiest and best big bands in the world.

In his book *Music Is My Mistress,* Duke Ellington wrote in 1973, "My son, Mercer Ellington, is dedicated to maintaining the luster of his father's image." As true as those words have proven to be, they provide only a hint of just how heavy a legacy, and at times a per-

sonal burden, was passed from father to son. Duke Ellington, after all, was one of the seminal figures not just of jazz, but of twentieth-century music. To his everlasting credit, Ellington has dealt with the

legacy on his own terms. By putting a number of personal imprints on the orchestra's music, he has established himself as a creative force to be reckoned with and in the process stepped out of his father's shadow.

One key to his success can be found in the way he approaches his role. After more than five decades in the business, Ellington today displays the same enthusiasm as he

did in the early 1930s when he was introduced to the likes of Dinah Washington, Paul Robeson, and Billie Holiday.

And only a man with unabashed love for music could maintain the bed and board routine that he does in his two-bedroom Manhattan apartment. "When the guys in the band come here, this apartment is almost like a dormitory," Ellington attests. "They can stay at the hotel if they want, but for the most part

I always have four or five of them up here. The full floor gets covered. We've got all kinds of convertible couches and extra beds. Some of them have sleeping bags. They come and hang here. It's like a big party. When my wife, Lene, who's a stewardess, is here, we sleep one less. I cook all the time myself. They come for the food."

As far back as he can remember, food has taken a place next to music as an important part of Ellington's life. Born in 1919, in Washington, D.C., he spent most of his first nine years in that city being reared by his grandparents since Duke Ellington and his wife, Edna, had essentially relocated to New York. "I had an affinity for eating," he chuckles. "I used to stay in the kitchen all the time. That's how I developed my interest." He maintained that interest during subsequent years jammed with

TASTY PLATTERS

- Duke Ellington Orchestra, *Digital Duke* (GRP)
- Duke Ellington Orchestra, *Black, Brown & Beige* (Bluebird)
- Various Artists, *The Music of Duke Ellington & Billy Strayhorn* (Stash)

diversity: studies at New York University, Columbia, and Juilliard; a hitch in the army; a stint as a semi pro football player; leader of the house band at the Savoy; disc jockey; musical director for Della Reese; record label owner; salesman; songwriter and arranger; road manager and trumpet player for the Duke Ellington Orchestra. He even served as a watchdog of talent for the likes of Billy Strayhorn.

"We had an apartment in New York when Billy Strayhorn made his first audition for Duke Ellington," the bandleader explains. "Ellington was on his way to Europe and he turned to me, after he listened to 'Lush Life,' the lyrics that Strayhorn had brought to him, and said, 'Take care of Billy, get him a room, and make sure he's cool until we get back.' I got him in the YMCA and Billy came up and had dinner with us the first night. And the second night he came back for dinner and never went back to the YMCA. He just stayed and remained a part of the family from that time on.

"If anybody verged on being a gourmet cook, it was Billy. We used to compare menus and surprise each other with dishes and not allow each other in the kitchen when one or the other was cooking so we wouldn't give away any of the secrets."

Besides keeping the music of

Soul Sole

Ellington's signature touch in Soul Sole is the crispy coat that covers each fillet. "I double-dip the fish in the coating mix," he explains.

Because Soul Sole keeps the cook busy, Ellington likes to team the dish with "something easygoing," like a simple one-layered macaroni and cheese, and a tossed salad as an opener.

Serves 6

- 4 eggs
- 2 cups cornmeal
- 2 cups flour
- 1 cup unflavored bread crumbs
- 6 large fillets of grey sole (approximately 6 ounces each), cut in half
- 2 cups or more olive oil
- 4 cloves garlic, minced

Crack the eggs into a large pie plate or a wide bowl, and beat well. Place the cornmeal, flour, and bread crumbs in a large paper bag and shake to mix the ingredients. Dip the sole, one piece at a time, in the egg and coat well on both sides. Place the sole in the bag and shake to coat. When all the fillets are coated, dip them in the egg and shake them in the bag a second time. In a large skillet or deep fryer, heat enough oil to cover the fish. When the oil nears the boiling point, add the garlic followed by the fish. It cooks quickly, about 2 to 3 minutes total, depending on the thickness of the fish. Drain on paper towels and serve.

Duke Ellington vital and restoring lesser-known gems to the band's repertoire, Mercer Ellington has added a large number of his own richly textured compositions to the book, from early pieces like "Blue Serge," "Things Ain't What They Used to Be," and "Moon Mist" to later works like "Music Is My Mistress" and "Danish Eyes." Besides seeing that the Ellington name and tradition continue and that his children have the means to carry it on, Ellington hopes to leave a legacy that will set him apart from his father. "I'd like to be remembered for the tunes I've written," he says. "The kind of music I've been writing is not the kind where I'm trying to get a hit from one song to the next. I just want to make some good music."

Ellington didn't inherit his culinary genes from Duke. "He swore he was the world's greatest cooker of eggs," laughs Ellington. "He loved to cook scrambled eggs and brag about it. But that was about it."

Though he "grew up on hog," the bandleader now tries to stick to chicken, fish, and the occasional veal dish. Salt and condiments are taboo. He'll sometimes prepare his "Soul Sole" as often as three times a week. "The boys in the band advertise it by saying, 'When we have grey sole, we don't want no company.'"

He doesn't possess the up-turned bell on his horn or the blowfish cheeks that Dizzy Gillespie does, yet trumpeter Jon Faddis, more than any other player alive, carries on the legend's bebop legacy. Tagged "the son of Gillespie" back in his teens because of an uncanny ability to mimic his idol's improvisations, Faddis is still linked with Gillespie as naturally as peaches go with cream. More than two decades after that bond first solidified, Faddis is engaged in the difficult mission of forging his own musical identity.

In spite of the perceptions, Faddis long ago established himself as a man with a mind of his own. Rather than settle for a medi-ocre arts education in the public schools in his hometown of Oak-land, California, he enrolled in a high school outside the city with an excellent jazz program. He shunned the potential glamour and inherent financial riskiness of the New York free-lance life to handle studio work behind the likes of the Rolling Stones, Frank Sinatra, and Luther Vandross. In 1971 he moved to New York as a member of Lionel Hampton's band and became a vegetarian. He's been one ever since. "It was during the Vietnam War," he points out. "There were moral reasons. Now it's not so much moral; it's more for health reasons."

Born in 1953, the youngest of three children, Faddis enjoyed a youthful passion for his mother's hamburgers, pork chops, and steaks overshadowed only by a love of jazz, specifically Gillespie's jazz. At ten, after three years of private lessons, membership in the school band, and listening to hours of

Pasta with Tofu and Fresh Tomato Sauce

Gone from Faddis's diet are the meats that he ate as a youngster in Oak-land. "If it was up to me, I wouldn't eat any cooked foods at all," Faddis says. "If I could get by on fruit, vege-tables and salads, it would be fine."

About his no-cook pasta sauce, Faddis says, "This recipe is normally done with fresh mozzarella, but I substitute tofu for health reasons. When you taste it, it's heaven."

Serves 6

1 pound firm tofu
7 medium-sized tomatoes, cut into chunks
5 cloves garlic, minced
Fresh basil ("As much as you can stand," says Faddis.)
Extra-virgin olive oil
Salt and pepper
1½ pounds amaranth pasta or Jerusalem artichoke pasta, available in health food stores
Parmesan cheese

Drain the tofu in a colander. Wrap in paper towels and press out a little of the liquid. Transfer the tofu to a paper towel–lined plate and allow to dry for 10 to 15 minutes. Cut the tofu length-wise into long, firm, bite-sized chunks. In a large bowl, combine the tofu and tomatoes. Add the garlic and basil. Add enough olive oil to cover the tomato mixture. Season with salt and pepper. Cover the bowl and set aside. Cook the pasta according to the pack-age directions, until al dente. While the pasta cooks, mix the sauce in the bowl. Place the drained pasta in a large serving bowl and pour the sauce over it. Mix well, being careful not to break the tomatoes and tofu. Serve with the Parmesan cheese.

Duke Ellington, Count Basie, and Earl Bostic at home, he became hooked on the trumpet star.

"There were some Dizzy forty-fives around the house," he says. "I remember coming home dur-ing lunch and practicing along with the records. When I was about eleven, I got a new trumpet teacher, Bill Catalano, who used to play with Stan Kenton. He told me Dizzy was the greatest trumpet player in the world, so immediately I started to go out and buy Dizzy Gillespie records. I'm just glad he didn't tell me Herb Alpert was the greatest trumpet player in the world as a joke."

At fifteen, Faddis was actually invited on stage with his idol to play "Satin Doll" and "Get That Money Blues." Dizzy had discov-ered his most faithful fan. It's a relationship that continues to this day, with Faddis joining in as a member of Gillespie's big bands whenever the occasion arises.

The years since he arrived in New York have included time with the Thad Jones–Mel Lewis Big Band and Charles Mingus, his stu-dio period, and, most recently, an effort to break free and create his own style. "I used to consciously try to play Dizzy things in a solo," he explains. "Now I just try to play what comes into my mind. If something Dizzy comes into it, I try to go in another direction with it. I figure there's been a lot of growth and I still have a lot of growing to do."

Faddis has endured brickbats for being too loyal to Gillespie's approach and too flashy in his technique. The fact remains that no trumpeter hits the high end as cleanly, effortlessly, and electrify-

ingly as Faddis, and few translate the nuances of hot emotions with as much fire. Being leader of his own groups has developed greater depth and flexibility in his attack, most notably in the middle registers. His attitude toward the music promises even better years ahead. "My philosophy is that there's no separation between who the person is as an individual and the music they produce," he says. "Music is sometimes a way to express many of the things that we hide from each other. That includes the good and the bad."

Nutritionally, salads, fruit, vegetables, and distilled water make Faddis a happy man. He and Gillespie both share a passion for fruit, in fact. "But Dizzy would go overboard," Faddis laughs. "He used to carry this big Acme juicer on the road with him. He'd see a fruit stand and buy a watermelon and five thousand peaches and nectarines and plums. At the end of the two days he was in town he'd have a big bag of fruit and couldn't give it away!"

TASTY PLATTERS

• Jon Faddis, *Legacy* (Concord Jazz)
• Milt Jackson, *Bebop* (East-West)
• Steve Turre, *Viewpoint* (Stash)

Art Farmer, the music's premier flügelhorn player, got his first heady whiff of the jazz life in Los Angeles immediately after World War II. When he and his late twin brother, Addison, a bassist, were still of high-school age, they set out on their own from their family's Phoenix home and lived in a series of rental rooms near Central Avenue in Los Angeles. The austerity of their accommodations didn't much matter, but the incredible bebop being played in clubs like Papa Lovejoy's, the Brown Bomber, the Last Word, and the Downbeat did. It seemed a West Coast extension of New York City's Fifty-second Street. Hampton Hawes, Howard McGhee, Charles Mingus, Gerald Wilson, and Wardell Gray all lived and performed in town. Soon-to-be giants Charlie Parker and Dizzy Gillespie passed through regularly. For an Arizona teenager who had played Duke Ellington and Count Basie tunes in a dance band and had seen the likes of Artie Shaw and Jimmie Lunceford in concert, this was indeed the City of Angels.

Los Angeles was also where Farmer and his brother learned an early lesson about the seriousness of employment—and food. "The first job we had when we moved there was working in a cold storage warehouse, until we got fired one day for throwing vegetables at each other," he recalls. "We had a potato war. We were very young and maybe we didn't take anything as seriously as we should have."

Music was the exception. The brass player, whose arsenal includes trumpet and flumpet—a cross between flügelhorn and trumpet—

landed work with Floyd Ray and Horace Henderson before joining Johnny Otis's band. The gig with Otis's band took Farmer to New York in 1946. At that time his priorities were absorbing the sounds on Fifty-second Street, taking private lessons, and surviving well enough to do both.

TASTY PLATTERS

- Art Farmer, *Something to Live for: The Music of Billy Strayhorn* (Contemporary)
- Art Farmer, *Portrait of Art* (Fantasy/OJC)
- Art Farmer, *Blame It on My Youth* (Contemporary)

"I was renting a room up in Harlem that had kitchen privileges and that's when I started to cook for myself," he remembers. "I was playing some, but I was actually making my living cleaning theaters at night after they closed. I used to work at Radio City Music Hall as a janitor. And I was studying with private teachers and not making a great deal of money. But I was able to eat fairly well by cooking simple things like red beans and rice, fried fish—things that anyone can cook. It just takes a little common sense: Don't leave the food on the fire too long."

Farmer returned to Los Angeles for a spell before settling in New

York in 1953, lured back by the chance to play in Lionel Hampton's band. By that time he had already worked with Wardell Gray, Jay McShann, and Dexter Gordon. His subsequent New York years found him in the company of many of the bebop masters he revered as a listener: Charles Mingus, Gerry Mulligan, Horace Silver, Gigi Gryce, Art Blakey. The Jazztet, which he co-led from 1959 to 1962 with saxophonist Benny Golson, and which was resurrected in 1982, was one of the most compelling and in-demand hard-bop outfits of the era. But by the mid-1960s, Farmer found himself dealing with a slow market for live jazz which made it extremely tough to earn a reasonable living. He began lining up work overseas and when he received a job offer from the Austrian Broadcasting System to perform as a soloist with the national network's studio orchestra, he took it. He moved to Vienna in 1968, and even though he is still on the road more than two-thirds of each year, he has called that city home ever since.

"Vienna is a place for me to unwind and study new songs," he says. "Once you reach a certain stature, where you are known to a certain extent, it doesn't matter that much where you live as long as the people who hire you know how to get in touch with you. If I was living in New York City, I wouldn't be working in New York City any more than I am now."

Although Farmer has seen a definite increase in the acceptance of jazz in the United States since those tight times in the 1960s, he finds that there is still a substantial gap between recognition for the music in Europe and in the States.

"The difference about being over here is that you can have a jazz concert in a little town that has only 10,000 people in it and there might be 500 people there, while in a town of 10,000 in the United States it might be hard to find anyone that had even heard of you. It seems that culture doesn't spread that well in the United States, at least jazz doesn't."

Farmer himself has done a yeoman's job of trying to spread the music. In addition to a full international performance schedule, his warm, honeyed sound on trumpet and flügelhorn has graced more than one hundred recordings. Farmer is a master of intimate, tender ballads, yet his introspection never feels exclusionary. Using lean, subtly lyrical phrasing on original pieces or underexposed compositions by others, he infuses his sound with a low-key passion that stirs sweet ballads and speedy boppers alike. His music is as comforting and evocative as any in jazz.

"My attitude toward music is similar to my attitude toward food or cooking," he explains. "If I cook something, I cook it for my own taste, and if I play something, I play it for my own taste. It's hard, because I only cook for myself. And as a creative musician it's difficult for me to think someone would like something that I do that I couldn't like myself. I find that the more effort I put into it, the more enjoyment I get out of it."

Farmer, who was born in Iowa, grew up in Phoenix on what he describes as his mother's "general American-style food: chicken on Sunday, fish, meatloaf, and stuff like that during the week." In the years since, he has simply adapted.

Chilled Cucumber Soup

Farmer's recipe for cucumber soup, which was given to him by his wife, is one dish that definitely will not put on the weight. It is easy to make, except you will need a food processor.

"It's refreshing and tasty," Farmer says, "but it's not a meal in itself. It's really great in front of broiled meats." The dish is quite similar to an Indian raita, *and Farmer fittingly suggests that it be served before such highly spiced food as may be found in an Indian meal. While many recipes for chilled soup call for chicken broth, this one bypasses it. The result: a very thick soup.*

Serves 4 as a soup course

- 1 medium onion, cut in half
- 2 cups plain yogurt
- 2 teaspoons white vinegar
- 2 teaspoons olive oil
- 15 or so mint leaves
- 1½ cloves garlic
- 1½ teaspoons salt
- 1 teaspoon fresh dill
- 2 cucumbers, peeled and seeded
- Fresh dill or parsley, for garnish

Using the shredding disk of a food processor, shred the onion. Remove the disk and replace it with the metal blade. Add the rest of the ingredients, except the cucumber, to the food processor bowl. Process until the mixture becomes smooth, about 20 seconds. (Be careful not to overprocess.) Remove the metal blade, taking care not to disturb the mixture. Reinsert the shredding disk. Cut cucumber to fit in the food processor tube and, using the plunger, shred the cucumber. Remove the mixture from the food processor bowl, scraping with a spatula, and place it in a bowl. Cover and refrigerate. Serve cold and garnish with fresh dill or parsley.

Be de bop, de bop de bop." That's trumpet player Dizzy Gillespie humming the introduction to tunes in Fifty-second Street venues like the Onyx Club and Three Deuces back in the 1940s. Legend has it that the term "bebop" was born from those unselfconscious introductory scats. Although some still disagree about the origins of the word, there's no jazz fan who will dispute this fact: John Birks Gillespie, along with soulmates Charlie Parker and Thelonious Monk, ranks as one of the certifiable founding fathers of bebop. That accomplishment is titanic in and of itself, but the trumpeter's career and influence have transcended stylistic advances.

With his infectious good humor, blowfish cheeks, soul patch under his lower lip, and often outlandish outfits, making him recognizable and welcome the world over, Gillespie is jazz's reigning international ambassador. Hollywood and Madison Avenue couldn't have conjured up a better one.

His road to the creative heights started early. Born in 1917 in the small town of Cheraw, South Carolina, the youngest of nine children, Gillespie was banging out "Coon Shine Lady" on the piano by age four. His father's death in 1927 brought hard times to the family, yet Gillespie's musical resolve and education continued. As a third-grader he was given a trombone to use in school, and he soon had his hands on a neighbor's trumpet as well. The story goes that he'd arrive at school in the morning with only the trumpet under his arm; his brother Wesley would be carrying his books.

When it came to music, Gillespie just wanted to play, whether it was for eight dollars a week in a Philadelphia club in the mid-thirties or for free food at the Minton's Playhouse Monday-night jam sessions in the forties. He would practice forever, always looking for that extra edge, the note or phrase that had never been played in quite that way before. And he succeeded. "When I played trumpet, they couldn't tell whether I was coming by land or by sea," Gillespie said about his early Philadelphia days in his fine autobiography, *To Be or Not to Bop*.

In Harlem clubs like Monroe's

Salmon and Hominy Grits

Grits, the coarse meal rendered from white hominy corn, is a truly beloved dish in the South. Despite this era of homogenization, they remain anchored in the cuisine of what history books call "The Old South."

"They'd been cooking this dish down South for years before I was born," points out Gillespie. "Canned salmon was one of the cheapest fancy foods you could buy at the store. A can would cost about fifteen cents."

As a youngster, like any child of the South, the trumpeter knew that Sunday breakfast would always include grits. With a pot of fresh coffee, some freshly squeezed orange juice, and warm corn bread, this substantial dish is indeed the center-piece of what's universally known as a "Sunday kind of breakfast." And like his bebop, the recipe hops in Gillespie's own inimitable phrasing.

Serves 4

- 4 eggs
- 2 (6½-ounce) cans pink salmon, bones removed
- Freshly ground black pepper
- 4 cups water
- 1 teaspoon salt
- ¾ cup hominy grits
- 1 medium onion, diced
- 2 tablespoons vegetable oil
- 12 strips bacon

"Bust the eggs in a [large] bowl and then put the salmon in there, stir it up, and put some black pepper in it," the trumpeter says. "In the meantime, make yourself some hominy grits [bring water and salt to boil in a large, heavy saucepan and slowly pour in the grits; reduce heat to medium]. When you're making the grits, be sure you stir 'em a lot because that gets the coarseness out of 'em. Stir 'em up, stir 'em up, stir 'em up; let it be real soft. [Cook until they taste done, are thick, and perfectly smooth—about 20 minutes.] In the meantime you're sautéeing the onions now, OK? [In a deep, heavy saucepan, sauté onions for a few minutes in the oil until they become just a little soft.] Now put the bacon in the pan [with the onions]; don't drain nothin'. Let that cook until it [bacon and onions] gets sort of done, yeah. Then right after that, pour them eggs and salmon that you beat into the saucepan [with bacon and onions and stir around until eggs set]. The eggs should be kind of juicy. Then you turn it down very, very low and put a top on it. You're not cookin'; you're just warming it up now. Now pour some grits on a plate and put that salmon [mixture with bacon and onions] on top and that'll make you slap your grandmama. It's a bad southern dish."

Uptown House and Minton's and then later on Fifty-second Street, Gillespie and friends created a music that stood the harmonies, melodies, and rhythms of the big band and swing eras on their collective ears. The lightning-fast improvisations they splashed over a constantly stretched harmonic foundation were as passionate as the rhythms were complex. Gillespie's full-bodied, often velvety trumpet sound is as gorgeous today as ever, even though he usually leaves the bulk of solo space to his bandmates now. Cab Calloway once called a Dizzy solo "Chinese music." Time-honored Gillespie gems like "Salt Peanuts," "A Night in Tunisia," "Groovin' High," and "Manteca" proved the big band leader embarrassingly out of touch and the trumpeter with the upturned bell daringly ahead of the times.

Bebop wasn't the only modern music in which Gillespie played a key role. He was the first American jazzman to recognize the potential of merging Afro-Cuban rhythms with jazz, a connection the recent documentary film *A Night in Havana* helps celebrate. And Gillespie remains a vibrant symbol of the forward-leaning jazz artist. In 1989, more than five decades after he began making listeners sit up and take notice of his novel ideas, he recorded a duet album with Max Roach that was stunning

in its adventurousness even by modern standards.

During the heyday of bebop, when he lived in New York, food wasn't a particular priority for Gillespie. "I didn't eat too much in those days," he recalls. "I was more interested in the music than anything else." Yet even though Gillespie wasn't exactly exchanging gourmet recipes with Thelonious Monk back in the late forties, he does recall one meal in Kansas City with particular fondness: barbecued ribs.

"We'd jam all day at the Booker T. Washington Hotel—that's where I first met Charlie Parker," he recalls. "Sometimes after work at night, 4:00 A.M., something like that, we'd go to Gates Barbecue. They'd stay open late. Well, Kansas City barbecue's about the best in the world. The sauce they made, whew, it was just tantalizing! Cayenne pepper, yeah man, they put it all over the meat. And they'd cook it outside! If somebody cooked me a great big barbecue like that now, I'd probably get sick."

Whenever Gillespie traveled in subsequent years, he made up for

his lean New York days by digging into the native dishes. And then his diet changed, dramatically. During the late seventies, he stopped eating meat completely. "My intestines wrote me a letter," he explains.

TASTY PLATTERS

- **Dizzy Gillespie/Max Roach, Paris 1989 (A&M)**
- *Oscar Peterson and Dizzy Gillespie* (Pablo)
- Various Artists, *The Bebop Revolution (1946–49)* (Bluebird)

"Then they gave me an official thank-you note." Diabetes, diagnosed during the mid-1980s, now keeps him away from sugars and fats as well. The days of enjoying Swedish meatballs and hefty pieces of vibraphonist Milt Jackson's peach cobbler are long past —to say nothing of barbecued ribs. Chicken, vegetables, and fish are high on the Gillespie diet now.

Fittingly for a man whose present is connected inexorably to his past, Gillespie digs back into his Cheraw childhood for a recipe his aunt used to make him every Sunday morning. Even though his wife of more than fifty years, Lorraine, does most of the cooking in their Englewood, New Jersey, home—he's still on the road for about three hundred dates a year— Gillespie does feel comfortable preparing this breakfast dish.

L
ove. That's it," Phillip Harper says, explaining what drives his band. "We love to play. We love to listen to the music. We love what the music does for us. When you come to hear us, that's what you're going to feel. It's like something that's just so great to us—and for me. It's like a religion. Religion is supposed to be about love. It's just a matter of getting that link happening with the music."

The Harper Brothers, with Phillip on trumpet and brother Winard on drums forming the core of their ensemble, make that connection by tapping into and re-invigorating the spirit and sound of the most deeply soulful hard bop of the 1950s and 1960s. The trumpeter/composer may argue that it's love that's the inspiration, but on a visceral level it's the sheer joy with which the Harper Brothers infuse their bebop that makes their music powerful and moving. Instead

TASTY PLATTERS

- **The Harper Brothers, *Artistry* (Verve)**
- **The Harper Brothers, *Remembrance, Live at the Village Vanguard* (Verve)**
- **Hank Mobley, *Peckin' Time* (Blue Note)**

of being weighed down by the tradition, they use it as a springboard to create jazz that manages to be respectful as well as gritty and new. Some have opined that they show their respect for bop roots by being overly imitative, a criticism Phillip Harper is happy to counter. "We're in different times now," he says. "There's no way you could listen to our band and then go back to the sixties and hear one of those bands and say it sounds the same. It can't. We have different influences on our lives right now that help make us sound different, whether we try to be or not."

The trumpeter was born in Baltimore in 1965, three years after his bandmate sibling, and raised in Atlanta from age eight on. Their older brother, Danny, a pianist, prodded both to immerse themselves in music.

"Winard and I are very competitive," Harper says. "He started around three years old, got his first drum set around five, and was already playing in clubs around seven. I didn't even get to it until I was ten, but I was practicing hard so I could someday be able to go and play with them. When I was about twelve or thirteen they started letting me play a couple of songs here and there. It got to the point where I could stand my ground."

All five children in the Harper family were raised in a no-nonsense household. Phillip found out early that this attitude extended to the kitchen as well. "I remember the first summer I tried to cook some eggs and they turned out awful," he says. "My mother made me eat them. So I made a promise to myself that I was going to have to learn to do it. I knew I had to get something happening in the kitchen."

Harper spends a great deal of time in the kitchen of his New Jersey home, sharing the cooking duties for his two young children with his wife, Michelle. He has continued with the little-meat/no-salt dietary guidelines established by his mother to deal with his late father's heart condition. And as a bodybuilder, Harper is doubly conscious of diet. He feels that what he eats and how he takes care of his body affect his playing tremendously.

"The trumpet is probably the most physical instrument there is," he says. "I found I'm strongest on the trumpet when I'm working out. If I lay off the gym for almost a month or so, I get weak on my trumpet no matter how hard I practice. Clark Terry knew I was working out and said, 'You're going to find later on that that's the best thing you could ever do for the trumpet.' You have to work out almost like a boxer in order to get the most out of the instrument. Miles was a boxer and so was Clark."

Harper's playing is certainly muscular when he chooses it to be, but it's just as often soft and cool. He makes his points economically, using a distinctive tone and an attack that's short on neither bite nor grace. There's an exciting tension underneath everything he plays. Harper's acknowledged influences, Kenny Dorham and Lee Morgan, two of bop's greatest trumpeters, had similar currents running through their playing.

For both Harper and Winard, who have played long periods with Art Blakey's Jazz Messengers and Betty Carter respectively, the concept of keeping a working band together is extremely important. The approach has already paid dividends: their live album *Remembrance* was a chart topper in 1990. More important, their sustained associations have helped shape them into original artists confident enough to go out on a limb in search of fresh ideas.

Listening to his words offstage and his music on, it's impossible not to hear the respect Wynton Marsalis holds for his musical elders. Yet those homages sound restrained compared to the praise the trumpeter heaps upon the cooks in his family.

On his mother: "When my mama wants to cook, it's very serious." On his great aunt: "Her okra gumbo was just killing in your mouth. Pies of all sorts, delectable, tasting truly epicurean. Her scrambled eggs had a certain type of tex-ture and humility." On his great uncle: "He cooks some red beans and rice, oh, Lord, have mercy!"

Stating his case emphatically and proudly has been a Marsalis trademark since the early eighties, when he burst onto the scene as a teenager whose extraordinary talents caused him to shine in both the jazz and classical arenas. Yet despite substantive classical triumphs, jazz is where his most memorable artistic, and cultural, contributions have been made. By standing up for the music's modern acoustic roots and questioning—some say proselytizing against—everything from the use of electronics to the pitfalls of commercialization, Marsalis has placed himself at center-stage in a heated debate about jazz's future. Nonetheless, opinion is close to unanimous that the trumpeter is the single most influential jazzman of his generation. While it's an exaggeration to claim that Marsalis brought jazz back from the dead, he has helped create a wider interest in the music and paved the way for scores of young musicians to find

Seafood Filé Gumbo

When Delores Marsalis talks about food, it's clear why her son claims her cooking skills are "very serious." She understands the subject as intuitively as the trumpeter understands where he wants to take his music.

"In New Orleans," she says, "the food is so improvised. There aren't set recipes. You throw in anything you want. Our town's so impoverished we use food as an expression, like music and art. That's why it's so hard for New Orleans's cooks to get real specific when they give out things like gumbo recipes. They all have their own. When I first started making gumbo, I used chicken wings and stew beef. I just kept adding and subtracting until I came up with this one."

10 appetizer servings

¼ cup cooking oil
¼ cup flour
2 celery stalks, chopped
1 small leek, cleaned and chopped
1 small yellow onion, chopped
1 small red onion, chopped
1 small bell pepper, chopped
3 cloves garlic, minced

⅛ pound hot sausage, cut into bite-sized pieces and browned
⅛ pound smoked sausage, cut into bite-sized pieces and browned
⅛ pound Italian sausage, cut into bite-sized pieces and browned
⅛ pound seasoned, cooked, or smoked ham
1 (8-ounce) bottle clam juice
1 cube fish bouillon, or 1 cup fish stock
Dash of oregano
Dash of savory
Salt and pepper
1 tablespoon filé powder
3 small cooked crabs, cleaned thoroughly
½ pound crawfish tails, peeled and cleaned
1½ pounds medium shrimp, peeled and deveined
30 oysters, shucked

Place the oil in an 8-quart pot and heat to medium-high. Add the flour a little at a time and stir until all of the flour has turned a dark brown color. "We call this a nutty brown roux. It takes me about 45 minutes to do this, but some people can do it really fast," Mrs. Marsalis says. Make sure the flour is nice and smooth but not burnt. If you want a thicker gumbo add more flour. Stir in the chopped vegetables and minced garlic, lower the heat to medium, cover the pot, and cook for 20 minutes. Add the sausages and ham, stir gently, cover and cook for another 20 minutes. If it looks thin, add a little more flour. In another pot, bring 2 to 3 quarts of water to a boil.

Increase heat under the vegetables and sausage to medium-high. Add the clam juice, stir to mix, lower the heat to a simmer, and cook for 10 minutes. Now add the boiling water until the liquid reaches two-thirds of the way up the pot. Add the fish bouillon (or stock) and stir. Add the oregano, savory, salt, and pepper. Pour some of the hot liquid (¾ cup) from the pot into a separate bowl and stir in the filé powder a little at a time. Mix until smooth and then add to the pot. Add the crabs, return to simmer, and cook for 15 minutes. Raise the heat to medium, add the crawfish tails and shrimp, and simmer for 10 minutes. Add the oysters and simmer for 5 minutes. Turn off the heat, cover the pot, and let it sit for 1 hour so that all of the flavors come together. Serve it over hot rice as an appetizer.

recording and performing forums for their tradition-inspired inventions. As a role model, he is emulated by many, which combined with his extensive charitable involvements and his media exposure has made the New Orleans native one of the rare jazz artists whose renown has transcended the genre.

His musical development has run a course parallel in accomplishment. Marsalis has grown into a bandleader, composer, and improviser who is cutting a stylistic swath worthy of the jazz greats he so admires.

Born in 1961, one of six brothers, Marsalis made room for classical music lessons during grammar school years. Even though Ellis, his piano-playing and -teaching father, kept several hundred jazz records in the house, the

TASTY PLATTERS

• Wynton Marsalis, *The Resolution of Romance (Standard Time, Volume 3)* (Columbia)
• Wynton Marsalis, *Soul Gestures in Southern Blue (Volumes 1–3)* (Columbia)
• *The Original Soundtrack from "Tune in Tomorrow"* (Columbia)

trumpeter paid little attention to jazz until he reached his teens. The music of James Brown, Kool and the Gang, Stevie Wonder, and Earth, Wind and Fire was what moved him. And then he took a closer look at his father's collection.

Marsalis listened to John Coltrane intently, enrolled in his father's school, worked in a funk band with older brother Branford, and performed with the New Orleans Philharmonic and New Orleans Civic Symphony. In 1979 he moved to New York to attend the Juilliard School. Soon after that he took over the trumpet seat in Art Blakey's Jazz Messengers. The rest seems like a blur of accomplishment. Grammy nominations and awards have become almost a foregone conclusion. In 1984 he won a pair, one each in the classical and jazz categories.

The layers of depth that Marsalis's music has taken on with the years provide a sharp counterpoint to the pure-toned, technically dazzling, but oftentimes icy bop and modal-derived workouts of his early recording years. Those bands had fire,

but the heat occasionally sounded more microwave efficient than flaming. In the late 1980s the trumpeter moved from mid-sixties inspirations to his Crescent City roots and hit artistic pay dirt. Using King Oliver, Louis Armstrong, and others as guiding lights, Marsalis is writing and arranging material that embraces the slinky and sensual, the relaxed and witty. It's a logical synthesis that's warm and emotional.

"I'm going to play in every style that I can learn," the bandleader says. "I'm not going to limit myself. I'm going to just deal with the fundamentals: blues, polyphonic improvisation, call and response, swing, grooves, perceptions of virtuosity coming from European music, form, conceptions of virtuosity coming from African music.

"I'm trying to make something of quality accessible to people without watering it down. What I'm trying to figure out is how to get more blues in the music, play more melodically, get more diversity in the music, so that somebody who doesn't know about the music can sit down and actually enjoy it."

Marsalis's schedule doesn't leave him much time at home for leisurely cooking or indulging in his favorite sport, basketball, but he does try to maintain healthful nutritional values and to instill them in his young sons, Wynton, Jr., and Simeon.

For years the bandleader for the "Tonight Show," epicure, and very possibly the best-known trumpet player in the world, Doc Severinsen offers this homespun advice on the subject of eating: "Don't trust anybody who doesn't like animals or good food."

It's counsel Severinsen volunteers in the same mock-serious spirit he has often used as Johnny Carson's spiffily dressed comic foil on the "Tonight Show," yet there's a hefty dollop of truth in it for him. A longtime pet owner and Thoroughbred and quarter horse breeder, Severinsen was raised to feel comfortable around animals. He had little choice, actually, since

there were cattle drives down the main street of his hometown. With a population under six hundred, surrounded by five-thousand-acre farms and ranches, Arlington, Oregon, was where Severinsen absorbed his first lessons in a life-

long gastronomical education that continues to this day.

"My mother used to make a lot of things they called 'soul food,'" the trumpeter recalls. "It was home cooking to me: greens, butter beans, chili beans, mac and cheese. We were pretty poor so we didn't get much meat. We got a little bit of hamburger and once in a while a little fried chicken. If anybody was sick or came to visit, you gave them a nice big bowl of beef stew."

Born Carl Severinsen in 1927, he acquired the nickname Little Doc because his father was the town dentist. Dr. Severinsen was also a classical violinist who exposed Little Doc and his sister and half-brother to as many kinds of music as the radio reception would allow.

"We lived out in the middle of nowhere and these little tiny table radios were the only musical entertainment we had," he remembers. "One day, Roy Eldridge came on the radio playing with the Krupa band. My dad ran into the house, grabbed me, pulled me into the office, and said, 'God, listen to this! That's the way you're supposed to play!'"

Severinsen became so good so quickly that he actually auditioned for Tommy Dorsey's orchestra when he was thirteen. He didn't make it,

but his admiration of and increased focus on players like Harry James and Louis Armstrong paid off soon enough when he hooked up with a big band led by Ted Fio Rito. Severinsen used the correspondence route to complete high school, did a hitch in the army, and then joined saxophonist Charlie Barnet's band. He moved to New York, befriended Barnet bandmates such as trumpeter Clark Terry, got married, started a family, and quickly learned to fend for himself.

"The first wife didn't care to cook and we couldn't afford to go out," he explains. "We had kids, so it was obvious if anybody was going to cook it was going to be me. I would call my mother and ask, 'How did you make this and how did you make that?' She'd teach me, and since most of my friends were Italian, I also learned to cook dishes from them. I got recipes from wives, mothers."

When the opportunity arose in 1949 to earn a steady income as a full-time member of the NBC staff orchestra in New York, Severinsen jumped on it. The work was anonymous and not particularly glamorous, but it did provide Severinsen with the chance to occasionally play with beboppers like Gerry Mulligan and Bob Brookmeyer. In 1962 he joined the "Tonight Show" band fronted by Skitch Henderson and five years later took over as musical director. When the show moved its base of operations to Los Angeles in 1972, he moved along with it.

Appearing nightly with Carson, Ed McMahon, and company has provided Severinsen with more exposure than he could ever have dreamed of when he was hustling for gigs in New York in the mid-forties, but it has also made him something of an enigma to jazz fans who question his credentials as an improviser. That he also spends a good deal of time appearing with symphony orchestras and with his own jazz-rock group, Xebron, muddies his jazz pedigree further. Severinsen doesn't concern himself, though, with fitting someone else's idea of what he should be. He simply thrives on the diversity. "I am a happy man and I hope it shows in my music," he says.

It does. The ten-second snippets of the "Tonight Show" band that television viewers hear before and after commercials capture only a small part of the skill that Severinsen the soloist possesses. His recordings with big bands and smaller ensembles are more telling. With a suede-smooth sound that's large and warm, Severinsen is as at home covering Herbie Hancock's "Maiden Voyage" as he is "I'm Getting Sentimental Over You." There's much more than virtuoso high-register fireworks to his playing. He uses an understated power to navigate the trickiest harmonic waters, stamping them with a mark every bit as personal as many of his jazz idols. The clarity and ease with which he creates belie the difficulty of much of the material he covers. And he has kept his competitive juices flowing over the years by surrounding him-

self in the "Tonight Show" band with consummate jazz artists like Ernie Watts, Peter Christlieb, and Conte Condoli.

On those days when the "Tonight Show" was being taped, Severinsen followed a consistent routine. After a breakfast of cereal, fruit, and juice, he headed to the gym to work out with weights or do some race walking, then returned home for a large lunch, oftentimes fish, potatoes, vegetables, and salad. He would leave his Hollywood Hills home by 2:30 P.M., tape the show, and usually

finish by 6:30. Before the day was over he would have spent at least two hours practicing his horn.

The bandleader shares the cooking with his wife, Emily, and their housekeeper, Ruth Salguero. Italian food is a special passion. "I feel, in the words of a great philosopher, 'The man who has not been to Italy is not a complete man.' More than two or three days without a good Italian meal is not a complete life. It improves my frame of mind and provides me with happiness and energy to perform my music."

Cocido

Nearly once a week, Severinsen also enjoys a bowl of cocido. *Of Spanish origin, this hearty soup entered the Severinsen household through housekeeper Ruth Salguero. "Besides being extremely healthy," says Severinsen, "this dish provides great protein."*

Often referred to as Cocido Español, *the thick stew can be made with either beef or chicken. This version combines three different cuts of beef with the usual wide assortment of vegetables and yucca, a Latin American tuber.*

Serves 6

Cooking oil
1½ pounds oxtails
1 pound beef chuck, cut into chunks
1 pound flank ribs or beef short ribs, separated and cut in half
1 cup beef stock or water
1½ pounds yucca (also known as cassava root), peeled and cut into chunks
3 medium carrots, cut into chunks
3 corn cobs, shucked and cut in half horizontally
2 large tomatoes, cut into chunks
2 celery stalks, coarsely chopped
1 large onion, thinly sliced
3 cloves garlic, minced
3 zucchini, cut into chunks
2 summer squash, cut into chunks
½ pound green cabbage, thinly sliced
1 bunch cilantro, finely chopped

Coat the bottom of a large, deep pot with oil, and in batches, so as not to crowd the meat, brown all of the meat, removing the browned pieces to a platter. When all of the meat is browned, return it to the pot. Add the beef stock (or water), and simmer, covered, for 1½ hours. Add the yucca, carrots, corn, tomatoes, celery, onion, and garlic. When the corn and yucca are cooked to your liking, remove them to a plate. (The corn should take about 5 minutes, the yucca 10 to 15 minutes.) Add the zucchini, summer squash, cabbage, and cilantro. Cook for 15 to 20 minutes, or until all of the vegetables are cooked to your liking. Return the corn and yucca to the pot, heat through, and serve.

For a player on the short list of the world's greatest trumpeters, Clark Terry is mighty modest about his accomplishments. "I've been playing for forty years, close to fifty, and I'm going to keep doing it until I get it right," he says with a laugh. Terry understates his impact. He has used his cushiony tone, graceful phrasing, and good humor to bolster some of jazz history's most important recording and concert sessions. Besides carving out his own identity in the bebop world, Terry has prodded stellar cohorts like Johnny Griffin and Oscar Peterson into some of their most adventurous and inspired performances, the sign of a truly charismatic original. Scores of players have looked upon Terry as a major influence, the late Miles Davis among them.

A fixture in the Duke Ellington band horn section for eight years during the 1950s, Terry had earned his seat through earlier stints with Count Basie, Charlie Barnet, and Charlie Ventura. Born in St. Louis in 1920, one of eleven children, Terry was exposed to jazz when he was only twelve by an older sister who was married to tuba player Sy McField.

"Sy was playing in a territory band known as Dewey Jackson's Musical Ambassadors," Terry recalls. "They used to rehearse at various members' homes and would allow me to go with Sy if I was a good boy—and I tried to be a good boy a lot. The thing that probably got me hooked on the trumpet was that one of the trumpet players, Louis Lattimore, used to own a candy store, and every time he saw me at rehearsal he gave me some candy. One of my favorite

Beer 'n' Beans

Terry's Beer 'n' Beans is a variation of the New Orleans standard he picked up from Billy Strayhorn. "Billy didn't care about what kind of beer covered the beans," he laughs. "He just liked the idea of using beer. All I know is that soaking and cooking the beans in beer gives them a different taste."

Serves 6 to 8 as a side dish or 4 as a main course with rice

- **2 cups kidney or pinto beans, washed and sorted through to remove any debris**
- **Approximately 2 (12-ounce) bottles beer**
- **1 or 2 meaty ham bones, or 2 smoked sausages (cut into pieces), or 3 or 4 turkey wings, or any kind of smoked meat that you prefer (or any combination that suits your taste)**
- **1 onion, quartered (optional)**
- **1 potato, quartered (optional)**
- **Salt and pepper**

Place the beans in a large pot and cover completely with beer. Soak the beans at room temperature overnight, adding more beer as needed. When ready to cook, place the beans and beer in a large pot, over low heat. Add the meat, onion and potato (if using), salt, and pepper. Add more beer or a mix of beer and water, if needed, to cover the beans. Cover the pot and cook for 3 hours, stirring occasionally to prevent the beans from sticking to the bottom.

candies in those days was Mary Janes, taffy with peanut butter down the middle. He used to bring me some Mary Janes, give me a couple of pennies, and tell me to watch his horn when they took intermission. I had been drawn so close to him through his kindness to me that on one particular occasion I grabbed the horn and started huffin' and puffin' just as they were returning from a break. He said, 'Oh my goodness, young man, you're going to be a trumpet player!' And I was stupid enough to believe him!"

Terry's rise to the top ranks of trumpeters didn't occur overnight. He moved out of St. Louis as a teenager, joined a carnival, was in the navy, and the navy band, from 1942 to 1945, then caught on with George Hudson's band prior to Basie. He remembers that the overt racial discrimination during his Basie and Ellington years in the 1940s and 1950s sometimes made the road a cruel place for musicians, especially when it came to lodging and food. "That was a way of life in those days," he says. "You rode the back of the bus and you were relegated to staying with 'Miss Jones.' But you still paid the same taxes!

"It wasn't always convenient to cook in your hotel room because you didn't always have facilities. We sometimes got lucky when we couldn't stay in the hotels because we were relegated to the rooming houses to stay with 'Miss Jones,' 'Miss Smith,' or 'Miss Green.' That usually meant there was some good food in the household. They were just regular families who'd decide to take a few of us in until we had all been dispensed around to different areas.

"It was ridiculous out in Las Vegas when I was with Duke Ellington's band. Duke's name was bigger than the sign 'Flamingo,' but he had to come through the kitchen with all of us to go to work. We couldn't stay in a hotel. We couldn't go to any of the swimming pools. It was hell."

A number of Terry's associates over the years, drummer Mousy Alexander and trumpeter Charlie Shavers among them, earned reputations for their culinary prowess. "Those cats used to carry their pots and pans and skillets and knives and forks and plates with them," Terry says. "And Ben Webster could cook any damn thing. He'd put the pots on for anybody who came through Copenhagen when he was living there. They call them 'scratch cooks.' Ben would go in the kitchen and put together anything from scratch." And Duke Ellington? "Duke never had to cook," Terry chuckles. "He always had a ton of ladies around to cook for him, or he'd go to fantastic restaurants."

Terry joined the "Tonight Show" band in New York in 1960 and stayed on the NBC staff for fourteen years. He kept his jazz trumpet and flügelhorn chops sharp through quintet work with trombonist Bob Brookmeyer and engagements with everyone from Thelonious Monk

TASTY PLATTERS

- Clark Terry, *In Orbit* (Fantasy/OJC)
- Clark Terry, *Portraits* (Chesky)
- Clark Terry, *Duke with a Difference* (Fantasy/OJC)

to Cecil Payne. Later, with his own big band and in gigs with smaller groups, he honed his articulate bebop to an even finer edge, all the while continuing the vaudeville-like persona of "Mumbles," the singing, goofing, entertaining alter-ego character he had created for himself years before. Terry is a composer and an educator of note, as well; he gives workshops year 'round and sponsors an annual jazz camp in Emporia, Kansas.

The trumpeter grew up in St. Louis on what he calls "ethnic food." Since his mother died when he was young, meals were prepared by whichever oldest unmarried sister was still living at home. "My dad was a common laborer," he says. "It was difficult for us to have any extra-fancy stuff, so we had a lot of staple things like potatoes, beans, and what they used to call 'cracklin',' the skin off the hog. Most poor black people who lived in the ghettos ate more or less basic food."

Terry learned about cooking primarily from his sisters and his wife of thirty-two years, who passed away in 1979. A diabetic for twenty years, he's particularly careful about what he eats.

PERCUSSION

Drummer Rashied Ali has made his mark in the music world in myriad ways, from running one of Manhattan's most progressive clubs during the 1970s to providing an outlet for many of the new jazz's best players by creating his own record label. Nothing Ali has done, however, has left a greater imprint on the public or on himself than the time he spent as a member of John Coltrane's intense ensemble in the final years before the saxophonist's death in 1967. Ali readily acknowledges the impact the legendary reedman has had on his life. Coltrane's outlook on music—and living—helped provide Ali with a foundation that has remained solid through good years and bad.

"It was unbelievable playing with him," Ali says about his 2½ years with Coltrane. "I learned so much. I learned about being a better person and about not having an ego. He never had anything bad to say about anybody else. If you could pick up on what was happening, then cool. If you couldn't, that was your problem. He let everybody do exactly what they felt they should. After being with him I learned that if you're a real giant, if you're really good at what you do, you don't have to be an asshole. The really good musicians are good people, too."

Ali and Coltrane shared the same hometown of Philadelphia but moved in different circles until the saxophonist asked Ali to join his band, the same year Pharoah Sanders joined, 1965. Born thirty years before, as a youth, Ali and his

younger brother Muhammad kept the two drum sets in the house busy. Omar, the other younger brother, played congas. "I got my first drum set from my uncle," Ali recalls. "I was eleven. I had a trumpet at first and my cousin Johnny, who is dead

TASTY PLATTERS

- John Coltrane, *Meditations* (MCA)
- John Coltrane, *Live in Japan* (GRP/Impulse)
- Phalanx, *In Touch* (DIW)

now, played drums. I liked the drums so much and he liked the trumpet so much that my uncle just switched instruments. Then my brothers started playing when I was fifteen or sixteen. My mom was very cool, especially for a person who

Chicken Anise

However, it's not from Ali's Alley, but rather from his wife, Patricia, that we get Chicken Anise, a strongly flavored dish finished with Oriental cooking techniques and flavors.

"I got this recipe years ago from a friend," says Patricia. "It's absolutely Rashied's favorite meal and something that I make for his mother, too. It's really quite easy to make."

Serves 4

4 tablespoons vegetable oil
1 whole large chicken, cut up into
    serving pieces
1 cup water
1/4 cup soy sauce
3 tablespoons sugar
1 teaspoon salt
1 teaspoon anise seeds, or
    approximately 1 tablespoon thinly
    sliced fresh anise
1 green bell pepper, seeded and
    thinly sliced

1 large onion, sliced
1/2 cup mushrooms, sliced

In a skillet that's large enough to hold all of the chicken without crowding, warm 2 tablespoons (or more if necessary) of the oil over medium-high heat. Add the chicken and brown well on both sides. Reduce the heat to medium and stir in the water, soy sauce, sugar, salt, and anise. Reduce the heat to a simmer and cook for 40 to 50 minutes.

During the last 10 minutes of cooking, in another skillet, warm the remaining 2 tablespoons oil. Add the green pepper and cook until the pepper begins to turn soft, about 4 minutes. Add the onion and cook for 3 more minutes, or until the onion is soft. Add the mushrooms and cook for 2 more minutes, or until the mushrooms are soft. Add the vegetables to the chicken mixture and simmer for a few minutes to blend the flavors. Serve over rice.

---

heard drums coming up from the basement all day long. The neighbors were kind of uptight, but they liked her because she was a nice lady. They didn't give her a hard time."

His mother, Dorothy Jackson, was head dietician and cook at Temple University and prepared all kinds of meals at home, from soul food to gefilte fish and potato pancakes. When he was sixteen she made sure Ali got a taste of another kind of cuisine: she enlisted him in the army. "I felt great about going into the army," he remembers. "I didn't want to go to school. My mom didn't want me on the street. When I got there, man, they got me up at six o'clock in the morning,

they had me running around, living in tents out in the cold weather. I begged her to get me out, do whatever she could do. She said, 'No, you're going to have to deal with it.' One morning they asked if anybody wanted to get into the band. I raised my hand and the rest is history."

Ali stayed in the army band in Nuremburg, Germany, for his entire three-year stint in the service. When he got out he moved back to Philadelphia, began playing in rock-and-roll and rhythm-and-blues bands, and then in jazz clubs in the city with Jimmy Smith, the Heath Brothers, Lee Morgan, and McCoy Tyner. He eventually worked his way to New York and

associations with freewheeling avant-gardists like Archie Shepp, Paul Bley, and Albert Ayler. The Coltrane period followed.

Ali's playing, with Coltrane and afterward, has always been riveting in its intensity. Coltrane matched and surpassed that tension by trading startling idea after startling idea with Ali. Their duo album, *Interstellar Space,* recorded less than five months before Coltrane died, is astounding in its sustained passion. Never a particularly loud player, Ali has long exhibited a deep, African-influenced sound, particularly on bass drum, and a fast, bristling cymbal style. He subsequently complemented musicians like Sonny Rollins, Jackie McLean, and Alice Coltrane, and now draws younger players like saxophonist Noah Howard and violinist Billy Bang.

"I like all kinds of music," he says. "I play whatever there is and I have fun playing. I don't care if it's rock and roll or bebop or Indian music. As long as I'm playing my drums, I'm satisfied and happy."

In 1974 the drummer opened his club, Ali's Alley, on Greene Street in Soho after a number of years of having difficulty landing gigs in New York. Situated in the same building in which he and his family lived, the loft club became a haven for artists like Frank Foster, Pharoah Sanders, and Jaki Byard who were also searching for a venue sympathetic to their music. Ali kept it operating until 1979, when he recognized that he was devoting all of his time to running the club and none to actually playing.

Ali's partner, bassist Benny Wilson, handled the food at Ali's Alley. "He was a hell of a cook," Ali says. "The food was a hit."

After Louis Bellson's wife of nearly thirty-nine years, singer Pearl Bailey, died of a heart attack in 1990, the veteran drummer could have easily dropped out of the scene. What Bellson did was much more in character; he returned to the road within a matter of weeks.

"It's the only thing to do," he says. "It's a wild thing. When we got Pearl to the hospital, I think she was already gone. When they finally told me she was completely gone, I went and sat with her in the emergency room for almost an hour and a half, just held her hand. Boy, she was giving me all kinds of vibrations, like 'don't just sit and mope, keep on going because there's nothing else to do but keep on going.' That's the way we lived our lives. She always used to say that there are two kinds of people, those who worry and those who care. Those who care get up and do something. I know she would have wanted me to keep on going, so that's what I did."

For nearly as long as he can remember, Bellson has plunged full speed into most every circumstance, the vast majority of them musical. "When I was three years old, my dad

took me to a parade," he remembers. "As soon as I heard the drum section I pointed my finger at them and said, 'That's what I want to

play!'" And since his father owned a music store in their hometown of Moline, Illinois, drums were soon among the instruments Bellson was playing. He and his three brothers and four sisters learned how to play just about every instrument in the shop. "Maybe I was seven when the four of us, me and my brothers, went out on the street one day, put a little cup in front of us, and started to play," he says. "Before we knew it people were dropping in quarters. Even the mayor came by and dropped in a quarter. At first my mother really chastised us for playing on the street, but when we showed her the cup that had about eight dollars in it, she said to go out and play some more. It was fun and we did it a few times, but after a while Dad said, 'Enough of that.' All eight of us had jobs in the music store and he didn't want us to neglect school and the store."

The employment provided for the family by Bellson's father's store was a godsend during the Depression years. The drummer, born Louis Balassoni in 1924, was actually giving lessons by age thirteen. He had already studied tap dancing, opera, classical music, and big band jazz by that time. At fifteen he came up with an idea that would change drumming forever: use two bass drums instead of one. While the concept was so revolutionary that it took years to gain acceptance from drum manufacturers, today the two-drum setup is widely used.

Bellson's professional career took off quickly. He turned first prizes in several national drum competitions into stints with orchestras led by Ted Fio Rito, Benny Goodman, Tommy Dorsey, Harry James, and Count Basie. It was an incredible musical education that also provided Bellson with culinary lessons on the side. Although both of his parents were fine Italian-born cooks, the drummer witnessed true passion for Italian food when he replaced Buddy Rich in Dorsey's band from 1947 to 1949.

"Tommy Dorsey loved Italian food," he recalls. "It's no exaggeration to say that we had to have it every day. Tommy loved Patsy's Restaurant in New York, and sometimes when he was on the road he'd call and tell him, 'Hey, Patsy, put a load on the next plane and send it to Illinois.' Or Pennsylvania, or wherever. The sauce, the macaroni, all the other stuff. Tommy would then call an Italian restaurant in the town where we were playing and say that we'd be coming in around one or two in the morning and to keep a chef there and the kitchen open. He'd pay for the rental of the restaurant, whatever it cost for the chef, and other than cooking the macaroni and heating the sauce, he'd ask for bread and a special salad. The whole band would usually go.

"At one time Tommy hired a guy named Sally Laperche who was a

Spaghetti à la Marinara

"Pearl was wonderful in the kitchen," says Bellson. *"She'd pick up different ways to cook wherever she went. Her mustard and collard greens were something else. She learned to make polenta and even taught my mom to mix in corn when she made zucchini.*

"This marinara sauce is mine. If my mother or Pearl were to make it, it would be more zesty. Pearl would brown up some spareribs first, then start the sauce from there, adding in the spareribs to slow-cook with the sauce. My recipe is pretty simple."

Serves 4 to 6

¼ cup olive oil
3 cloves garlic, chopped
1 large (28-ounce) can Italian plum tomatoes
1 large (28-ounce) can whole tomatoes
Salt and pepper
Sprinkling of chopped fresh basil
1 pound high-quality Italian spaghetti, such as De Cecco
Freshly grated Parmesan cheese

In a large saucepan, warm the olive oil. Add the garlic and cook for 1 minute. Add the tomatoes, breaking them up with the back of a wooden spoon. Season with the salt and pepper. Reduce the heat and simmer, uncovered, for 1 to 2 hours, stirring occasionally. Add the basil during the last 15 minutes of cooking. Cook the spaghetti according to package directions, until al dente. Drain well and toss with sauce. Serve with the Parmesan cheese.

pretty good trumpet player and a great cook. Tommy brought one of those big road vans that had a small kitchen in the back and he had Sally cook Italian food for the band."

In 1951 Bellson joined Duke Ellington's band. During his two years with the orchestra he made his presence felt not only with his fervid drumming, but also with several compositions that Ellington used, "Skin Deep," "Ting-a-Ling," and "Hawk Talks." He left Ellington in 1953 to tour with Pearl Bailey, went on to play with various "Jazz at the Philharmonic" troupes, and soon started his own bands, big and small, which he has been leading ever since. He maintains big bands on both coasts, composes and arranges prolifically, and squeezes in clinics whenever possible.

Few drummers in the history of jazz have combined Bellson's sentient, immaculate touch, relentless zeal and drive, and penchant for drama and diversity. His ability to swing profoundly, though, is what ultimately has led Bellson to be revered by colleagues and fans alike.

"The biggest compliment for me is when the guys say, 'Louie, you really swung the band,'" he says. "That's better than saying, 'Louie, that was really a great solo.' That's putting the cart before the horse."

Bellson's diet was broadened immeasurably not only by years on the road, but by his late wife's cooking. The author of her own cookbook, *Pearl's Kitchen,* she used to prepare a wide range of dishes, taking special care that Bellson got plenty of greens and beans.

When he was in his late teens, Andrew Cyrille made a decision that may well have deprived the chemical industry of one of its hippest members. He switched from college to the Juilliard School. "I was studying chemistry at St. John's University, but I was gigging at night with jazz musicians," the drummer recounts. "I couldn't be up half the night and then go to class the next day carrying twenty credits. Somebody said, 'What are you doing here when you can play like that?'" Cyrille passed the Juilliard entrance exam and then met with a dean at St. John's. "I remember the counseling he gave me: 'You can go to Juilliard, but remember, you might lose your soul. Be careful. You can always come back here.' So I left and never looked back."

There would be no setup for a midlife crisis for Cyrille, a percussionist of unparalleled stylistic range, musicality, and listening skill. "Teachers at St. John's would say to me, 'Get your degree in chemistry or biology and you can play music on the side,'" he recalls. "But I wasn't that kind of person. If I did it, I was going to do it all the way. I didn't think of music as a hobby. And I would have had to become a research chemist. I didn't want to be in a laboratory making aspirin.

"With the drums I can do all that. I can be creative. I can research. I can be traditional. Whatever I want to do with my job I can do.

"I have really had a rich life as far as music is concerned. I'm not a millionaire. I'm not a wealthy person,

TASTY PLATTERS

- Charlie Haden, *Liberation Music Orchestra* (MCA/Impulse!)
- Anthony Braxton, *Eight (+3) Tristano Compositions 1989* (hat Art)
- David Murray, *Sunrise, Sunset* (Red Baron)

but I work. I can pay the bills. I'm not starving. I meet great people. I travel around the world. I do what I want to do, more or less. And I have a job that I love. I could have done something else with my life, but I think I made the right decision."

Certainly anyone who has heard Cyrille's compositions or drumming during the last thirty years reaches the same conclusion. He may be best known for his eleven-year association during the sixties and seventies with Cecil Taylor, the seminal avant-garde pianist, yet Cyrille's collaborations and the contexts in which he plays have been so varied that he serves as a model for jazz musicians who want to transcend idiomatic barriers. Illinois Jacquet, Kenny Dorham, Nigerian drummer Babatunde

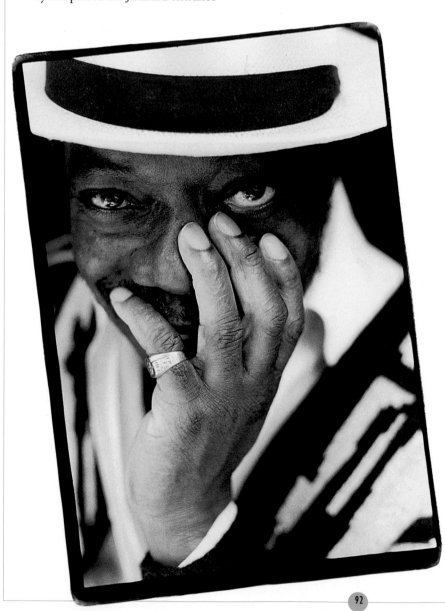

Chicken Drumsticks

One dish the drummer still enjoys making is spice-rubbed chicken drumsticks coated with a mustard glaze. "I call them Andrew's Chicken Drumsticks," he laughs. Mashed potatoes and a green vegetable are Cyrille's preferred accompaniments.

Serves 2 to 4

4 meaty chicken legs, without thighs
Salt and pepper
Few pinches cayenne pepper
1 teaspoon garlic powder
1/2 teaspoon paprika
1/2 teaspoon oregano
Safflower oil
4 tablespoons Dijon-style mustard

Preheat the oven to 350°F. Remove the skin from the chicken legs. Mix together the salt, pepper, cayenne, garlic powder, paprika, and oregano. Rub the spice mixture over the chicken, pressing it into the meat. In a deep skillet, over medium-high heat, warm the oil, until hot but not smoking. Add the chicken (don't crowd) and brown it well on all sides. Remove the chicken from the pan and, using a cooking brush, generously coat the legs with the mustard. Place the legs in a baking dish (again, not crowding), cover, and bake for 35 to 45 minutes, or until the juice runs clear when a leg is pierced.

Olatunji, and choreographer Michael Bennett are but a few of the artists outside avant-garde circles with whom the drummer has worked. Drum duets, a choral theater group, big band ensembles, and playing solo for dancers scratch the surface of settings in which he has appeared.

Much of the drummer's inspiration for eclecticism comes from his upbringing. Raised in Brooklyn during and after World War II, he was brought up in a household that was catholic in its musical tastes. His Haitian-born mother exposed Cyrille and his four sisters and brothers to Haitian sounds at local club meetings and dances, but never forced that music on them. "I remember my mother singing nursery rhymes to me either in Haitian patois or French, but it wasn't something I heard day in and day out," he says. "I heard more American music than Haitian. We used to listen to John Gambling's radio program, 'Rambling with Gambling,' every morning before I'd go to school and he had songs like 'Good Night, Irene.' Then I played all those things like John Philip Sousa when I was in the high school band at St. John's Prep."

Cyrille had already gotten a taste of those sounds with his grammar school drum-and-bugle corps. He expanded his scope immensely when he began playing local gigs of every description as a teenager. "In a cosmopolitan city like New York, where you have so many different kinds of ethnic groups, you have to know how to play polkas, American marches, the bunny hop, calypso," he says.

Cyrille was soon absorbing the fine points of swing and bebop in the company of Coleman Hawkins, Jacquet, Dorham, Mary Lou Williams, and Freddie Hubbard. His subsequent years with Cecil Taylor established him as an innovator whose approach is impossible to pin down. He'll employ minimalism, bombast, and sweet grooves as readily as he'll experiment with the sonic possibilities of a drumstick clacking against a tile floor or a cymbal shuddering when it's bent inside out. If it's out of the ordinary and it feels like it should work, Cyrille will try it.

"I try to bring genuineness, realness, to the instrument all the time," he says. "There's dedication there, a respect for what it is that I've inherited in order to play some of the things I do, and a respect for the musicians from the past who gave their lives to the instrument.

"There are three components in making great music. The first is technique, how you physically master the instrument. The second is concept, how to put this technique together to get the music you need to fit any given situation. How do you bring that idea to life? That's the third component, the spiritual part. How do you make what you have on paper and in your mind come to life, like a great actor or a great singer? How do you make it believable? That's the spiritual part of it."

Given his family's roots, it's not surprising that Cyrille was raised on Caribbean fare, dishes his mother prepared like rice and beans, yams and green plantains. The drummer's diet has changed a number of times since those days, with a decided leaning now toward poultry and shellfish and away from red meat. His wife, Candy, does most of the cooking in their Little Ferry, New Jersey, home, but Cyrille is far from a stranger to the kitchen. In fact, for years when he was single he collected recipes from a television cooking show. He's frank, though, about the extent of his culinary creativity. "When I was living alone, most of the time I would cook for survival, so I wouldn't go hungry," he notes. "I'm not a gourmet cook."

Lester Young. Charlie Parker. Miles Davis. John Coltrane. Chick Corea. Pat Metheny. These six players represent some of jazz's most significant schools of the past sixty years, six players with whom drummer Roy Haynes has worked. Called the father of modern jazz drumming, Haynes, it can also be said, is a living link between bebop and contemporary jazz. His drumming connects the music's stylistic dots every time he sits behind his set.

Haynes was born in 1925 and grew up in the Roxbury section of Boston. His childhood prepared him for a life of extremely varied eating habits. Much of the cuisine in the house was Caribbean since his parents were from Barbados, but he also went out of his way to eat in the city's Italian section. He loved kosher food as well. "I lived across the street from a synagogue," he remembers. "They'd let me put out the lights at certain times and I used to eat in there a lot."

Musically, Haynes picked up on the jazz of the day from his older brother. "He was brilliant," he says. "He knew about Count Basie, Duke Ellington, Billie Holiday, and had their records as a teenager. Around the house I listened to everything. I knew the lyrics to most of Bing Crosby's songs. We always had the radio playing. I had good ears. In fact, the first drumsticks I picked up were my brother's. I was eight or nine. I had the feeling I wanted to play and just went at it.

"I started playing around town when I was a teenager, still in Roxbury Memorial High School. I used to play at Art's Grill on Essex Street in Boston. They had danc-

Derby Day Lobster

Haynes's Boston and Caribbean roots have imparted to the drummer a love for seafood. New England's most famous crustacean, Americanus homarus, *receives several twists with his Derby Day Lobster. Steamed in beer and dusted with seasonings, this is a relatively spicy lobster that may remind some of the famous Maryland steamed crabs.*

Haynes's dish was born in the late fifties, when the drummer and a group of friends, all living in Manhattan's Chelsea section, would gather on the first Saturday in May to watch, and maybe invest a dollar or two on, the Kentucky Derby. "We had a Derby Day celebration in Chelsea right through the sixties," Haynes says. "When I moved out to my home on the Island, we continued to have it out there."

Serves 8 to 10

2 (12-ounce) bottles beer
8 to 10 (1- to 1¼-pound) lobsters
4 bay leaves
Dried sage, dill, and Old Bay Seasoning, to taste
1 teaspoon garlic powder
1 tablespoon crab boil seasoning mix
Tabasco sauce

In a pot large enough to hold the lobsters, add the beer, and then the live lobsters. Distribute the seasonings as evenly as possible over the lobsters, moving the lobsters in the pot if necessary. Cover the pot and bring the beer to a boil; after 5 minutes move the lobsters around in the pot to cook them evenly. Continue to cook for 10 to 15 more minutes, until the lobsters are bright red and cooked through.

ers, singers. The war was on and a lot of sailors and soldiers would hang out. The music would start at one o'clock in the afternoon and go to one in the morning. Those places in downtown Boston had very good food. I was really into eating Boston cream pie. It was one of my favorites.

"There was also the Paradise in Bowdoin Square, owned by Italians in an all-Italian neighborhood. That's when they made pizza the old way, in brick ovens. They used to put olive oil on it so it tasted different, naturally. During intermission, that's what we'd do, eat pizza."

Haynes went from pizza and music with Boston bandleaders like Sabby Lewis to a two-year stint starting in 1945 with Luis Russell's big band. From there he spent another two years with Lester Young's ensemble before going on to the bebop and New York–style pizza served up on Fifty-second Street and clubs like the Three Deuces, where he played behind Charlie Parker, Miles Davis, and Dizzy Gillespie. The balance of his career is crammed with associations with a veritable *Who's Who* of jazz: a long period with Sarah Vaughan; dates with Eric Dolphy, Stan Getz, John Coltrane, and Thelonious Monk; his own Hip Ensemble during the 1970s; and, later, trio work with stars like Chick Corea and Pat Metheny.

The drummer's style has always been ideally suited to accommodate any and all circumstances. His sticks or brushes are in perpetual motion, shifting an accent here, altering a rhythm there, tickling the snare or pounding the bass drum unexpectedly, all with perfect logic, precision, and power. The drum set is Haynes's stage prop which develops the theater he and his bandmates are creating all around them. "I'm just trying to reach people," he explains. "With my music and my playing, I just try to paint a picture and tell a story about life and feelings."

Contrary to his claim—"I'm now a senior citizen; I cool out a lot"—Haynes is as busy as ever, collaborating with vital young artists like Metheny, tenor saxophonists Ralph Moore and Craig Handy, and his own son Graham, a trumpet and cornet player. When he's not touring or appearing in New York clubs, which include Condon's and the Blue Note, he tools around his hometown of Roosevelt, on Long Island, in his sports car or on his ten-speed bike.

TASTY PLATTERS

- Roy Haynes/Pat Metheny/ Dave Holland, *Question and Answer* (Geffen)
- Eric Dolphy, *Out There* (Fantasy/OJC)
- Oliver Nelson, *Blues and the Abstract Truth* (MCA/Impulse!)

The drummer/composer shops for grains and herbs for a recipe as earnestly as he strives for the perfect sonic impact of bass bow upon cymbal. This commitment has paid dividends both in the kitchen and on the bandstand: Hemingway's organic diet has left him feeling healthier and stronger, and his often-intricate free-jazz experiments have enhanced his reputation as one of jazz percussion's most potent and exciting voices.

"I embrace a trend that isn't particularly popular, what I call 'new music,'" he says. "It's a way of synthesizing the many influences and ideas that are occurring all at once around the world and putting together a music that

TASTY PLATTERS

- **Bass Drum Bone**, *Wooferlo* (Soul Note)
- **Reggie Workman**, *Images: The Reggie Workman Ensemble* (Music & Arts)
- **Gerry Hemingway**, *Special Detail* (hat ART)

defies definitions and categories. On the one hand, I'm not really a jazz musician, but then again, I am a jazz musician. I'm not really what some people refer to as the classic academic twentieth-century composer, but I certainly have a hell of a lot to do with that. And I'm

certainly an improviser, but that doesn't necessarily mean that all I do is improvise music.

"I'm only concerned with creating things that I think are fresh, exciting, and interesting, that move music forward. It's sad to me that a majority of the business now is very much concerned with recreating and replicating what has already existed. I'm interested in ideas, in things that make me think. I'm interested in music that hits me hard in the soul. I'm into music that when I hear it, I'm really moved. Every time I perform, I'm after moving people."

Hemingway often does just that,

whether in a solo concert or in collaboration with stalwart jazz adventurers like Anthony Braxton, Earl Howard, and Anthony Davis. His creations are never retiring, and in order to create music that's thick with new ideas, he draws from the world's cultural landscape: American rock and influences from Africa, the Far East, and the Caribbean. With an uncanny sense of swing and tempo as his bedrock, Hemingway utilizes an eclectic variety of shifting rhythms to propel material that runs the gamut from chunky and dark to lanky and lighthearted. Where some avant-garde jazz gets bogged down in stilted pretentiousness devoid of heart, Hemingway's music opts for the route that's both challenging and fun.

He approaches his nutritional habits with a similar thoughtfulness. For more than a decade, he and his wife, Nancy, have relied on a regimen of organic food and vitamin supplements. Hemingway was exposed early to healthful eating habits and good music when he was growing up in Connecticut. His mother was the primary cook for the drummer and his brothers, using her two hundred–odd cookbooks as a guide to American and French cuisine, all of it fresh.

The theater and classical music Hemingway was exposed to at a young age gave way to Jimi Hendrix and the Mothers of Invention. By eleven he was working out with a

Potato and Pea Curry

"Good ingredients," says Hemingway, "make all the difference." He strongly recommends using ingredients that are not only fresh, but also organic.

Hemingway's recipe for Potato and Pea Curry is one of the many Indian-inspired dishes that he cooks and likes to serve as part of an Indian repast.

Serves 4 to 6 as part of a larger Indian meal

2½ pounds Idaho potatoes
2 Red Delicious apples
12 Medjool or Bahri dates

ONION-AND-PEA MIXTURE

1 tablespoon *ghee* (clarified butter)
   or cold-pressed peanut oil
1 teaspoon salt
¾ tablespoon black mustard seeds
¼ teaspoon *asofetida,* available in
   Indian markets (optional)
2 crushed dry red chilies
1 tablespoon cumin seeds
1½ cups fresh shelled peas
2 medium-sized yellow onions, diced
1 sprig minced curry leaves,
   available in Indian markets
1½ teaspoons dried mint leaves

SPICE MIXTURE

1 teaspoon salt
1 teaspoon cumin seed
½ teaspoon coriander seed
¼ teaspoon clove powder
¼ teaspoon nutmeg
½ teaspoon turmeric
3 fresh green chilies
1 large clove garlic
1 large marble-sized cube of fresh
   ginger (approximately 1 inch long
   and ¾ inch thick)
3 tablespoons *ghee*
½ cup fresh coriander (cilantro)
   leaves

Cut the potatoes into even ¾- to 1-inch cubes. In a medium-sized saucepan, cover the potatoes with water and cook until tender, being careful not to overcook. Peel, core, and chop the apples into ¾- to 1-inch chunks and set aside. Pit and dice the dates. Set aside.

To prepare the onion-and-pea mixture, in a large skillet, over medium heat, warm the *ghee* (or peanut oil), salt, and mustard seeds, until the mustard seeds turn gray, about 1½ to 2 minutes. Add the *asofetida* (if using), chilies, and cumin. Lower the heat and simmer for 1 minute. Add the shelled peas, onions, and curry leaves. Stir and cover. Cook until the onions become translucent, about 20 minutes. Stir in the mint leaves. Remove from the heat and keep covered.

To prepare the spice mixture, grind all the dry spices in a mortar. Add the chilies, garlic, and ginger and mash them into the spices. In a large saucepan, over medium-low heat, combine the *ghee* and the spice mixture and cook for 2 minutes, stirring continuously. Add the reserved apples and stir to coat. Cover, reduce the heat to low, and simmer until the apples are semi-soft, about 10 minutes. Add the dates and cooked potatoes and stir to coat with the spices. Stir in the onion-and-pea mixture. Remove from the heat and add the coriander leaves. Keep covered. Serve warm, not hot!

---

snare and cymbal. The money he earned as a golf caddy paid for the second half of the set. At seventeen he discovered jazz.

"Charles McPherson used to say to me, 'You are your own culture, by what you encounter and what you make,'" Hemingway recalls. "I was raised in a real white suburban culture, but I ended up being included in a whole 'nother community that had nothing to do with it. It was because I created that myself. I found it by way of the radio and the records I bought."

New Haven was where Hemingway made many of his most impor-

tant musical connections: pianist Anthony Davis; trumpeter Leo Smith, who encouraged him to delve deeply into jazz history; bassist Mark Helias, who with Hemingway and trombonist Ray Anderson would later form the group Bass Drum Bone. A semester at Berklee College of Music, more than two years of studies with Boston-based drummer Alan Dawson, and course audits at Yale in big band orchestration and at Wesleyan College in Javanese, South Indian, and West African music all laid the groundwork for his move to New York in 1979, where he has lived ever since.

His studies of South Indian music with Ramnad Rhaghazan led to his interest in that region's cuisine. "He was a marvelous cook," the drummer recalls. "We never used recipes. I always watched what he did and took it in. Ever since then, that's the way I've always worked in the kitchen. I never, ever wrote anything down. I always just did it off the top of my head. It was the way I was approaching music at that time, the improviser's spirit. Whatever strikes you at the moment, whatever happens to be in the spice rack, you swing with that one way or another."

Among his peers, Milt Jackson's reputation for culinary excellence is exceeded only by his renown as the pioneer of bebop vibes. As a charter member of the groundbreaking

Modern Jazz Quartet, he built his name on stage and in the studio as the world's premier jazz vibraphonist. Back in hotel and rooming house kitchens, he was honing his cooking skills.

Jackson, also known as "Bags," hooked up with Dizzy Gillespie's big band in 1945 and soon went on to work with Thelonious Monk, Tadd Dameron, Howard McGhee, and Woody Herman. Around 1950, when Jackson joined Gillespie's smaller group, he discovered his second vocation.

"That's when I really got into cookin' on the road," he recalls. "I've always been a very finicky eater

TASTY PLATTERS

• **Milt Jackson, *The Harem*** (Music Masters)
• **Milt Jackson/John Coltrane, *Bags and Trane* (Atlantic)**
• **The Modern Jazz Quartet, *MJQ 40* (Atlantic Jazz)**

from having had asthma when I was little. My taste buds never changed. The solution on the road was to be able to cook myself. Dizzy loved the way I cooked. He was always asking me to cook something wherever we were. I could usually make him

happy with my fried chicken and some biscuits, or grits and eggs in the morning. We'd always try to find a place with a kitchen. I'd make homemade dishes for the guys, things like pork chops, sometimes

a roast lamb or roast beef, and a lot of corn bread."

Born in Detroit in 1923, Jackson had a rather unorthodox inspiration that taught him about rhythm: his mother tenderizing beef. "She'd hit it with the hammer," he remembers, "and I played the rhythm on my father's guitar." He heard his first live jazz in the late 1930s when he was still in high school and he caught the big bands of Ellington, Lunceford, Basie, and Calloway whenever they played in the city's ballrooms on Monday nights. The music he grew up with, though, was gospel. He studied voice and harmony and sang in several of the city's gospel choirs. Jackson's family's church affiliations, in fact, had a lot to do with his later culinary inclinations.

"I learned to cook from my mother," he explains. "She was a great cook. The church women were the greatest when it came to cooking. Every Sunday, the Women's Auxiliary Board of the Church of God and Christ would designate who was going to cook for the congregation after the service ended. Man, all those sisters could cook like you'd never believe! Ham hocks, turkey with corn bread dressing, candied yams, roast beef, Southern dishes, all kinds of greens and all kinds of pies and cakes. It was like a big feast every Sunday.

"In the church kitchen, there'd be six, seven, eight women cooking. They'd start before the people would come to the church and then when the services were over, there would be these big tables in the basement. The whole congregation, ninety to a hundred people, would go down to eat and talk. They'd stay for two or three hours. The best meals in my life were on those Sunday afternoons. The church tradition influenced me in a lot of ways."

While Jackson's music owes a more obvious debt to Lionel Hampton and Lester Young than to Mahalia Jackson, there has always been an element of church-on Sunday fervor in his playing. It surfaces whether he's barreling through a hard-bop burner or playing a wistfully lyrical ballad. Years in the form-conscious Modern Jazz Quartet and later as leader of his own looser-limbed groups established Jackson as a disciplined improviser whose mallets slide across the metal with swinging, bluesy grace. His own "Bluesology" is a classic of the genre. A listener need search no farther than the voluminous Modern Jazz Quartet recording catalogue to discover that Jackson has set the standard on his instrument for inspiring ensemble simpatico. "It's just like a doctor is dedicated to healing," Jackson says, explaining his artistic philosophy. "It's a therapeutic process through the music. I like to feel that we bring a lot of enjoyment to people through it."

Even though he maintains a low-cholesterol diet now and his wife, Sandra, handles most of the cooking in their Teaneck, New Jersey, home, the vibraphonist still whips up a fair number of pastries. "Making sweets has become a hobby with me," he says. "It carries over

Peach Cobbler

"Milt, you're the master of the inner layer," said drummer Joe Harris after eating some of Jackson's peach cobbler. He was referring, of course, to the dessert's soft middle crust.

"It's the kind of thing that cooks best under a slow fire," says the peach-cobbler master himself. "By cooking it slow and low, just like my mother did, it won't burn and the inner layer won't become soggy."

Serves 6

CRUST

2 cups flour, sifted

1 teaspoon baking powder ("You don't want a big rise")

⅓ cup sugar

¼ teaspoon salt

½ cup (1 stick) butter

⅓ cup vegetable shortening

About ¾ cup half-and-half or milk

FILLING

7 cups sliced canned peaches, packed in syrup, or ripe, fresh peaches

¼ cup sugar, plus an additional ⅓ cup if using fresh peaches

½ teaspoon nutmeg

½ teaspoon cinnamon

1 cup (2 sticks) butter

Preheat the oven to 325°F. Butter an 8-inch square baking dish. To prepare the crust, sift the flour, baking powder, sugar, and salt into a large bowl. Using a wooden spoon, and in small pieces, alternately cut the butter and shortening into the flour mixture, until it resembles cornmeal in consistency. Slowly add the half-and-half (or milk), mashing the mixture with a fork and

using only enough liquid to make the dough soft. Turn the dough out onto a floured surface and, with your hands, knead for 30 to 45 seconds. Separate the dough into 2 portions, making 1 portion slightly (10 to 15 percent) larger than the other. Set aside.

To prepare the peach mixture, if using canned peaches, drain the syrup from both cans, reserving ¼ cup. (If using fresh peaches, make a sugar syrup by combining ⅓ cup water and ⅓ cup sugar in a saucepan. Bring the mixture to a boil, stirring continuously, then lower the heat to a simmer and continue to stir for 5 minutes or until it coats the back of a wooden spoon. Remove from the heat and cool.) Place the peaches in a large bowl and sift the sugar, nutmeg, and cinnamon over them. Mix well. Pour half the peach mixture into the prepared baking dish and dot with half the butter. Roll out the smaller portion of dough and place over the peaches. Pour the second half of the peach mixture on top of the layer of dough. Lightly drizzle the peach syrup (or sugar syrup) over the peaches. Dot with the remaining butter. Roll out the remaining piece of dough so that it is large enough to slightly overlap the baking dish, and crimp the edges. Place the dough on top of the peaches, allowing the excess to hang over the edge of the baking dish. Place a large dish or bowl on the rack below the baking dish to catch drips, and cook for 1 to 1½ hours, until the top crust is lightly browned all over. Serve with vanilla-spiked whipped cream, ice cream, or as Jackson likes it, "just plain."

from learning from my mother when I was small. I used to watch her and got her to teach me." No

fewer than a dozen musicians expected Jackson to contribute his peach cobbler recipe.

No instrument in jazz is more capable of wreaking havoc with the delicate balance of an ensemble than the drums. Few are better at keeping that balance than Paul Motian. His disciplined skills as an instrumentalist as well as his freethinking as a conceptualist have made him the drummer of choice for some of the most influential jazz artists in his-

TASTY PLATTERS

- **Paul Motian, *Bill Evans* (JMT)**
- **Paul Motian, *On Broadway, Volumes 1 and 2* (JMT)**
- **Bill Evans, *Waltz for Debby* (Fantasy/OJC)**

tory, Bill Evans, Paul Bley, and Keith Jarrett among them.

Not surprisingly, Motian has also maintained a balanced dietary regimen for much of his professional career. It wasn't always that way, though, particularly when he moved to Manhattan in 1954.

"I remember going down to the Lower East Side and buying potato pancakes for ten cents," Motian laughs. "I didn't do any cookin'. I was young and indestructible. I could eat anything.

"When I was playing with Bill Evans in the early sixties and was on the road, I ate hamburgers, grilled cheese sandwiches, chocolate milkshakes, that kind of junk food. When I was playing with Keith Jarrett, it was still the same

thing. My consciousness started to get raised later on in the mid- and late sixties. It was during the time with Keith Jarrett that I started to become aware that maybe this stuff ain't great. I started trying to cook for myself. Luckily, I had a good basic diet, that Middle Eastern diet, yogurt and that kind of stuff."

Motian's parents were born in Turkey, so his mother's Middle Eastern dishes were on the stove when he was growing up in Providence, Rhode Island. The music in the air was Armenian, Turkish, Arabic, and Egyptian. "My parents had the old seventy-eight records that you cranked up on the machine, the one with the big spiked nail on the end," he recounts. "When I started going to school, I started hearing other stuff and buying seventy-eights. In high school I used to listen to Symphony Sid broadcast from Birdland in New York City. I had my ear glued to the radio and then I would send away for those records—Bud Powell, Max Roach, Lester Young. This was in the mid-1940s."

Motian actually began playing when he was twelve or thirteen. He got an early taste of the road after high school as a member of a big band that traveled around New England and entertained at resorts in places like Lake Winnipesaukee, New Hampshire. In Providence he spent his earnings on admissions to theater shows to hear stars such as Jimmie Lunceford, Count Basie, and Duke Ellington and for records that featured Buddy Rich, Gene Krupa, and Max Roach. He signed on with the navy during the Korean War, went to music school while he was in the service, and settled in Manhattan when he was discharged in 1954. Manhattan has been home ever since, and that's where he began his real education, going to hear drummers like Denzil Best and Shadow Wilson in downtown clubs.

Motian eventually appeared on a number of albums with Bill Evans and with Keith Jarrett, yet those represent only a small portion of his recording output and his list of collaborators. The drummer regularly plays with the best of jazz's cutting-edge practitioners, from Geri Allen and Charlie Haden to Bill Frisell and Dewey Redman. He also leads his own bands and writes prolifically. As a stylist, no one is more adept than Motian at capturing a piece's nuances and creating a field of unexpected colors and off-kilter changeups for his soloists. He constantly performs that most sought after of drumming feats: laying down a swarming rhythmic base that implies the melody without belaboring the obvious.

"Whether it's 'in' or 'out,' as long as it's what I consider good music, I love it," he says. "It could be a cowboy song. I couldn't even imagine doing anything else. I feel the best when I'm playing. When I'm not, I'm like a fish out of water.

"I hope the music touches people, that they get something out of it. When I was a kid and listened to music, I got a lot of inspiration and joy out of it. I hope people get that when they listen to my music or my drumming."

Ospok Showfreh—Armenian Lentil Soup

Motian maintains an exercise regimen that includes brisk walks through Central Park. He eats healthily, as attested to by Ospok Showfreh, his mother's recipe for Armenian lentil soup.

"My mom used to make this when I was a kid," he explains. "I don't think this is exactly the way she did it, but it's close. It's the kind of recipe where it's all right to improvise."

Serves 3 to 4

1 pound lentils
3 tablespoons butter
1 large Spanish onion, diced
Salt and pepper
5 1/4 cups water
1 tablespoon lemon juice
1/2 pound string beans
1/2 pound cooked green peas

Wash the lentils until the water rinses clean. Drain and set aside. In a large soup pot, over medium heat, melt the butter and sauté the onion, just until soft. Add the lentils and season with the salt and pepper. Add the water and the lemon juice. Slowly bring the mixture to a boil, then reduce the heat and simmer until the lentils are tender, about 1 hour or slightly longer. Add the string beans and simmer for 15 to 20 minutes, or until the string beans are tender. Add the cooked peas. Adjust the seasonings to taste. Add more water if the soup appears dry. "As I said," Motian reiterates, "it's okay to improvise. So add other vegetables." Note that carrots, celery, and zucchini all work well in this soup. However, one must be aware of the various cooking times inherent in the different vegetables. Note that carrots and celery should go in 5 minutes or so before the string beans while zucchini should be added about 5 minutes after the string beans.

He's known as *El Rey*—"the King"—yet Tito Puente is simply not the crown-wearing type. Even if he were, the native New Yorker would be too busy to put it on. Puente's concert and recording schedule makes a door-to-door Bible salesman's life seem restful by comparison, so preparing a relaxed meal for himself at his home in Tappan, New York, is rarely in the cards for him these days. Puente is on the road constantly, refining the union of jazz and Afro-Cuban music pioneered by Machito, Mario Bauzá, and Dizzy Gillespie and adding luster to the titles he earned years ago—King of Latin Music, King of Latin Jazz, King of Mambo, and King of the Timbales. Fittingly, he recently served as musical director for the film adaptation of Oscar Hijuelos's novel *The Mambo Kings Play Songs of Love.* When he's not on the bandstand, he's oftentimes receiving an award. His star can now be found on the Hollywood Boulevard Walk of Fame.

Born in New York City in 1923 to Puerto Rican natives, Puente was the oldest of two children. His father was a foreman in a razor-blade factory; his mother, a non-musician, nonetheless provided the family's artistic inspiration. Puente was enrolled in piano and dancing classes at a very young age, for good reason. "I was always banging on boxes and walls and windows," he recalls. "I was seven years old."

Puente was too young to turn down the *escabeche* and *habichuelas coloradas* that his mother prepared, but he did have his own ideas about what to eat. "I only ate that stuff when my mother made it," he says. "I really wanted to eat American food."

Musically, Puente stayed truer to his roots. After several years of playing around his Latin neighborhood, he dropped out of high school at fifteen for a winter job with a rhumba band in Miami Beach. From there he was able to make a number of trips to Cuba to absorb the sounds. When he returned to New York, he became a member of the band led by Jose Curbelo, generally acknowledged to be the city's first "Mambo King." Just before he joined the navy for three years he got a taste of the big time during a brief stint with Machito's Afro-Cubans. It whet his appetite for arranging and composing, which skills he honed at the Juilliard School and later with leaders like Miguelito Valdes and Marcelino Guerra. By 1949 he had his own ensemble, the Picadilly Boys, a pun on *picadillo,* a meat and vegetable hash.

Puente's hot mambo sound, soon expanded to big band size, became

TASTY PLATTERS

- Tito Puente, *Puente Goes Jazz* (Fresh Sound)
- Tito Puente, *Goza Mi Timbal* (Concord Picante)
- Tito Puente, *Out of This World* (Concord Picante)

the rage during the fifties and early sixties. Latinos in many of the country's major cities jammed ballrooms and clubs like Manhattan's Palladium to dance to the band

Ensalada de Bacalao

On his trips to Puerto Rico, when he doesn't get caught up in fatty foods, Puente enjoys bacalao *salad, made with dried salt cod and onions. "In New York it was something my mother used to make around the Christmas holidays and during the summer," he says. "It's a really typical Puerto Rican dish."*

Serves 6

- I pound dried salt codfish
- 2 large onions, thinly sliced
- 4 large tomatoes, peeled and sliced
- I cup olive oil
- ½ cup vinegar
- Salt and pepper

Soak the codfish overnight in water that amply covers the fish, draining the water and adding fresh water a couple of times. When ready to cook, drain the codfish again, then place it in a large pan of boiling water. Cover and simmer for 15 minutes. Drain and rinse in fresh, cold water. Let cool, then peel off the skin. Remove any bones and, using a fork, shred the codfish. Set the shredded fish on a large platter and cover with the onions and tomatoes. In a small jar with a tight-fitting lid, combine the oil and vinegar. Season with the salt and pepper, then shake well and pour over the fish. Chill for an hour or 2. Serve cold.

that had overtaken Machito's and Tito Rodriguez and his Mambo Devils in popularity. Puente poured out a steady stream of hits. His 1958 album *Dance Mania* remains one of Latin music's biggest sellers.

Despite immersing himself in the heated riffs and cross-rhythms of the mambo, Puente still kept up with the bebop of the day, performing at Fifty-second Street clubs and even recording an early fusion album, *Puente Goes Jazz.* He has continued to work both sides of the street ever since, maintaining both salsa and Latin jazz bands and collaborating with Latin superstars like Celia Cruz and Eddie Palmieri and with jazz giants like Gillespie. Puente's renown spread wider when Carlos Santana recorded a pair of his songs during the seventies, "Oye Como Va" and "Para los Rumberos." It helped the *timbalero* reach a wider audience, a primary goal.

"I'm trying to get some recognition for our music," he says. "That's one of the reasons I'm traveling so much, so that people all over can hear our music. I'm trying to spread the rhythms, the cultural roots, of the Latin-American people."

With more than one hundred albums and nearly five hundred compositions to his credit, Puente is a one-man musical juggernaut. His Latin jazz is built on a foundation of torrid polyrhythms and a driving Latin *clave* beat that acts as a launching pad for free improvisation. Whether it's John Coltrane's "Equinox" or Chick Corea's "Spain," a jubilant Puente can be found in the center of the action standing at his timbales, setting the syncopations, and often gesturing with his patented, flamboyant, sticks-circling-over-his-head move. He's also the King of Excitement.

Puente laments that his diet over the years hasn't been more consistent and health conscious, a circumstance he's working hard to change. Since neither he nor his wife get a chance to prepare many home-cooked meals, he has to rely on restaurant cuisine.

"Latinos are always into fats," he says. "You go to Puerto Rico, baby, you put on pounds right away. You can get into that bag without realizing it in a place where everybody eats the same.

"The problem with the road is that you can't get the food you're accustomed to getting. When you're hungry, you eat anything. But I'm not into rice and beans. I watch my diet now. I'm eating more intelligently now. I'm into salads and fish."

Don't count on Max Roach to become nostalgic about the cuisine he experienced back in the late forties and early fifties when he was helping to create a new music in Manhattan clubs like Monroe's Uptown House and Minton's Playhouse. Even if the drummer was gastronomically inclined then, which he wasn't, he would have been hard pressed to fit eating well, let alone cooking, onto his overflowing artistic plate.

"On Fifty-second Street with Charlie Parker and everybody, we were kind of catch as catch can," Roach recalls about his dietary habits. "Nobody really got into cooking. You can only do so much. If you're really going to master an

TASTY PLATTERS

• Max Roach, *Deeds, Not Words* (Fantasy/OJC)
• Max Roach, *To the Max!* (Mesa/Blue Moon)
• Clifford Brown/Max Roach, *Daahoud* (Mobile Fidelity)

instrument and deal with music in all its aspects, you don't have time to do anything else.

"Miles [Davis] and I roomed together when we worked with Charlie Parker and we never even thought about cooking. Cooking wasn't a thing that you really talked about. We were too busy trying to keep up with Charlie Parker."

In the four decades since he established a reputation as one of jazz's most influential musicians, helping nurture bebop through its infancy, drums have had no greater champion than that of this instru-

mentalist, composer, and arranger. And while he has made time to become acquainted with the family stove, creating fresh music, not exotic meals, remains his focus. "Cooking is not really that difficult," he maintains.

Roach was born in 1925 and raised

in Brooklyn. "I grew up during the Depression," he says. "Rough times. We ate what we could get. Everybody cooked in the family. People were very inventive. It was the art of making the most out of the least."

Inspired by a mother who sang gospel music and an aunt who

taught him how to play the piano, Roach soaked up the sounds emanating from his home, the radio, and the city around him. He played drums in the high school marching band, had a brief stint when he was sixteen as a replacement in the Duke Ellington Orchestra, and made his recording debut at nineteen with Coleman Hawkins. It was the start of a lifetime of incredible collaborations. Charlie Parker, Dizzy Gillespie, Miles Davis, Clifford Brown, Sonny Rollins, and Thelonious Monk shared the bandstand with the drummer during the 1940s and 1950s. The 1960s found him politically active, married to vocalist Abbey Lincoln for a few years, and composing hard-hitting works like the "Freedom Now Suite."

In the early 1970s Roach joined the faculty of the University of Massachusetts at Amherst, in the department of music and dance. He now holds a part-time position there as an adjunct professor. As befits a visionary who perceives no boundaries between disciplines, Roach has spent the last two decades working with a wide range of artists in every conceivable format. Collaborating with playwright Sam Shepard, avant-garde jazzmen Cecil Taylor and Anthony Braxton, choreographer Alvin Ailey, and the Kodo Drummers of Japan, and creating music for breakdancers, rappers, symphony orchestras, and television and film scores just scratch the surface of his endeavors.

In every setting, from his earliest bebop experiments with Charlie Parker through his percussion ensemble M'Boom to his current Double Quartet and work with his daughter, Maxine, and the Uptown String Quartet, Roach has carved out a lead role for the drums, which historically had been relegated to more of a background instrument in jazz. He has been called an architect of percussion, constructing well thought out and unexpected forms that support richly diverse textures, colors, and dynamics. Never coldly technical or overly ornate, Roach's charged drumming and compositions are melodic masterpieces that inevitably inspire bandmates to greater emotional heights.

"The drummer sets the mode," he says. "The rhythm section identifies what's going on. That's what it's all about. You have to know who you are, what you are, what your job is, and try to be creative within those boundaries. It ain't easy.

"I just try to stay in the continuum of Louis Armstrong and Duke Ellington and Charlie Parker and be creative within those boundaries. Those great musicians and composers developed a unique and personal individuality. I'm always striving for my own perfection within the continuum."

Like many other musicians, the drummer has adjusted his diet over the years. "I could eat anything I wanted to eat," he says, "but you become aware of health foods and the fact that you're eating too much cholesterol. Of course, I know some people who've been eating fried chicken and all that stuff who are up in their early hundreds. I guess it's constitution, and psychological.

"My wife and I don't eat that heavily. We eat salads and fish and stuff. As you get older you start trying to take care of yourself."

Fried (Pan-Simmered) Corn

The drummer's fried corn harkens back to those days when his family needed to make the most out of the least. "We'd eat this when the corn was in season," he recalls about this popular Southern recipe. "Now that I spend every summer in a place like Amherst in western Massachusetts, I can easily pick up fresh corn and bring it home so I can make this dish."

Serves 4 as a side dish or 2 as a main course

  8 ears fresh white corn
  ¾ cup vegetable oil
  1 cup onion, diced
  1 large garlic clove, minced
  1 cup sweet red pepper, diced
  1 cup green pepper, diced
  ½ cup celery, diced
  1 teaspoon jalapeño pepper,
    finely chopped
  Salt

Shuck the corn and slice the kernels from the cob. In a large skillet, heat the oil over medium heat. Sauté the onion and garlic for 5 minutes, or until they become transparent. Add the corn, stir in the red and green peppers, celery, and jalapeño pepper. Reduce heat to medium low, cover the pan, and cook for 30 minutes, stirring occasionally. Remove lid from skillet and cook over medium heat for an additional 20 minutes. Remove from the stove and salt to taste.

Arthur Taylor has come full circle. More than three decades after leaving America for Europe, the drummer is home again, in the Sugar Hill section of Harlem, New York. Making several hundred recordings with the greatest players in jazz and establishing a reputation as the quintessential bop and post-bop drummer weren't enough for Taylor. He felt he still had something to prove to himself right back where he got his start.

"I was anxious to get back to the United States so I could come back to Harlem, so that the people could react and I could know how good I really was," he says. "When you get to Harlem, you can't be fooling around. They don't want to know about that funny stuff."

Taylor needn't have worried. The respect he had earned as a drummer before he left New York had only grown deeper by the time he returned as both an oft-recorded musician and a published author. His book, *Notes and Tones,* comprising Taylor's frank interviews with peers like Miles Davis and Don Cherry, remains one of the most insightful documentations of the personalities behind the music. His recorded musical output is matched by that of only a handful of cohorts.

TASTY PLATTERS

• **Arthur Taylor, A.T.'s Delight** (Blue Note)
• **Bud Powell, *Time Was*** (Bluebird)
• **Red Garland, *Soul Junction*** (Fantasy/OJC)

Taylor's fulfillment now comes in part in less tangible ways. "The Prestige label sent me the complete recordings I had done with them," he explains. "I was the only guy alive. Monk, Charlie Rouse,

Thad Jones, Red Garland, Paul Chambers, John Coltrane, Gene Ammons, Bud Powell, George Duvivier. They're all gone, so naturally the music has changed." Thinking of the youthful members of his own ensemble, he notes, "I try to pass on things that I learned and did with those men to these young men." Taylor's voluminous storehouse of cultural and musical knowledge, past and present, is among the reasons why he has been asked to host his own radio show in New York through the years.

Born in 1929, the drummer saw the fortunes of Harlem ebb and flow as he was growing up. When Taylor was in grammar school, a crowd of one hundred thousand celebrated Joe Louis's world championship in the streets of Harlem. Adam Clayton Powell, Jr., was elected New York's first black congressman when Taylor was in high school. Even though the Depression and World War II didn't treat Harlem kindly, his parents, through rough times and smooth, put enough food on the table for Taylor and his sister. Since his father was from Belize and his mother—the cook in the family—from Jamaica, the fare was tinged with a West Indian flavor.

His father also made sure that

Taylor was nourished culturally, bringing him along to the Paramount and Harlem theaters to hear the likes of Buddy Rich, Count Basie, and Billie Holiday. For Christmas, 1948, his mother bought him a set of drums, and by the following spring he was playing locally in a quartet with his neighbors Sonny Rollins and Jackie McLean. "We were known as the guys from the Hill," he recalls. "People like Bird used to come up to see us."

In 1952 Taylor began an association with pianist Bud Powell that lasted three years. "The only thing that I really wanted to do was play with Bud Powell," he admits. "That was my highest ambition." He didn't stop there, of course. After a decade of working with the most inventive jazz artists on the scene, he went to Europe in 1963 with Johnny Griffin and Kenny Drew for a three-month stint. He stayed seventeen years, ten of them in Paris, seven in Liège, Belgium. It was in Europe that he learned to cook, picking up tips from his colleagues.

"Johnny Griffin is an excellent cook. We would go to Europe and the fans or guys' wives would meet us and take him right to the store to get what he wanted to cook. I'd say to Johnny, 'We don't have to play. We can come here and you can just cook. We can live off that.'"

Taylor's diet was greatly influenced by a conversation he had with pianist Walter Davis, Jr., in the late 1960s. "He had become a vegetarian and he told me about the dangers of eating meat," the drummer remembers. "He had spoken about the slaying of the animal, the mixing of animal blood

Taylor's Wailers Chicken

Taylor, who mostly cooks for himself, prefers to eat only once a day. "Sometimes in the morning I'll have tea or coffee, maybe a piece of bread, and some fruit," he says. "If I eat at night, it might be a green salad, some brown rice with sautéed onions, and fried shrimp."

On those occasions when he's cooking for guests, he'll often prepare one of his favorite dishes, an original creation he's dubbed Taylor's Wailers Chicken. It's a chicken and vegetable roast perked up with Szechuan hot sauce.

Serves 4

- 1 cup white wine, plus extra for basting (approximately ⅔ cup)
- 2 tablespoons canola oil
- Juice of 1 lemon
- 1 tablespoon Dijon mustard
- 1 tablespoon Szechuan hot sauce
- 2 large tomatoes, minced
- 2 cloves garlic, minced
- 1 teaspoon marjoram
- Salt and pepper
- ¼ pound string beans, trimmed
- 8 small new potatoes, quartered
- 1 (3-pound) chicken, cut into serving pieces

In a deep, ovenproof skillet, mix together the wine, oil, lemon juice, mustard, hot sauce, tomatoes, garlic, marjoram, and salt and pepper to taste. Add the string beans, potatoes, and chicken. Mix to coat and marinate for at least 1 hour. To cook, preheat the oven to 350°F. Bake for 1 hour, or until the potatoes are tender and the chicken is cooked through, stirring and adding a little more wine (about 3 tablespoons) every 20 minutes.

with human blood. He frightened me to death. I didn't look at meat for six or seven years."

On the bandstand Taylor applied lessons picked up from many of the musical legends he accompanied. Charlie Parker in particular offered advice to which the drummer still adheres.

"He gave a lot of nice tips," Taylor recounts, "one of which was, 'The audience is never supposed to know how you do this, because if they know, they don't have to come and see you.' That's exciting to me, because people have to really become involved to realize that they can't figure out what's happening. In a club it's one thing to play for an audience where everybody sits there and claps, but nobody hears you. It's better when you stun them so much that they forget to clap."

Taylor is a powerhouse behind the drum set, one who also dearly values shifting dynamics and subtle colorations. He has always challenged his bandmates, from John Coltrane to his young collaborators, Willie Williams, Vincent Herring, and Abraham Burton, to take their ideas as far as possible. His tacks vary, from a lazy Sunday afternoon groove to a white-hot rhythmic flurry. There's never any excess with Taylor, just an endless string of precise explosions that keep the soloist's train of thought —and the song—on course.

As for the drummers of today, Taylor is not all that impressed by what he hears. "Younger drummers put me to sleep, in a sense, because they just think that it's going ring-ding-a-ding or boom-boom-boom," he says. "It's more than that. It's got to come from the heart. It's not all in the head."

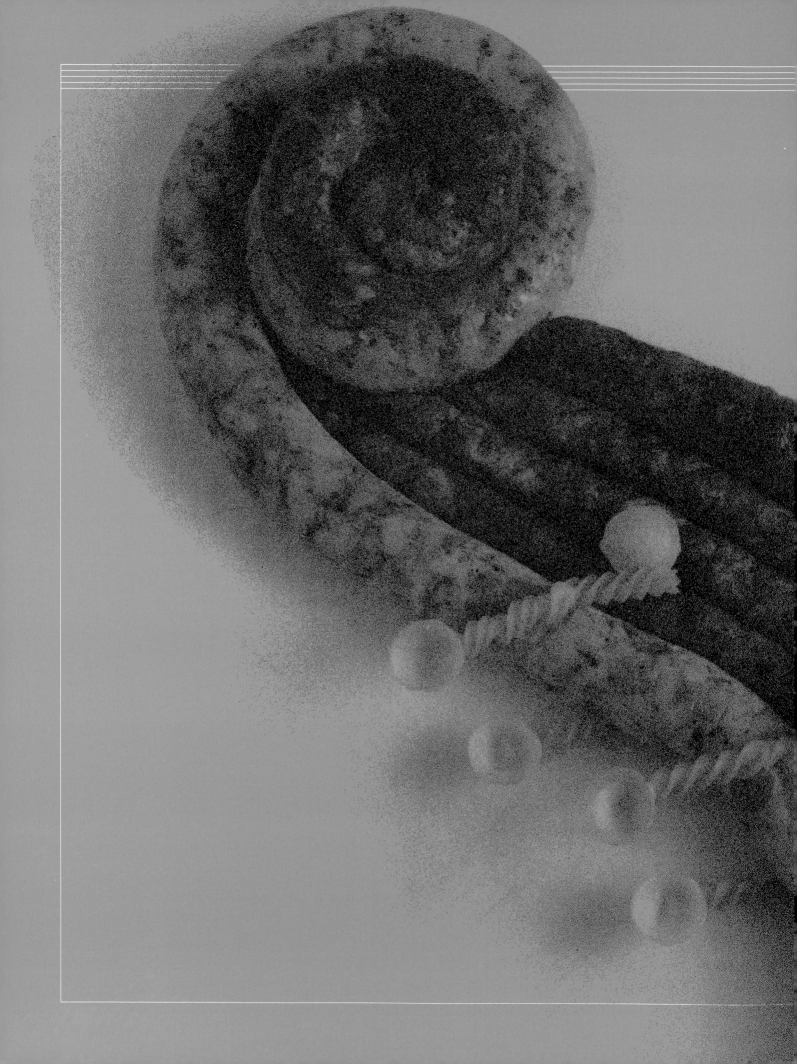

STRINGS

It's small wonder that Ray Brown feels comfortable with both his improvisational and gastronomical decisions. Among the *crème de la crème* of jazz bassists, Brown has time and again proven his impeccable, swinging taste in the company of the music's most demanding masters, Dizzy Gillespie and Oscar Peterson among them. Since both of his parents cooked professionally, he was already knowledgeable about good food long before he was navigating the changes in Dizzy's "Salt Peanuts." He especially revered the culinary prowess of his father, a chef on the railroad.

"Imagine if you played the piano and Oscar Peterson was your father," he says. "If somebody asked you, 'What did your father play that you liked?' you'd say, 'You've got to be kidding!' I lived in a house where my mother didn't have to call us to come inside, wash up, and eat. Everybody was there waitin'. That's how good the food was."

Brown was born in 1926. The section of Pittsburgh where he was raised was a melting pot. "During the holidays, my father sometimes used to make gumbo and take pots of it over to different neighbors," he remembers. "It was a mixed neighborhood, Polish and Italian and black. They traded wines and different kinds of foods."

The popular music on the radio at the time was Fletcher Henderson and Louis Armstrong, sounds that Brown loved. He studied bass at Schenley High School and moved to Buffalo in search of gigs soon after graduation. He was armed with confidence about how to play and what to eat, which he soon enough got the opportunity to test. Trumpeter Gillespie took him on the road in 1945, just when bebop was beginning to shake the jazz world by its foundations. Brown's life clicked into fast forward, with challenges on stage by night and in hotel room kitchenettes by day. He recorded "One Bass Hit" with Gillespie in 1946. During the late forties he worked regularly with Gillespie and bandmates Milt Jackson, John Lewis, and Kenny Clarke, players who

TASTY PLATTERS

- Ray Brown, *Something for Lester* (Fantasy/OJC)
- Ray Brown/Jimmy Rowles, *As Good As It Gets* (Concord Jazz)
- Ella Fitzgerald, *These Are the Blues* (Verve)

were to become three-quarters of the Modern Jazz Quartet. He married Ella Fitzgerald in 1948 and toured with her before getting divorced four years later.

From 1951 to 1966, interrupted occasionally by "Jazz at the Philharmonic" tours and other collaborations, Brown teamed with pianist Peterson and guitarist Herb Ellis in a trio that became legendary for both its endlessly fascinating interplay and its easy grace. The anticipation Brown brought to the improvisational mix at times seemed telepathic. It's a talent that keeps him possibly the most in-demand bassist in jazz.

And, then, there's his effortless swing. Nobody, but nobody, swings like Ray Brown.

"You're either gonna swing or you're not," Brown asserts. "It's like saying, 'I'm going to be white or black today.' You don't make an effort to do it. It doesn't come like that. I wish it did, but it doesn't."

Not only is Brown endowed with a wonderfully unhurried sense of time, he has cultivated a tone that's plump and immaculate and pitch that's utterly perfect. It adds up to a groove too rich to ignore, one that he adjusts to fit straight bop, big band swing, the blues, and modal pieces alike. His succinct, almost conversational lines, elastic beat, and smoothly shifting dynamics never fail to inspire his bandmates. His arco playing, that is, with the bow, is unrivaled. And as a leader, Brown leaves plenty of room for his sidemen to roam. Longtime group members Gene Harris on piano and Jeff Hamilton on drums have made fine use of that space over the years.

On the music and business fronts, Brown is a man of many hats. Since he moved to Los Angeles in 1966, he has maintained both a busy studio and an international touring schedule. He plays regularly with Peterson, the Philip Morris Superband, and Triple Treat, a trio with pianist Monty Alexander and Herb Ellis. Off stage, he has written several bass instruction books, produced concerts, and run a video and recording company. In the late 1980s he even tried his hand as part-owner and booker of a Santa Monica jazz club/restaurant called the Loa. "If you ever get the chance to do it," he laughs, "pass."

Even though his wife, Cecilia, takes care of most of the cooking, Brown nevertheless considers himself "a bit of a gourmet. . . . If you flew me to any city in the world," he says, "I could take you to some great restaurants."

Japanese-Style Grilled Oysters with Cognac

Although at a loss for the name of the Tokyo restaurant that serves oysters flamed in cognac, Brown well remembers the various dishes he sampled at that Japanese steak house.

"The Japanese like to cook everything on a grill right in front of you," the bassist points out. "At this restaurant they'd sometimes start out with crab, cook it with a little butter and fresh asparagus. They also did something with fresh oysters as a first course, something you'd order before dinner. I've learned to make them at home. They're fantastic."

Serves 4 to 6 as a first course

3 to 4 dozen large oysters, shucked
¼ cup (½ stick) butter
2 tablespoons olive oil
Salt and freshly ground pepper
½ cup cognac

Place the oysters in a colander and rinse them well, then place them on paper towels to dry. In a cast-iron skillet that is large enough to hold all the oysters without crowding (it may be necessary to do this in shifts), warm about half of the butter and oil, being careful not to burn the butter. When the skillet is very hot add the oysters and quickly sprinkle them with the salt and pepper. (They cook quickly, so work fast.) After about 90 seconds, the oysters should have a little brown "crust" on the bottom. Flip, add the remaining butter and oil to the skillet, and sprinkle the oysters with more salt and pepper. When the oysters are brown on both sides, turn off the heat, pour the cognac evenly over the oysters, and ignite with a match. Shake the skillet until the flame dies. Serve immediately.

Guitarist Charlie Byrd has a special place in his heart for Brazil. And with the kind of introduction to that country he received during his visit there in 1960, it's no surprise.

"We played out first engagement in Fortaleza," he remembers. "We drove down to Bahia and then had a flight cross-country to Belo Horizonte. It was a little ol' plane, I think a DC-3. Well, it stopped for lunch; we landed at this

with Stan Getz, is credited with helping to ignite the American love affair with the bossa nova in the sixties. Yet while the guitarist has spent many subsequent years using the sounds of Brazil as a springboard for his own inventions, he's a musician who doesn't restrict himself to one idiom. His years spent in New York's bebop scene during

the early fifties and, later, his intensive classical training have shaped Byrd into an artist who flourishes

in several distinct worlds. He even composes scores for films, television, and dance groups. "I get a kick out of all of them," he says.

Born in 1925, Byrd grew up in southeast Virginia, where blues was the predominant music he heard on the radio. But it was Les Paul's warm, technically dazzling electric sound that fueled an early infatuation with guitar. Byrd had hopes of playing major-league baseball, but those dreams slowly fell by the wayside as his guitar skills became sharper and sharper.

His father, who gave him his first lessons and owned the town's general store, had an influence on Byrd that transcended the musical sphere. Not only was the store his practice space, it was the unofficial town social club where young Byrd and his three brothers learned to appre-

little farmhouse. The farm matron had this big buffet lunch for all of the passengers on the plane, all of the Brazilian specialties, black beans, *feijoada.* It was one of the most wonderful meals I've ever had in my life."

Even though that charming stopover has yet to be repeated, Byrd continues to return to Brazil for reasons more musical than culinary. *Jazz Samba,* the 1962 pop chart–topping album he recorded

---

Bacalhau—Portuguese Fish Hash

When your tastes run from grilled and southern fare to Brazilian feijoada *and Portuguese* bacalhau, *a fish hash, it's not hyperbole to proclaim, as the guitarist does, "I love food. I've never found any that I don't like."*

Byrd's creative touch in his Portuguese bacalhau *recipe is substitution of fresh cod for the traditional salt cod. Why the switch? "It's better for my diet," Byrd explains.*

Serves 4

4 tablespoons olive oil
¾ pound potatoes, sliced into thin ovals
4 tablespoons chopped onion
4 large cloves garlic, minced
1 pound fresh cod, broken into 1-inch cubes

Salt and pepper
1 cup fresh basil or dill, chopped
2 lemons, cut into wedges

In a large skillet, over medium-high heat, warm the oil. Add the potatoes (Note: To speed the process, you may parboil the potatoes beforehand) and cook for 10 to 12 minutes, stirring frequently, until the potatoes begin to soften. Add more oil if the potatoes are sticking. When the potatoes begin to soften, add the onion and garlic and cook for a few minutes, until the onion softens. Add the fish and cook for 5 minutes, stirring frequently, until the fish loses its translucency. Season with salt and pepper. Transfer to a large platter. Sprinkle with the chopped basil (or dill) and garnish with the lemon wedges.

ciate Tidewater specialties like oysters, clams, crabs, and catfish stew, dishes that his father prepared in large batches for periodic parties. Those get-togethers were among the few occasions at which his mother didn't lay out her down-home southern fare, meals often graced with the perch, bass, and catfish her sons caught in the freshwater pond near their house. "We didn't throw much away," the guitarist laughs.

Jazz played an increasingly significant role in Byrd's plans when he set out on his own in his late teens. As a member of the Southern Colonels band at Virginia Polytechnic Institute, he became comfortable with the big band sound. He then joined an army orchestra overseas during his World War II hitch, spent time playing with the great Gypsy guitarist Django Reinhardt in Paris, and upon his return to the States became a regular for several years on the stages of Manhattan clubs.

And then he dropped out of the jazz scene completely.

For six years, beginning in 1950, he concentrated on classical guitar, even studying with the legendary Spaniard Andrés Segovia. When he went public again in 1956, he had become a master of both the classical and jazz idioms. Those worlds have remained separate for Byrd, with his acoustic guitar the only overt link between the two. He also put the electric instrument away for good when he returned.

"There's a great benefit in practicing classical music," he says. "There's an awful lot to learn from it, being that it's written

TASTY PLATTERS

- Charlie Byrd, *Byrd at the Gate* (Fantasy/OJC)
- Stan Getz/Charlie Byrd, *Jazz Samba* (Verve)
- Charlie Byrd/Herb Ellis/ Barney Kessel, *Great Guitars at the Winery* (Concord Jazz)

down and composed by masters. The study of jazz music is more a search for your own emotions. In classical music there's structure and technique to be learned and someone else's work to draw from. In jazz you can listen to a lot of records and hear plenty of hot licks, but eventually you're on your own if you're really serious. I like both of these feelings."

The Brazilian tinge that Byrd added to his repertoire in the sixties is a natural extension of the sensibility that moves him toward both structure and experimentation. Whether he's improvising with jazz guitar cronies like Barney Kessel and Herb Ellis, being featured with the National Symphony Orchestra, or playing a samba with Brazilian guitarist Laurindo Almeida, Byrd's mellow-toned instrument comes across as unostentatious, tender, and rich in dynamic range. His swing is subtle but sure, and his most powerful improvising can sneak up on a listener during his wonderfully melodic strolls.

The guitarist now lives in Annapolis, Maryland, still near plenty of water. Byrd prides himself on the cooking skills he picked up from his mother, which he uses and refines during the six months or so each year that he's not on the road. "I try to eat a lot of salads and a lot of fish," he says. And some of the fish he catches himself from the sailboat he takes out onto Chesapeake Bay.

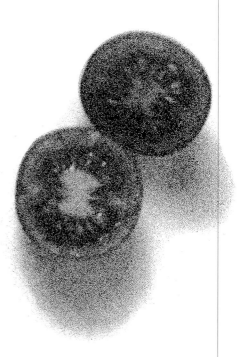

Jefferson Airplane and Jimi Hendrix, not bebop, were the rage when Larry Coryell moved from Seattle to New York in the mid-sixties. Intent on immersing himself in the city's jazz scene, the guitarist instead discovered a powerful concoction of rock, blues, and jazz that was too intoxicating to resist. His plans—and creative direction—thus altered, Coryell was soon on the leading edge of a new genre that would effect the course of jazz for years to come: jazz-rock.

It was a heady time, when non-musical events like eating were necessary distractions rather than priorities.

"Between Beatles records, Bob Dylan's records and gigs, we'd grab a bite here and there and that was it," he recalls. "I didn't think about food. I was thinking about music. Food was like number fifty-seven on the list. We would have egg creams at the Gem Spa. We were on acid trips. The Lower East Side, no shoes, hair down to our butts. Food was some kind of weird wiggly worm thing."

Coryell arrived from Seattle armed with a pyrotechnic style that was ideal for this new amalgamation. His band, fittingly called Free Spirits, was in the vanguard of those that married rock's raw electric energy with complex jazz harmonies. Before long he joined vibes player Gary Burton, turned out what many consider the first fusion recording, *Duster*, and further cemented his credentials as a lead-

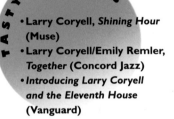

ing proponent of electrified jazz with his blockbuster band, the Eleventh House. During the next two decades, Coryell went on to make music that consistently defied expectations. Classical, mainstream jazz, fusion, and even folk are now fair game for the guitarist. All of which is a lengthy leap from the course it seemed he might follow when he was growing up.

Born in 1943 in Galveston, Texas, Coryell moved with his family to the small town of Richland, Washington, when he was seven. He began playing piano at four but switched to toy ukulele and then guitar by his early teens. "I just had a natural love of music," he explains. "I gravitated toward it, like certain charged metals get attracted to a magnet." The radio was an early source of inspiration. "They'd play five or six country songs and then something by Chet Atkins, and I'd say, 'What was that? That guy can play! He's no hick.'"

Molly's Shrimp and Pasta

"As you get older, you get more interested in food," the guitarist says. *"A great meal is an event that's meant to be focused upon. Thanks to Molly, I'm getting into the sublime details associated with food."*

These *"sublime details"* can be traced to March 1986: *"It was the first time Molly cooked me dinner. She made shrimp and pasta. It's a special favorite of mine."*

Serves 4

- 1 handful fresh parsley
- 4 cloves garlic
- 1 teaspoon freshly squeezed lemon juice
- 1 cup (2 sticks) butter or margarine, at room temperature
- Sea salt and freshly ground black pepper
- 1 pound rotelle (wheel-shaped) pasta
- 1 red bell pepper, seeded and sliced into long thin strips
- 1 green bell pepper, seeded and sliced into long thin strips
- 2 tablespoons olive oil
- 1 pound shrimp, shelled and deveined

In a food processor fitted with a steel blade, mince together the parsley and garlic. Add the lemon juice and the butter and pulse until you have a smooth green butter. Season with the salt and pepper. Begin to cook the pasta, according to the package directions, until al dente. In a large skillet, melt some of the green butter and sauté the red and green peppers, until soft. Remove the peppers from the pan. Add the olive oil to the pan and sauté the shrimp over medium-high heat for about 2 minutes, or until just white all the way through. Drain the pasta and place in a large serving bowl. Immediately add the shrimp and toss together. Stir in the peppers and the remaining green butter, tossing everything until it is coated with the green butter. Season with the pepper. Serve immediately.

Coryell moved to Seattle to study journalism at the University of Washington, played in jazz and rhythm-and-blues bands, dropped out of school, and moved to the Big Apple in 1965 with visions of Barney Kessel and Tal Farlow floating in his head. Instead, he was pulled toward fellow jazz-rock improvisers like Chick Corea and John McLaughlin and avant-gardists like the Jazz Composers Orchestra. His career has ever since been fueled by the eclectic: either acoustic or electric guitar duos and trios; adaptations of works by Debussy, Ravel, and Stravinsky; collaborations with Charles Mingus and Wayne Shorter;

and formation of his own bebop-based quartet.

Coryell has always had the technical facility to succeed in such wide-ranging stylistic efforts. On both electric and acoustic guitar he maintains a thick, mahogany tone and light touch, yet even on his purest jazz ventures Coryell gives the impression of being a volcanic rocker ready to explode. He now leans to the slower, intricate harmonic and melodic possibilities offered in various jazz-based settings, as well as the disciplined, structured challenges of classical works.

"My music is definitely based on the jazz traditions or the jazz fun-

damentals that I was exposed to growing up, but it branched out into classical and fusion," he says. "I love what Bobby Hutcherson said when somebody asked him why he plays, 'I just can't help it.' I really think that's a very good way to put it. There was something with my destiny.

"And of course as a Buddhist, I play music as proof of my Buddhist practice and to try to create a better world, a more perfect world."

Coryell is a member of the Nichiren Buddhist sect, a branch of Buddhism that uses chanting as a basic tool. His consciousness about food has been raised in recent years, as well. Coryell has developed a deep respect for food and especially for the family meal with his wife, Molly, and his daughter, Allegra. While Molly handles most of the cooking, the guitarist is very much involved in what goes on the table in their Westport, Connecticut, home.

"When we are at home we primarily eat organically grown fruit and vegetables, free-range chicken, and farm-raised fish," he says. "We also like Brae beef. Essentially we try to ingest as few chemicals as possible. We make our own fruit and vegetable juices and grind our own coffee beans.

"Dinner is a time of coming together for us. We almost always eat together as a family when we're at home. Molly has a wonderful style that carries over to the dinner table. The food is presented in a setting that includes fresh flowers and candles. After years and years on the road with the inconsistencies of eating habits due to crazy schedules, I cherish the meals we have at home."

Count bassist Richard Davis among those who savor different tastes, musical or culinary. In fact, if the music world had an address for players who thrive on the eclectic, he'd no doubt be at the door welcoming kindred spirits inside. Bass professor at the University of Wisconsin in Madison, the Chicago-born Davis has performed with as diversified a menu as you'll find on anyone's résumé: Eric Dolphy, Barbra Streisand, Igor Stravinsky, Sarah Vaughan, Van Morrison, Sun Ra, Antonio Carlos Jobim, Archie Shepp, Bo Didley, and Leonard Bernstein and the New York Philharmonic. A driving, dark-toned stylist who swings even harder now than he did back with Zoot Sims and Benny Goodman, Davis is one of music's most passionate and inventive bassists, a player who moves comfortably from the abstractions of free jazz to the heat of bebop grooves. His philosophy has served him well: "I believe in open broad-mindedness toward music."

Much the same holds true for his attitude toward food. Years spent on the road and in Manhattan have served to widen his tastes. He loves the food of Japan as much as he does a warm bowl of home-cooked beef stew. Early on, though, he developed a first-hand appreciation for a meal that's still a favorite—barbecue.

"My father—I was raised by foster parents—owned a barbecue restaurant on the South Side of Chicago, on Forty-seventh and Champlain, Johnson's Barbecue," Davis recalls. "I spent a lot of time there, from scrubbing the floors to managing it. It was a real joint, open until four in the morning. My father had the business going from about 1942 to 1950. There was lots of money being spent at that time. Everybody was working. We couldn't open until twelve noon because we had to cook up enough meat for the people lined up, waiting to get their orders in."

Davis excused himself from the grill at Johnson's Barbecue often enough to study the bass at Chicago's Jean Baptist Point DuSable High School, alma mater of jazz greats Gene Ammons, Nat "King" Cole, and Johnny Griffin. After stints with the Youth Orchestra of Chicago and the Chicago Civic Orchestra, Davis joined Ahmad Jamal's trio in Chicago in 1952, moving to New York two years later where he worked for nine months with pianist Don Shirley. "Then the scuffles came," Davis says with a laugh.

Johnson's Barbecue had made him an aficionado of ribs, yet the move east taught the bassist a few culinary tricks he didn't know. "Working in some of the best restaurants as a musician, sometimes you'd get to know the cook and watch what he could do," he explains. "I picked up on a chef at the Embers on Fifty-fourth Street on the East Side where I was playing with Don Shirley. This chef was taking the skin off the top surface of the ribs, in the concave part. Do you know why? To keep people from splashing themselves with sauce when they pulled the skin off the ribs."

Some of Davis's most memorable road meals came between 1957 and 1962, when he was touring with

TASTY PLATTERS

• Richard Davis, *Now's the Time* (Muse)
• Elvin Jones/Richard Davis, *Heavy Sounds* (MCA/Impulse!)
• Clifford Jordan/Richard Davis/James Williams/ Ronnie Burrage, *Four Play* (DIW)

Sarah Vaughan's ensemble. They would play four or five shows daily at theaters like the York in Baltimore, the Howard in Washington, D.C., the Royal in Chicago, and the Apollo in Harlem on bills that would include groups like Miles Davis's sextet with John Coltrane and Cannonball Adderley. "There was always some lady's house in the neighborhood near the theater where the band could get a meal," he recollects. "And there was always southern food in the black neighborhoods. On Saturday nights there was almost always a Chitterlings Night dinner. Word would get out to the bands and, a lot of times, signs would be posted at the theater: 'Dinner—$1.50,' with the name and address of the house listed. You'd run into a lot of good cooks."

Davis was also a proponent of setting up meals in the hotel room, a decision often based on finances and the threat of discrimination. "When you travel a lot, you save money if you can cook," he says. "And why should you go into a restaurant and be embarrassed when you can stay in, get a hot-plate, and have a ball with friends? Cooking was kind of a necessity.

"When we were traveling with Sarah Vaughan and would get to Las Vegas, I remember Sir Roland Hanna, the piano player, and Percy Brice, the drummer, had a kitchen in their room. I would shop, Roland would cook, and Percy would clean up."

Rib stories seem to run throughout much of Davis's long career. One of his favorites involves bassist Jerry Jermott. "It was back in the sixties sometime when I was living in New York," he says. "Jerry asked

Red Beans and Rice

Red beans and rice is still the traditional Monday luncheon dish in New Orleans, and like jazz, another Crescent City staple, it has been given a new twist in its trek up river. Most Creole recipes use a teaspoon each of black, cayenne, and white pepper as well as finely chopped green bell pepper, but, with a nod to daughter Persia, Davis's version of this Monday main dish lays low with the peppers. Today, one often finds red beans and rice as a side to dishes such as smoked sausage, pork chops, chicken, or even barbecued ribs.

Serves 6 as a main course or 10 to 12 as a side dish

- 1 pound red beans, washed and sorted through to remove any debris
- 2 pounds smoked pork butt, cut into small cubes
- 2 cups finely chopped onion
- 4 cloves garlic, finely minced
- 2 teaspoons onion salt
- 2 cups rice

Cover the beans with a generous amount of cold water. Let sit overnight. Drain the beans just before using. Put the drained beans in a large pot and cover with enough fresh, cold water to reach 2 inches above the beans. Add the pork butt, onion, garlic, and onion salt. Bring to a boil, stirring frequently, then reduce the heat to medium and simmer, stirring occasionally, until the beans are tender, about 1 1/2 hours. If necessary, add more water as the beans cook.

In the last half hour of cooking, in a medium-sized saucepan, bring 4 cups of salted water and the rice to a full boil, stirring frequently. Reduce the heat to low, cover the pan, and simmer for 25 to 30 minutes, or until all of the water is absorbed. Remove from the heat and allow the rice to sit for a few extra minutes to add fluffiness. To serve, mound some rice in the plate and spoon a generous amount of red beans on and around the rice.

me if I felt like some barbecue and I answered, 'Sure, man.' I'll never forget it. He flew down to Texas in the morning and was back that evening with slabs of ribs. It was one of the most incredible things I'd ever heard of."

In 1977, Davis moved from New York to Madison to join the University of Wisconsin faculty, a post he has maintained ever since. He teaches jazz string bass, European classical bass, black music history, and combo improvisation. Although he still tours occasionally with players like Hanna, Ricky

Ford, Cecil Bridgewater, and Ronnie Burrage, Davis primarily sticks close to home these days. A major reason is to spend as much time as possible with his children, Persia and Joshua. As a single parent, Davis has no choice but to handle most of the cooking chores. "I enjoy it because it gives me another activity to do with my daughter, who loves to cook," he says. "I cook simply and have some meals that are kind of special. Persia likes rice a lot."

Electric bassist Mark Egan believes there are inexorable links among the ways he plays, eats, and lives. The New York–based artist, a cornerstone of guitarist Pat Metheny's band during the late 1970s and one of contemporary jazz's most influential stylists, works hard to maintain a harmonious relationship with music, diet, and daily life. His philosophy permeates all three.

"When I pick up the bass neck, it's a very deep feeling," he explains. "I really have a lot of respect for the instrument. I don't want to play anything jive. I treat it as a sacred thing. It's endless, mastering the music and taking it as far as I can in my lifetime. One of the ways to do that is to eat right and be healthy. But even aside from eating well and being physically fit, you've got to be a good person, strive to be good, to be able to communicate something. You've got to be at peace with yourself."

In order to achieve that peace, Egan is consistent and disciplined in his physical and nutritional habits. When he's home, he works out four or five times a week at a YMCA in Manhattan. On the road, he runs or seeks out a gym. "To be a really good player, it's sort of like being in the Olympics," he says. "You really have to be in tune and in shape to tap the energy that's in there. I eat a lot of fruit and vegetables. For the last fifteen years, I've been really aware of foods and additives. I know

what's good and what's bad. I was into a heavy macrobiotic thing for quite a while, but then I tapered off because it was too extreme. Then I got into a vegetarian thing and now I've leveled off to more natural food: fish sometimes and a little bit of chicken."

The bassist clearly understands balance and interplay in music, as well, which has been appreciated not only by Metheny, but by artists like saxophonist David Sanborn and the late composer/arranger Gil Evans, each of whom worked with Egan. His longest-standing collaboration is with drummer Danny Gottlieb, with whom he co-leads

the group Elements. The pair first met in the early seventies when they were both attending the University of Miami. Elements's wide-ranging, fusion-oriented book of material puts Egan's talents in espe-

TASTY PLATTERS
- Elements, *Forward Motion* (Antilles)
- Pat Metheny, *American Garage* (ECM)
- Gil Evans, *Farewell Gil Evans* (ProJazz)

cially sharp focus. Often wielding a fretless bass that makes his full sound even more cavernous, Egan will shun the bassist's traditional background role to step in front of the impressionistic atmospherics of Elements, pumping hard grooves and improvising so his colors shift continually. When he leads, melody is often his inspiration.

"For me, it's a deep spiritual source that the music comes from," he says. "What I want to do with manipulating these sounds is to try to make it as pure as possible and create uplifting music that is inspiring and inspired."

Born in 1951 and raised in Brockton, Massachusetts, Egan grew up in a family that encouraged his musical efforts. His father played trumpet, primarily in navy bands, and his mother played piano. Trumpet, in fact, was Egan's first instrument. "I can remember playing it on a tune like 'A Tisket a Tasket' while my mother was ironing and she said, 'Oh, that was good, Mark.' I said, 'No, it was horrible.' I was in the fourth grade, about ten. My parents were always totally supportive. They got me lessons and I played in the elementary and junior high school orchestras, then in high school. I was about sixteen when I started to play bass."

Basic meat and potatoes was the fare in the Egan household. His mother handled most of the cooking for the family of six, although his father enjoyed cooking beef stew or chicken on occasion. One family activity has stayed with the bassist through the years—fishing. His grandparents owned a home on Cape Cod, and the Egans would spend long days on sports-fishing boats angling for tuna, bluefish, and

Morty's Gourmet Brown Rice and Tofu

"You might have gathered I'm sort of a health nut," Egan says. A follower of Harvey and Marilyn Diamond's book, Fit for Life, *the bassist likes to begin the day with the cleansing properties of fruit followed by a salad at lunch. Dinner is often a mix-and-match meal with the likes of brown rice, tofu, fish, mixed vegetables and a salad—especially cabbage salads.*

The spirit of combining nutritional, lowfat ingredients is evident in Egan's contribution, Morty's Gourmet Brown Rice and Tofu. An original creation, it's a successful kitchen experiment inspired by the meals served in the many vegetarian restaurants Egan seeks out while he's on the road.

Serves 4

4 1/2 cups water, preferably
   spring water
3 tablespoons sesame oil
2 cups short-grain brown rice
2 tablespoons curry powder
Reduced-sodium soy sauce
1 package instant miso soup,
   available in health food stores or
   Japanese markets
1 pound extra-firm tofu
4 tablespoons extra-virgin olive oil
1 tablespoon fresh dill, or
   1 teaspoon dried dill weed

2 tablespoons Mrs. Dash
   seasoning mix
2 tablespoons rice wine vinegar

To prepare the rice, in a medium-sized saucepan with a tight-fitting lid, bring the water to a boil. In a medium-sized skillet, heat the sesame oil. Add the rice, stir to coat with the oil, and cook, stirring, for 5 minutes. Add the rice and the oil to the boiling water. Add the curry, 2 tablespoons of the soy sauce, and the miso soup mix. Stirring constantly, boil for 5 minutes. Reduce the heat to a simmer, cover, and cook for 40 minutes, or until all the water is absorbed.

To prepare the tofu while the rice is simmering, cut the tofu into 2-by-4-inch pieces that are approximately 2 inches thick. In a frying pan with a tight-fitting lid, over medium heat, warm the olive oil. Add the tofu cubes and sauté for 1 minute. Add the dill and Mrs. Dash seasoning mix. Flip the cubes when lightly browned on 1 side, being careful not to overcook them. When the tofu cubes are almost cooked (lightly browned on all sides), add the rice wine vinegar and 1 tablespoon of the soy sauce. Cover, turn off the heat, and let sit with top on until the rice is ready. To serve, place the tofu mixture on top of the rice. Season with the soy sauce.

striped bass. If anything, the years have made Egan an even more avid fisherman. He annually embarks on a camping and fishing trip to Quetico Provincial Park in Ontario, Canada, with several buddies, including saxophonist Bill Evans. The group endures two-mile portages

with canoes through swampland in order to find lakes filled with four- and five-pound trout, northern pike, and small- and largemouth bass. "It's everything you wanted to do when you were a Boy Scout," Egan laughs. "It's like the camping expedition of your life."

Thirty years spent living in Los Angeles didn't change Herb Ellis's country-boy inclinations. The guitarist called "Orange" by his peers still likes his jazz the way he remembers hearing Charlie Christian play it back in the forties: unadorned, straight-to-the-point, and flawlessly graceful. And he still likes his food down-home hearty, even though nowadays his diet keeps him from indulging in the rib-sticking fare he ate on his family's North Texas farm.

Ellis and his wife now reside in a planned community in the Arkansas Ozarks. "Where we live is peaceful," he says. "We're enter-

TASTY PLATTERS

- **Herb Ellis, *Roll Call* (Justice)**
- **Herb Ellis/Red Mitchell, *Doggin' Around* (Concord Jazz)**
- **Monty Alexander/Ray Brown/Herb Ellis, *Triple Treat III* (Concord Jazz)**

ing that time when we can use it." The guitarist claims that he's slowing down, yet for a man born in 1921 he maintains a pretty heavy schedule. He tours half the year and offers clinics at colleges and music schools as often as possible.

There weren't any guitar clinics for Ellis to attend when he was growing up in rural Farmersville, forty miles north of Dallas. Cotton and onions were the crops, country music the king. He picked up the rudiments of string instruments on the banjo when he was five, accompanied by his older brother on guitar. When a guest left a guitar at the house, Ellis claimed it for his

own. He was seven. "I taught myself to play," he says. "I played old-time country songs like 'Home on the Range' back then." Jazz came into the picture when some of his roommates at North Texas State University played a Benny Goodman record that featured Charlie Christian's electric guitar. "A few days later it hit me how much I loved what I had heard," he recalls.

Ellis got his first professional break with Glen Gray's Casa Loma Orchestra in 1944, parlayed it into a stint with the Jimmy Dorsey Band, and in 1953 took a gig that would change his life: He replaced Barney Kessel in the Oscar Peterson Trio. He stayed with the legendary pianist for five years. A year with Ella Fitzgerald led to a long period of TV studio work for Steve Allen, Regis Philbin, Danny Kaye, Joey Bishop, Merv Griffin, and a number of other Hollywood hosts. Ellis stayed active in the jazz field, though. He began a longtime collaboration with Joe Pass in the early seventies, joined Great Guitars with Kessel and Charlie Byrd, and later became a member of

Triple Treat with bassist Ray Brown and pianist Monty Alexander.

A classic duet album with Pass, *Two for the Road,* is a showcase for Ellis's relaxed electric guitar style. His lines on this mid-seventies disc are immaculate, melodious, steeped in the blues, and always swinging. "I've found a way of playing, just swing music, a little Charlie Christian and Charlie Parker and Lester Young," he points out. "I want to always play that way. I don't think guitarists now are grounded enough in the total rhythmical field, the swing of the thing. They're interested in how many notes they can play, how grand and florid they can make it. Just get down to where the real feeling is, that's the main thing to me."

While Ellis's approach to music has remained rock steady, age and the road have caused him to change his eating habits. In his youth, huge breakfasts of eggs, sausage patties, hash-browns, and biscuits with syrup or gravy were the norm. Although dinner was relatively light, lunch was an event. Fried chicken, chicken-fried steak, black-eyed peas, red beans, pork, and

Quick Pizza

"I really love good Mexican food," Ellis says. *"There was so much great stuff in Los Angeles. I grew to love that hot, spicy, really flavorful food."*

This passion for flavor and spice tinged with a touch of heat inspired the recipe he's dubbed Quick Pizza. It's an easy-to-make pizza that derives its unique taste from the addition of salsa to the tomato sauce and a topping that includes sliced jalapeño peppers.

Serves approximately 4

Pizza dough to fit in a 12-inch
   pizza pan, either homemade,
   store-bought, or purchased from
   a pizza shop
Cornmeal for sprinkling on
   pizza pan
¾ cup tomato sauce
¼ cup spicy Mexican salsa

2 teaspoons oregano
1 teaspoon red pepper flakes
1 cup grated Monterey Jack cheese
   (with or without jalapeños)
1 small onion, finely chopped
1 small (4-ounce) can diced
   jalapeños, or to taste
Chopped black olives (optional)

Preheat the oven to 500°F. On a floured surface, roll out the dough and fit it onto a pizza tile or a pan that has been lightly sprinkled with cornmeal. Curl the edges. Mix the tomato sauce with the salsa and spread over the dough. Mix together the oregano and red pepper and sprinkle over the sauce. In order, evenly distribute the cheese, onion, jalapeños, and olives (if using) over the sauce. Bake for 10 to 15 minutes, or until the crust is browned on the bottom and the sauce is bubbly. Let cool for a minute, then slice.

turnip greens were on the table on any given day, with cake and pies for dessert. "After we finished the noon meal, we'd often lay down and take a rest for a half hour or so before heading back to work," Ellis remembers.

The guitarist admits that his diet during his early years on the road wasn't the world's best. "I ate whatever I wanted to eat," he says. "You get conscious of your diet when you have to be. Up until that time, you just let the good times roll. You eat as much ice cream as you want. I was at the peak of my eating and I was still slim when I was with Oscar Peterson. I did a lot of exercise then. I played golf a lot with Ray Brown. I don't play nearly enough now."

Jane Hall had a fine idea several years ago: she convinced her husband Jim, arguably the world's greatest living mainstream jazz guitarist, to take a course near their Manhattan apartment called "How to Boil Water." "I thought it would be fun for him—and for me," she laughs.

It was more than fun for the guitarist; he soon became a cooking convert. "We went almost literally from boiling eggs to fancy stuff like the *ribollita*," he says.

Hall hadn't been a complete stranger to cooking, even though his wife, a psychoanalyst and composer, handles the bulk of meal preparations. He took care of himself as a bachelor for years and as a youngster growing up in Cleveland often made himself breakfast. "It wasn't until I got on the road and went to foreign countries and met Jane that I even realized there was such a thing as exotic, interesting food."

Born in 1930, Hall moved to a new WPA housing project in Cleveland with his brother and mother when he was about ten. Inspired by an uncle who sang and played "hillbilly" guitar, he started taking lessons on the instrument. By junior high school, when friends provided him with his first exposure to Benny Goodman and Charlie Christian, he was hooked on jazz. Soon his days were spent going to school, caddying on a local golf course, and working in a bowling alley. At night he played music and heard live jazz. That routine stayed much the same after he enrolled at the Cleveland Institute of Music.

While the food in Cleveland may have been unexciting during the 1940s, the jazz scene more than made up for it. "There was a lot going on considering it was just a midwestern town," Hall says. The list of players he heard in his hometown when he was in his teens is amazing. At the Café Tijuana he saw Ella Fitzgerald and Charlie Parker with Max Roach and Miles Davis. At Lindsay's Sky Bar he caught Stan Getz and Art Tatum. At the Palace Theater he heard Duke Ellington, Artie Shaw, and Nat "King" Cole.

Just as important were the associations he made with locals like Benny Bailey, Fats Heard, Joe Dolny, and Tony DiNardo. During that period he formed a group

TASTY PLATTERS

- **Jim Hall, *Jim Hall's Three* (Concord Jazz)**
- **Sonny Rollins/Jim Hall, *The Quartets Featuring Jim Hall* (Bluebird)**
- ***The Complete Recordings of the Paul Desmond Quartet with Jim Hall* (Mosaic)**

called the Spectacles; all the band's members wore glasses.

On stage and off, Hall was learning about the jazz life. "There were a couple of musicians' meeting places, Italian or Chinese restaurants where we'd go after work," he recalls. "They were kind of hangouts. The guys would show up there and we'd tell stories until daylight."

After graduating from music school, Hall left Cleveland for Los Angeles and then New York. Ever since, he has immersed himself in situations that are rich and varied in style and format as jazz itself. Ben Webster, Bill Evans, Sonny Rollins, Ron Carter, Itzhak Perlman, Bill Frisell, and Art Farmer are but a few of his collaborators over the

Ribollita—Tuscan Vegetable Bread Soup Baked with Cheese

Hall's culinary sensibilities have sharpened immeasurably since his youth. "Ohio in those days was like living in the Dark Ages," he laughs. "The food wasn't all that thrilling."

One favorite dish that Hall learned to make at his "How to Boil Water" course at New York's New School was ribollita, a Tuscan bread-and-vegetable soup. "I've made it about a half-dozen times," he says. "One time I made it for John Abercrombie and his wife. It was amazing to me to realize that I could just follow a recipe and it would work out all right. I got over being intimidated by the whole thing."

Serves 8

- ½ cup olive oil, or more if needed
- 2 large onions, halved, and thickly sliced crosswise
- 4 carrots, thickly sliced
- 3 ribs celery, thickly sliced
- 3 large cloves garlic, minced, and 2 whole cloves garlic
- 2 small zucchini, sliced
- 1 red bell pepper, sliced (optional)
- ½ teaspoon rosemary
- 1½ pounds fresh spinach, stemmed and washed
- 1 (20-ounce) can cannellini (white) beans, drained and rinsed
- 6 fresh plum tomatoes, cut into long strips, or 1 (17-ounce) can imported whole plum tomatoes, drained and halved
- 2 teaspoons salt
- 12 thin slices Italian or French bread
- 2½ to 3½ cups high-quality chicken broth
- ½ cup freshly grated Parmesan cheese
- Freshly ground black pepper

In a large casserole, over medium heat, warm 3 tablespoons of the olive oil. Add the onion and sauté until wilted, stirring often, about 7 to 9 minutes. Add the carrots, celery, and minced garlic, and sauté for 2 to 3 minutes, tossing the vegetables around the casserole to coat them with the oil. Add the zucchini, red pepper (if using), and rosemary and toss and cook until the zucchini begins to wilt slightly, about 4 to 5 minutes. Remove the mixture to a bowl. Place the spinach with water clinging to its leaves in the casserole. Cover and steam over medium heat, turning the leaves over with a wooden spoon after 3 minutes. Continue to steam until the leaves wilt, about 2 to 3 more minutes. Using a slotted spoon, remove the spinach to a colander, allowing the water to briefly drain into the casserole. Pour the spinach liquid in the casserole into the bowl holding the sautéed vegetable mixture. Coarsely chop the spinach and add it to the vegetables. Stir in the beans, tomatoes, and salt, and toss to combine. Correct seasonings if necessary; the flavor should be assertive.

Preheat the broiler. Arrange the bread slices in a single layer on a baking sheet. Toast until golden brown on both sides, about 1 minute per side. Lower the oven temperature to 400°F. Arrange a layer of the vegetable mixture on the bottom of the casserole and set 6 slices of the toasted bread in one layer over the vegetables. Spread half of the remaining vegetable mixture over the bread, top with the remaining toast, and then top this with the remaining vegetable mixture. Smooth evenly. Add enough broth just to come to the top of the vegetables, making sure that the very top is dry. In a small skillet, over medium heat, warm 4 tablespoons of the olive oil, until fragrant. Add the whole garlic cloves and simmer for 5 minutes. Discard the garlic cloves and drizzle some of the oil over the uncovered top layer of vegetables. Place the casserole in the oven and bake until the top is golden, about 30 to 45 minutes. Allow to stand for 5 minutes before serving. Serve in large, shallow soup bowls with a sprinkling of olive oil, Parmesan, and pepper on top.

---

years. And even though he took a three-and-a-half-year break from the road in the mid-sixties to join the house band for the "Merv Griffin Show," he never really lost touch with the jazz world.

No guitarist listens more intently and reacts more imaginatively than Hall. Those qualities, along with the bluesy swing that simmers underneath every note he plays, are at the core of his popularity among his peers. Hall's precise sound on both acoustic and electric guitar is feathery and warm. He can be a swift stylist, yet even his speediest lines are graceful, melodic, and laced with subtle emotion. His ideas are economical, but never at the expense of harmonic opulence. Listening to Hall play guitar is like sipping a smooth, intriguing sum-mer drink. It may be impossible to figure out all the ingredients, but it ultimately doesn't matter since it goes down so easy.

"I try to stay open to new things and still keep my values," Hall says. "The music is a means of self-expression. I like to win over the audience and then take them someplace with me. It's the same as being a painter, poet, or writer."

Using strength, physical and inner, to meet challenges head on has played a major role both in Mark Helias's life and in his steady rise to the upper echelon of jazz bassists. The New Jersey native relishes a test, be it on the playing field, in "bucket of blood" clubs, or in a jazz world where traditionalists haven't always appreciated his freewheeling approach to improvisation and composition. Nowhere is his attitude more telling than when he discusses his gradual evolution from serious athlete to serious musician.

"I played everything," he says. "Basketball, football, baseball. I

TASTY PLATTERS

• Mark Helias, *Desert Blue* (Enja)
• Mark Helias/Gary Thomas/ Bobby Previte/Christy Dorn, *Corporate Art* (JMT)
• Ray Anderson, *Wishbone* (Gramavision)

was a long-distance runner in high school. Mostly the joy of it is what I get off on. It's kind of like that transformation in your psyche that occurs when you're really playing. To me, the sports thing led right into music. I always felt this connection with athletics, the joy part and the physical, the concept of elevating and extending yourself, trying outrageous moves, outrageous harmonies."

Helias still plays basketball at a Manhattan YMCA, not far from the apartment he shares with his wife, Marie-Claude Nouy. Athletics have never been difficult for the bassist. Breaking into music was.

Born in 1950, Helias had already tried his hand at drums, guitar, and electric bass by the time he got serious about learning acoustic bass at twenty-one. "I was working in factories, part-time Manpower stuff, manual labor," he explains. "Then I decided to actually play some schlock music. I auditioned for this really silly group, worked a weekend, and made ninety dollars in three nights. I realized it would take me four days to make that bread in a warehouse or loading freight cars. So from then on, whenever I needed money, I would work in some kind of nonfulfilling musical job. But it got better."

Although not right away. The commercial country groups and soul bands Helias hooked up with put him in some shaky scenes. "We played these really rough bars," he says. "There was a lot of heavy drinking, a lot of violence, a lot of machismo. A couple of times I had to hide behind the amp."

Helias didn't receive much musical encouragement at home. His education at Livingston College and Yale School of Music was self-motivated. "My parents' tastes in music ran from Percy Faith to Mantovani," he laughs. "When I was about four or five, my oldest brother

was deep into the 'Hit Parade' so I was listening to all that early rock and roll. I was about eleven or twelve when I started to buy records. I remember the first Cecil Taylor record I bought, *Unit Structures*. When I put that on in the house, it was rough. The same year—I was seventeen—I got *Are You Experienced?* by Jimi Hendrix. Between those two they thought, 'Our son has obviously lost his mind.'"

What that listening did was set the stage for an approach to music. Associating at Yale with experimenters like Anthony Davis and later in New York with Anthony Braxton and Dewey Redman, Helias discovered that he felt most comfortable playing alternatives to the more traditional branches of jazz. His hardy, large-toned bass swings and keeps perfect time with the best of them, assets he takes into a world of settings, from the "no wave" funk of the Slickaphonics to Latin-leaning ensembles to wildly adventurous forays with cronies like Gerry Hemingway and Ray Anderson. His intricate melodic writing is similarly eclectic, spanning a range of genres yet always offering fresh slants on texture, harmony, and color. And Helias doesn't restrict himself to the jazz sphere; piano sonatas and compositions for string quartet are also in his portfolio.

"I need music as a completion, just like anyone needs who does a kind of work that makes them complete, like a scientist or a writer," he explains. "I feel like it ennobles us somehow, just like a good carpenter or a good me-chanic. It's not selfish to dig what you're doing. I just try to bring total integrity to the music."

Helias's mother did her best to make him feel comfortable in the kitchen. "I was always there when the dinner was cooking," he remembers. "I was three, four, five, six. I had this real tight hang with my mother. I don't recall her specifically teaching me how to cook, so I guess I picked it up by osmosis."

Twice-Cooked Pasta with Seafood

To Helias, cooking is more than an avocation. "It's an extension of artistic expression to make people appreciate food and also kind of an expression of the culture," he says. "If you grew up in the South, there's that whole cuisine aspect of the culture that's so vital."

Helias, who works much of the time at home, likes to have dinner ready for his wife when she returns from work. "I oftentimes whip up quick pasta dishes that are very good and easy to make," he says. One of them is his recipe for Twice-Cooked Pasta with Seafood. "I think it began as an improvisation which became codified with further experimentation, although I do it differently every time."

Serves 6 to 8

2 pounds fresh plum tomatoes, or
  1¹/₂ (28-ounce) cans of imported
  plum tomatoes
Bay leaf
Extra-virgin olive oil
1 medium or large Spanish onion,
  chopped
2 to 3 shallots, chopped
2 to 3 cloves garlic, minced
1 small (6-ounce) can tomato paste

Pinch each of oregano and thyme
Freshly ground black pepper
1 small green bell pepper, seeded
  and chopped
Small bunch scallions, trimmed
  and chopped
1 pound shrimp, shelled and deveined
¹/₂ pound sea scallops, cut into
  bite-sized pieces
¹/₄ pound mussels and/or octopus
  (optional)
³/₄ cup Italian parsley, chopped
³/₄ cup dry white wine, such as
  Pinot Grigio
Pinch of saffron soaked in ¹/₂ cup
  warm water (optional)
2 to 3 pinches of either cayenne
  pepper or chili powder
2 to 3 teaspoons filé powder
1¹/₂ pounds fusilli, preferably
  DeCecco brand
2 tablespoons butter, cut into
  small pieces
1¹/₂ ounces cognac or Spanish brandy

Coarsely chop the tomatoes (by hand). In a large saucepan, combine the tomatoes and the bay leaf and simmer slowly. Coat a large skillet with olive oil. Add half of the onion, shallots, and garlic and cook, stirring, until the onions are soft. Stir in the tomato paste, then add the oregano, thyme, and black pep-per. Increase the heat to high, stir for 1 minute, then add to the saucepan with the simmering tomatoes. Reduce the heat to medium and add more olive oil to the skillet. Add the green pepper, and cook for 3 minutes, until it just begins to soften. Add the scallions and the remaining shallots, onion, and garlic. Cook for an additional 4 minutes, or until all of the vegetables are almost soft, then increase the heat to high and quickly add the shrimp, scallops, and mussels or octopus (if using), parsley, a pinch more of thyme, and the wine. Cook for 2 to 3 minutes until the wine reduces slightly and thickens. Reduce the heat to medium-low. Add the saffron water (if using), and cook until the seafood is cooked through, about 3 to 5 minutes. Add the seafood mixture to the simmering tomatoes. Stir in the cayenne pepper or chili powder and filé powder.

Preheat the oven to 375°F. Cook the fusilli according to the package directions, until al dente. Stir the drained pasta into the simmering sauce. Blend well, then place this mixture in a large casserole or baking dish. Dot with the butter and sprinkle with a shot of cognac or Spanish brandy. Cover the dish and bake for 30 minutes, or until everything is cooked through.

When you've lived as long and rich a life as Milt Hinton, "the Dean of Jazz Bassists," it's only natural that you aim high when compiling a wish list for future generations. "I'd like to see the world get a little better, see people respect each other, love one another, and listen to good music," he says. "That's why they call me the Judge; I sentence everybody to thirty days of listening to good music."

Hinton has been meting out his sweet brand of justice to audiences for over six decades during a career filled with thousands of one-nighters, studio dates, jazz clinics, and more than six hundred recordings. Armed with a luscious, thumping tone and a seemingly innate sense of swing, Hinton is one of music's most consistently open-minded improvisers, anchoring bands of any style for any occasion, from Cab Calloway, Billie Holiday, and Jackie Gleason to Paul McCartney and Branford Marsalis. The bassist is also a respected photographer and author; his autobiography, *Bass Line,* filled with his photos, is arguably the warmest and most illuminating book ever written about the jazz life. Hinton has donned the hat of cultural historian, educating younger generations about the pains and joys of creating a new art form in America. And many of his remembrances revolve around food.

Born in 1910 in Vicksburg, Mississippi, Hinton migrated north with his family to Chicago when he was nine years old. "My grandmother had to run the house," he recounts. "We didn't make much money, but it was fabulous compared to what it was in Mississippi.

My mother, my two aunts, and one uncle lived at home. Each morning they left their twenty cents on the dresser, so that was eighty cents. My grandmother had to take that and cook for all six of us. I was the guy who had to go to the store, a little store in Chicago where we could get

credit. I'd get ten cents worth of mustard greens, five cents worth of sweet potatoes, a nickel's worth of rice, and some meat bones. My grandmother could season that up and it tasted like caviar. She was a magician. I keep trying to capture that."

Hinton's mother bought him a violin when he was twelve. In high school he switched to tuba in order to play in the brass band but eventually settled on the bass. When his playing became good enough scores of free-lance gigs led to longer stints with violinist Eddie South, trumpeter Jabbo Smith, and drummer Zutty Singleton. In 1935 bandleader Cab Calloway hired Hinton. The bassist stayed with him for sixteen years.

New York's Cotton Club usually was home for the Calloway band for half the year, with the balance being spent on the road. "They were adventurous times," Hinton recalls. "Segregation was rampant then, in the thirties and forties. We couldn't stay at certain

Millionaire Meatloaf

Hinton honed his cooking skills on the road with Calloway's band, which is where Millionaire Meatloaf originated, a recipe best told in the bassist's own words:

"Since we often couldn't even sit in restaurants, Cab, being a very engineering man who tried to keep us out of as much of that stuff as possible, bought an electric stove, a big thing that you could put a roasted turkey in. It had three compartments. We had a case made for it and we carried plates and knives and forks. Most theaters in those days had kitchens, but if they didn't we could use our stove and cook our dinner between shows. Several guys in the band would team up to cook. Tyree Glenn, the trombone player, and I liked to cook together. We would get up early and go to the store, set up the kitchen down in the basement of the theater and cook. Tyree liked a thing called Millionaire Meatloaf. We called it that because it wasn't cheap at all.

"It had one pound of ground beef, a pound of sausage meat and a pound of veal, ground up. We mashed it all up, put in salt and pepper and powdered garlic, took five or six slices of bread, crumbled them up and mixed it in there. Then we put in one egg. For three pounds we'd use up one large onion, one large green pepper, and two sticks of celery, chopped up fine. You mixed it in, kneaded it like you knead bread, and formed it into a loaf. We'd put a slight amount of butter on the bottom, cover it and let it cook at 350 degrees for an hour during shows.

"When we came off the first show, we'd put in a can of tomato purée and let it cook for another half hour or so. In the other two compartments we had some baked rice and something green. After the second show, about 5:30 or 6 o'clock, all the guys in the band had their own plates and knives and forks and they'd come back and have a wonderful dinner. We made Cab get in line just like everybody else. He couldn't go to those restaurants either."

hotels and we had to eat in certain restaurants. We loved music and played and entertained people. That was the thing we felt most comfortable doing regardless of the conditions under which we did it.

"We sort of laughed at the stupidity of segregation. But being American citizens, we tried to obey the law, whatever the law was. When we went down south and had to go in a certain entrance to get in a railroad station, we did that. And we still laughed about it.

"Cab did everything in the world to avoid the segregation for us. The first thing he did was hire Pullman cars. We traveled by train from theater to theater, starting at the Strand Theater in New York right on to Newark, Philadelphia, Pittsburgh, across the country like that, Ohio to Detroit to Chicago, Omaha to California. One week at a time. It took about two or three months. We had a huge baggage car and Cab had a baggage car with a big Lincoln in there. We had these big H and M theatrical trunks. When we stepped off the train, it was just like we had stepped out of a bandbox. Everybody was very dapper.

"We couldn't stay in white hotels and the black hotels were almost nonexistent or very bad, so we stayed right in the Pullman car.

"The one-night stands where we had to take a bus through the South, that was where we really caught hell. We'd ride all day to get to tobacco warehouses, old churches, dance halls, armories. My wife, Mona, sometimes was the only girl who traveled with us. While we were at the dance, she would go down through the black neighborhood, make friends, and tell them that we didn't have any place to stay. They'd say, 'Mrs. Smith will take two musicians over there, Mrs. Jones will take two over here.'

"And then Mona would say, 'You know, the fellas got right off the bus to play and didn't have anything to eat. If I go out and buy five or six chickens and pay you, will you help me cook them up? You can see the second half of the show for free.' So at intermission Mona would come down with a clothes basket full of chicken sandwiches and potato salad and say, 'Okay, fellas, Dizzy, you and Chu Berry are staying at Mrs. Jones's. Foots, you and Lamar Wright are over at Mrs. Smith's house. Now give me a dollar and a quarter for this food.' And this was the way we existed at times."

From his last year with Calloway in 1950 up until the mid-sixties, Hinton was one of New York's busiest studio musicians, teaming with just about every giant in the music business at one time or another. When he's not on the road with myriad all-star ensembles, he still returns to the studio.

The bassist is the primary cook in the family and even has his own kitchen in the basement, which also houses a photographic darkroom and a studio.

Taking care of business has always gone with the territory for Preservation Hall Jazz Band banjo player Narvin Kimball. The New Orleans native, born in 1909, prides himself on giving every venture, from the artistic to the domestic, nothing less than its rightful due. That philosophy, instilled in him by his father, Henry, a bass and sousaphone player, has earned Kimball a reputation as one of the champions of the traditional New Orleans jazz created decades ago by the likes of King Oliver, Bunk Johnson, and Louis Armstrong.

"My inspiration was almost inevitable because my father was a musician," he says. "So that development came very easily. But there were things that he told me particularly that I found to be of great value in later years. He was a stickler for what was right as far as music was concerned.

"He talked to me about the general carriage of a musician and how most times you unconsciously express your feelings of what you are from the way that you act. He told me if you sit up and hold your instrument with dignity and play it with pride, that's the way you'll be

looked upon. In other words, the mannerisms of a musician should be the general characteristics of a man being a gentleman. That's what I want to be. That's exactly what I have tried, and am trying, to do."

Anyone who has ever seen Kimball perform can attest to his success in following his father's advice. Before he became one of the original members of the Preservation Hall Jazz Band in 1961, he led a group known as Kimball's Gentlemen of Jazz. The Preservation Hall Jazz Band provides him with the ideal outlet for his music, which has stayed true to the New Orleans tradition honed at parades, dances, funerals, and picnics. The band's feel-good mix of spirituals, rag-

time, marches, and the blues is rougher-edged and more free-spirited than the relatively strait-jacketed Dixieland sound to which it's often compared.

Kimball's banjo and soulful vocals play a key role in maintaining the music's jubilant mood. Besides keeping the harmonic base solid and the rhythm steady, his resonant strumming turns up the heat on

TASTY PLATTERS

- **Preservation Hall Jazz Band,** *New Orleans, Volumes 1–4* **(CBS)**
- **Louis Armstrong,** *The Hot Fives and Sevens* **(Columbia Jazz Masterpieces)**
- **Dr. Michael White,** *Crescent City Serenade* **(Antilles)**

songs like "Bourbon Street Parade," and, of course, "When the Saints Go Marchin' In." Kimball's reedy-sounding tenor voice puts a wonderfully fresh face on everything from "Lonesome Road" to Ellington's "Mood Indigo."

Kimball built his first instrument out of a cigar box before he was in high school. "My father would bring me some of the strings that his band's banjoist would break," he recalls. "I made a little neck and put the strings on in the manual training department at school and just plucked on it. That eventually led me into getting a ukulele. Then I went to the banjo."

At seventeen he joined his father in the Fate Marable band on the Mississippi steamboat *Capitol.* But the decision to join wasn't easy. "One evening when I came home my mother told me that my father had called and wanted me to be in

St. Louis on Sunday morning," he remembers. "It was my second year of college, about two weeks before final exams. I said, 'That's impossible. I can't go.' He told me that this was an opportunity."

Kimball went on to play with Sidney Desvigne's Orchestra and Papa Celestin's Original Tuxedo Orchestra, both pre-swing era big bands that relied heavily on stock arrangements. He actually didn't pick up the banjo from 1937 until 1963. He relied exclusively on bass, the instrument he used onstage in a 1945 concert with Louis Armstrong.

Music didn't pay most of the bills during those years; the United States Postal Service did. Kimball served as a letter carrier by day from 1938 until 1973 and a musician on as many nights as he could. "In thirty-six years at the post office, I was late three times," he says. "Never was I not paid for a day's work."

Kimball does all the cooking at home and prides himself on his culinary skills, which he picked up early. "When I was about nine or ten years old, I first learned to make something in the kitchen that was worthwhile: mayonnaise," he says. "I told my mama, 'I can make that!'"

Creole Gumbo with Filé

Gumbo, a dish that's more of a technique than a specific formula, embodies the New Orleans penchant for turning fresh local ingredients into a memorable event. Kimball points out the differences in the various gumbos: "Creole gumbo is made with okra. Okra gumbos never use filé powder. Okra and filé will both thicken a dish, so you'd only use one anyway."

Kimball's gumbo style comes from watching his wife and mother prepare it. "You're not really taught to make gumbo," he says. "It's something that comes from your desire and aptitude."

Serves 20, more or less

1 picnic ham, approximately 8 pounds
2 (6-ounce) packages commercial crab boil
2 pounds chicken gizzards, chopped
18 fresh crabs
5 pounds Creole hot sausage
6 green bell peppers, chopped
3 onions, chopped
8 scallions, chopped
1 (28-ounce) can peeled, chopped tomatoes
4 pounds split chicken wings
Salt and pepper
4 (.87-ounce [245 grams]) packages chicken gravy mix, or 1 cup flour and ²/₃ cup vegetable oil (If using the flour and oil, read the entire recipe first and prepare the roux before assembling the gumbo.)
5 bay leaves
6 pounds shelled and deveined shrimp
filé powder

In cooking gumbo you must think in terms of your major pot, what Kimball calls "the central pot," one that can hold about 12 to 14 gallons. In the central pot, cover the ham with water, add 1 package of crab boil, and boil the ham until the skin and fat become soft. Remove the ham from the pot, cut off and discard the skin and fat, and dice the meat into 1- to 1½-inch chunks. Set aside. Strain the water and save. In another pot, add enough water to cover the chicken gizzards. Add the remaining package of crab boil and gently simmer the gizzards for 1 hour. In another pot, cook the crabs in boiling water to cover for 5 minutes. Save this water. Let the crabs cool, then detach the claws, crack the leg joints, and clean the crab bodies. Set aside. In a large skillet, cook the sausage until crisp. Remove the sausage, leaving the fat in the skillet, then cut the sausage into chunks. Add the green peppers, onions, and scallions to the sausage fat and cook for 5 minutes or so, until the vegetables begin to soften. Add the crabs and tomatoes, mashing the tomatoes until they are soft. Simmer the crabs and vegetables for 30 minutes. Add the crab-and-vegetable mixture, diced ham and sausage chunks to the central pot. Season the chicken wings with salt and pepper. Add oil to the skillet and brown the wings on all sides, then add them to the central pot. In the same skillet as the wings were browned, season the gizzards with pepper and cook for 1 minute only, to encase the gizzards in the seasonings. Add the gizzards to the central pot. Add a total of 4 quarts of the ham and crab water to the central pot (you may have to add tap water to make it 4 quarts). Add the 4 packages of chicken gravy mix to the pot. (Alternatively, make a medium brown roux by heating the vegetable oil in a large skillet and then quickly adding the flour [all at once] to the hot oil. Mix it together quickly and cook, stirring for 30 minutes or so until it's reddish brown. Let it cool.) Stir the packaged gravy (or roux) and the bay leaves into the central pot and bring to a boil. Reduce the heat and simmer for 1 hour. Add the shrimp during the last 10 minutes of cooking. Serve in large bowls over plain white rice. Pass filé powder if the gumbo isn't thick enough.

In a world where honest hard labor and the appreciation of opportunity are often viewed with jaded cynicism, the career of Cecil McBee seems a throwback to an era steeped in the values of the work ethic. McBee has become one of jazz's premier bassists both because he seized the chances presented to him and because he devoted himself fully to applying his talents when doors were opened.

Born in 1935 and raised in Tulsa, Oklahoma, the bass player got into the habit of earning his own way at

TASTY PLATTERS

- The Leaders, *Unforeseen Blessings* (Black Saint)
- Cecil McBee/John Hicks/ Elvin Jones, *Power Trio* (Novus)
- Cecil McBee/McCoy Tyner/ David Murray/Roy Haynes/ Pharoah Sanders, *Blues for Coltrane* (MCA/Impulse!)

an early age. Working part-time at a farmer's produce market from when he was nine until he was sixteen helped pay the family bills. Listening to every kind of music that Tulsa had to offer helped establish his direction. McBee absorbed it all, country and western, gutbucket blues, jazz, and rhythm and blues. He heard yet another kind of music in his own home: his uncle's gospel quartet often used the living room as rehearsal space to practice harmonies modeled after groups like the original Five Blind Boys of Alabama.

McBee's first big opportunity came in high school when he dis-

covered the bass in the school's instrument room. He put down the clarinet forever. "It was just there laying on the floor and I picked it up," he recalls. "I remember, even to this day, the first note. Just thinking about it still feels right. I tried to play an old boogie-woogie–type blues and I think I was close. Every day during lunch hour I'd go down to the music room and play. I was

persistent. Pretty soon I was good enough that word was getting around town that there was this new bass player, a kid bass player."

McBee went from performing at junior proms to playing at a strip joint called the Flamingo Club that featured rhythm and blues to a club by the name of Clarence Love's Lounge, where he became house bassist. And then he switched gears. Prodded by his high school music teacher, Clarence Fields, he enrolled at Central State College in Ohio in 1953.

"I really wasn't a good student, but I got in," he recounts. "It was the greatest thing to happen to me. The scholastic environment demanded something from me internally. The parameters of my life expanded. I learned about the world and about how to relate to people. I realized the potential of achievement and that I was part of a bigger world, one that was unfolding. I jumped into books. I knew I was behind the other students and worked on my deficiencies. I had better not fail; I couldn't let my mother and Mr. Fields down. My mother worked too hard for me to come home a failure."

It took McBee nine years to graduate, not because he was a slow learner but because he opted to interrupt his education each year in order to earn money washing dishes and washing cars.

After a hitch in the service, during which time he played in the army band, he moved to Detroit and immersed himself in its invigorating musical climate. A stint with Paul Winter in New York in 1964 led to his making that city his permanent home and to subsequent work with Denny Zeitlin, Grachan Moncur, Jackie McLean, Charles Lloyd, Yusef Lateef, and Alice Coltrane. His career of collaborations with an eclectic range of stylists was under way.

McBee's versatility is only one reason why everyone from Sonny Rollins to Abdullah Ibrahim loves having him behind them. His swing has an easy, graceful confidence to it that belies the strength and lightning speed he can apply at

Sautéed Salmon

"I grew up on Oklahoma food," the bassist says. "Oklahoma was designated as a territory for the red man and slaves, and here I am. When I was growing up we ate a lot of my grandmother's food, good quality food." Then there were the Tulsa barbecue restaurants whose sauce helped set Tulsa's barbecue apart from any other city's. To this day, McBee orders his barbecue sauce from a Tulsa restaurant called Wilson's.

He's both proud and humble when discussing his own culinary skills. "People who know me know that I'm one for quality foods," he says. "But it's also embarrassing for me to say that I'm considered a good cook."

McBee, who does most of the cooking for his wife and two children in their Manhattan home, also utilizes his skills at the family's summer house in Maine. "We get a lot of salmon up in Maine," he explains. "If I don't cook it on the grill, I like to prepare it in a skillet. And if I can't find salmon, my recipe also works with swordfish or tuna." According to McBee, this dish goes well with steamed, red-skinned potatoes, asparagus, and a crisp white wine, such as an Italian Pinot Grigio, or a California Sauvignon Blanc.

Serves 4

2 pounds salmon, swordfish, or tuna fillets
Approximately ⅓ cup flour
Salt and pepper
3 tablespoons butter
2 tablespoons high-quality cooking oil
½ cup fresh parsley, finely chopped
Lemon wedges

Wash and dry the fillets. On a plate or a large piece of waxed paper, combine the flour, salt, and pepper. Dredge the fillets in the flour mixture. In a skillet large enough to hold all of the fish, over medium-high heat, warm 2 tablespoons of the butter and the oil. Transfer the fillets to the hot skillet and cook until the underside of each is crisp, about 5 minutes. Gently flip and cook the other side for 4 to 5 minutes, until the underside is crisp. Remove the fillets to a warm platter. Lower the heat to its lowest possible setting and add the remaining tablespoon of butter to the skillet. Add the parsley, swirling the pan, and cook for no more than 1 minute. Pour the butter over the fish and serve immediately with the lemon wedges.

a moment's notice. And his stout tone, a rich-sounding aural buoy, is always true, whether the vehicle is bop-oriented, free, or modal. A virtuoso on his instrument, McBee similarly writes solid, exciting compositions that make use of a kaleidoscope of rhythms, tones, and textures. With his own groups or with others, the bassist has been in the midst of some of the most stirring jazz created from the sixties to the present.

After spending more than three decades perfecting his craft, McBee is justifiably pleased with what he has accomplished. "I'm proud of what I do," he proclaims. "I'm an American musician playing American music."

hether you bob your head, snap your fingers, or tap your feet, it's the swing in a song that makes you move to the beat. Duke Ellington composed "It Don't Mean a Thing If It Ain't Got That Swing" back in 1932, and the tenet still makes sense today. Acoustic bassist Rufus Reid's definitely got that swing.

His influences on bass are among the deepest swingers the music has ever known: Milt Hinton, Ron Carter, Richard Davis, Paul Chambers, Ray Brown. But it was a saxophone player with whom Reid worked early in his career, Eddie Harris, who provided him with the words of wisdom on the subject that the bassist uses as his credo to this day. "I learned an awful lot from Eddie because he played a lot of different styles," Reid points out. "But one thing he always said was, 'Whatever you do, don't ever stop swinging.' If I haven't learned anything else, I've learned there has to be something groovy and swinging in my presentation. Otherwise I'm not really doing what I can do best. Swing is something that a lot of people take for granted."

No one who has ever heard or played with Reid takes his penchant for swing for granted. He has

TASTY PLATTERS

- **Rufus Reid,** *Perpetual Stroll* **(Sunnyside)**
- **Stan Getz,** *Serenity* **(EmArcy)**
- **Dexter Gordon,** *Nights at the Keystone, Volumes 1–3* **(Blue Note)**

teamed with many of jazz's giants, from Dexter Gordon to Bobby Hutcherson to Andrew Hill. His tone, fat as a blimp and springy as a trampoline, leaves an unmistakable

burnish on every song he plays, whether it's in quick bebop changes, the locomotive power of a big band, or the high-wire maneuvers of free jazz. His peers think so highly of him that he was chosen to conduct a fourteen-member all-star acoustic bass ensemble honoring Milt Hinton on his eightieth birthday. And he has little problem attracting students to his courses at William Paterson College in New Jersey, where he is director of jazz studies and performance.

Reid has crammed in a lifetime of accomplishments since his early days in Atlanta, where he was born in 1944, and in Sacramento, where he spent most of his childhood. His first instrument wasn't bass, but trumpet, which he took up at twelve. By high school he had hooked up with a soul and rock band. "We did proms and high school dances," he recalls. "I dread to think what we sounded like, but it was fun."

Reid also got an unforgettable taste of manual labor back then, during the summer break from school. "I was hanging around without a job," he says. "I was a kid who needed some bread and we didn't have much money. In California, when you're a kid of

Pasta from Bari

Like so many jazz artists, Reid's tastes and tastebuds have been expanded by frequent trips abroad, especially to the many summer festivals in Europe. While his recipe for the aptly named Pasta from Bari is a taste-perfect recollection of a dish he discovered in Bari, Italy, while on tour with the Dizzy Gillespie/ Phil Woods All-Stars, some of his stateside Italian improvisations haven't turned out quite so well.

"There was this one pasta dish that we had in a small town," recalls Reid. "It was a knockout. Sweet with herbs and olive oil. I wrote everything down. Came home, made it . . . and it wasn't even close. I went through so many virgin and extra-virgin olive oils trying to get it down."

There's no problem with his memory, technique, or ingredients in Pasta from Bari, however.

Serves 4 as a main course or 8 as a first course

> 1 pound ziti, preferably imported
>
> 3 sun-dried tomatoes (not packed in oil)
> ¼ pound fresh mozzarella, cut into slices or bite-sized pieces (if necessary, substitute packaged mozzarella)
> 1 cup cherry tomatoes, halved
> 1 bunch fresh basil, chopped (approximately 1 cup, or to taste)
> ¼ cup extra-virgin olive oil
> 1 or more large cloves garlic, crushed

Begin to cook the ziti according to the package directions. While it is cooking, prepare the sauce.

Cover the sun-dried tomatoes with a small amount of boiling water and let sit for 2 minutes. Drain and cut into small pieces. In a nonreactive bowl, mix together the mozzarella, cherry tomatoes, basil, sun-dried tomatoes, olive oil, and garlic. Set aside.

When the ziti is ready, remove it from the pot and drain well. Toss the ziti with the mozzarella mixture, until the pasta is well coated.

fifteen or sixteen, there wasn't a whole lot you could do, but there was always the opportunity to go out to the fields to pick tomatoes or corn, which I did one summer. I remember getting up at the crack of dawn to go downtown to catch the truck. Talk about serious— twelve-, fourteen-hour days of bending over, picking, and getting dirty! Man, I was beat. I couldn't wait to see the bed."

At home, Reid's mother turned out dishes like ham hocks, collard greens, and sweet potato pie. He also got the chance to sample the different ethnic foods cooked by the mothers of his Japanese and Italian friends. When he joined the air force in his late teens and was stationed in Montgomery, Alabama, as a member of the band, the culture shock he experienced wasn't culinary.

"I had all kinds of friends in Sacramento, all colors and shapes," he points out. "It was great. There was a lot of bigotry, but as I look back it was nothing compared to what so many people had to deal with. When I got to the service in Alabama, segregation was a way of life. It took me back. I rode on the first integrated bus in Montgomery. I saw all hell break loose. There were bombings. It was a wild time, but very important. This was also the time that my ideas of music and being a musician started to come together."

Reid switched to bass while he was in Montgomery and started listening to jazz seriously. Later, after being transferred to Japan, he studied with a classical bassist in Tokyo. He knocked around some when he got out of the service in 1966 before landing at Northwestern University, in Chicago, where he earned a degree in performance. The Windy City is where Reid made his first substantive contacts in the jazz world. The reputation he started earning there has become more and more stellar ever since.

In the mid-1980s Reid settled in the New York area, and he now lives in Teaneck, New Jersey, with his wife, Doris, and son, Michel. While Doris handles most of the cooking, Reid takes on a fair share himself, smoking turkey and brisket on the grill or preparing shrimp in a mustard sauce for a dinner party.

KEYBOARDS

Whether the lessons are about food, culture, or philosophies of life, belief in the power of education has deep roots for Geri Allen. This belief took hold in the one-room Tennessee schoolhouse where her grandmother taught, became firmer in the Detroit elementary school where her father was principal, and continues to spread to this day in the halls of Howard University where she teaches, and more importantly onstage, where the pianist is intent on passing along what she has absorbed.

Allen's propensity to delve deeply into her heritage has helped put her at the forefront of modern jazz composers and improvisers who share a vision of the future that's grounded solidly in the past.

"My whole family is really education-based," she explains. "Everybody says, 'You must go to school. You must be educated.' It's been a strong push for me."

Learning hasn't been limited to the classroom. Allen, who was born in 1957 and raised in Detroit, got to know her way around the kitchen by following the leads of her mother and father, both excellent cooks, and by trial and error. "They let me destroy a couple of meals once or twice," she laughs. Her musical education was similarly hands-on.

"My parents made sure my brother and I checked out many different aspects of the arts, including the visual arts and dance," she says. "I took to music." Her father was a record collector, so the sounds of Charlie Parker, Duke Ellington, Billie Holiday, and Milt Jackson were part of her life at a young age. She started playing piano at seven. By fourteen she was taking advantage of one of Detroit's most highly regarded cultural programs, the Jazz Development Workshop, which exposed her to artists like trumpeter Marcus Belgrave. "It put everybody together. The young people had the opportunity to sit next to stellar, veteran musicians, learn their crafts, and hear their stories," she recalls.

Allen began frequenting Detroit's jazz clubs while she was a student at Cass Tech High School, but given that city's rich musical diversity, she didn't confine her listening to jazz. Hers was an open-minded approach, which served her well as she developed her own music. "There was always a lot to draw from there: Motown, Reverend Franklin's church with the young Aretha Franklin, Little Stevie Wonder, the staunch bebop tradition," she says. "I found that there were musicians doing all those things, sort of moving through the whole environment. I didn't get a sense of snobbery, of one being better than another. One of Marcus Belgrave's golden rules is that in order to be a great musician you have to be versatile, and in order to be a great artist you have to be a great musician. Being an artist means being an original, somebody who does things their own way. It assumes that you have a foundation, and the foundation means embracing all those things that are available to you."

Allen kept building on her foundation, playing for theater groups, at bar mitzvahs, ethnic weddings, clubs, churches, and dance classes.

Cream Cheese and Peach Pie

"I've always been really open about foods," says Allen. "When I got to Howard University, I got a sense of all these different foods from other cultures. There were Ethiopian restaurants, foods from the Caribbean, and different Spanish and French cuisines. Washington had many international flavors to sample."

Yet Detroit is the inspiration for her Cream Cheese and Peach Pie. "My mom, Barbara Jean Allen, learned to make this pie from her sister Nanita Long," she says. "It's really just a simple family recipe."

Makes 2 pies

- 2 (8-ounce) packages cream cheese, at room temperature (*Note*: Use 3 packages for thicker, richer pies)
- 3 large eggs, separated
- 1 (14-ounce) can sweetened condensed milk

- Juice of 1 lemon
- 1 large (29-ounce) can sliced peaches in syrup, drained
- 2 homemade or store-bought graham cracker crusts, baked and cooled to room temperature

Preheat the oven to 350°F. In a large bowl, beat the cream cheese until smooth. Beat in the egg yolks just until incorporated. Add the sweetened condensed milk, lemon juice, and sliced peaches. Pour equal amounts of filling into the two pie shells and smooth the tops with a rubber spatula.

In a medium-sized, grease-free bowl, beat the egg whites until they hold firm peaks. Spread the egg white over the filling and bake for 10 to 15 minutes, just until the meringue begins to brown. Transfer the pies to a wire rack and let set for about 1 hour before serving.

terrain of the avant-garde. She also revels in tempos and meters that change continually, harmonies that are taut and inventive, and textures, melodies, and rhythms that seem incongruous, unpredictable, yet in

the end perfectly logical. Although her spare, often splintered piano phrases have on occasion been called studied and dry, she evokes the full range of emotions in her music, especially in the company of current bandmates Anthony Cox, Wallace Roney, and Pheeroan akLaff. Her lyrical side is brought out particularly brightly when she's with bassist Charlie Haden and drummer Paul Motian.

"I'm living my music as I live my life," she says. "I'm motivated by the changes life presents. There are many different choices, and balancing those choices is the sweetest challenge. I like to experience music in the same way."

Allen experienced one of those changes in March of 1990 when her daughter, Laila, was born. Before their daughter was born Allen and husband Rabb would sample the many Caribbean restaurants near their Brooklyn home. However, the Southern/Midwestern cooking that Allen was raised on gave way long ago to a more organically based diet that now has been refined even further to include Laila's needs.

She solidified it further when she earned a degree in jazz studies at Howard University in Washington, D.C., in 1979, and later a master's degree in ethnomusicology at the University of Pittsburgh. By the time she moved to New York in 1982, she was ready to apply her knowledge to her music. She recorded with Oliver Lake's reggae-funk band Jump Up soon after she arrived, paid the bills by playing soul for six months with former Supreme Mary Wilson, and began collaborating steadily with experimenters like Lester Bowie and Joseph Jarman. She had found a family of kindred spirits that would

keep expanding. For a time Allen also became part of the M-Base movement, a loose coalition of mostly Brooklyn-based players that has been working since the 1980s to forge a fresh conceptual synthesis of modern and classic jazz with the most vibrant elements of contemporary popular music.

These disparate affiliations have inspired Allen to come up with a sound that's simultaneously challenging in the novel directions it travels and reassuring in its acknowledgment of roots. She employs international rhythms and soulful riffs in her pieces as naturally as angular bop or the open-spaced

Neither gumption nor a sense of humor have ever been in short supply in the personality of composer/arranger/keyboard player Carla Bley. They are among the many traits that have made her one of jazz's most entertaining and original artists.

By the time she was six, with her mother ill and confined to bed, Carla was already cooking for herself and her father in their Oakland, California, home. "My first very funny big mistake was making an apple pie," she recalls. "The recipe said to put shortening in the pie crust. I thought that meant baking powder. That was sort of funny. And, needless to say, there were many cases of 'food poisoning.' It was awful but I was just a kid and tried to cook as well as I could. I made most of my mistakes before I was ten."

After Bley's mother died when Carla was eight, her father occasionally hired live-in help. The composer remembers one woman's cooking vividly. "Every night she'd cook roast beef with gravy," Bley says. "You'd pour the gravy on the white bread. The white bread was the potatoes. It was really pretty insane. The food was not happening at all when I was a kid."

Even though she was born in 1938, the jazz and popular swing and dance music of the late forties and early fifties weren't part of her childhood. There was only one musical genre in Bley's life until she was nearly a teenager. "It was church music from the age of three, when I used to sing 'This Little Light of Mine' and hold out a dish and get money, until around twelve, when I played solo piano for Youth for Christ. That was it. At thirteen I became a stodgy athe-

TASTY PLATTERS

- **Carla Bley, *Dinner Music* (ECM/WATT)**
- **Carla Bley, *The Very Big Carla Bley Band* (ECM/WATT)**
- **Charlie Haden, *Dream Keeper* (Blue Note)**

ist and left the church." Bley left home a year later. When she was fifteen, music became more important to her than studying history and math. She quit school and went to work in a music store. In the early sixties she moved to New York to break into the jazz world, supporting herself as a cigarette girl, usherette, and hatcheck girl, and later as a fledgling composer.

Bley quickly found herself immersed in the free-jazz movement of the day in New York. With musicians like Archie Shepp, Michael Mantler, Roswell Rudd, and former husband Paul Bley, she became active with the Jazz Composers' Guild, a group that evolved into the Jazz Composers' Orchestra Association (JCOA), a nonprofit organization that commissioned new works. Her reputation grew as a writer who had a totally original slant on the music, which attracted commissions from heavyweights like George Russell, Gary Burton, and Charlie Haden.

Bley's book of material, much of it recorded on her own label, WATT, has since become voluminous. Her pieces, which often carry unusual titles such as "Sex with Birds" and "The Girl Who Cried Champagne," evoke a range of moods and employ a seemingly endless variety of styles. Her syncopations can be funky or goofy, tangos twisted and lyricism completely off-kilter. Bley's unique sense of instrumentation is often wryly humorous, yet always precise and economical. She'll employ a tuba as the meat of one song, a raucous, clattering trombone as foil to two earnest saxophones on another. Her keyboard playing, whether on acoustic piano, organ, or synthesizers, leans toward the spare and lyrical.

"The music changes, just like one night we have Mexican food and the next night French food," she says. "I just want to explore new tastes. I become infatuated with something for a while and just keep doing it."

The period Bley calls her "quiet storm" period, during the mid- to late 1980s, wasn't particularly well-received by critics, although the musician believes that her attempt to create music that would make people relax and feel good was misunderstood. Standard big band orchestra is a love now. "Bebop is

Soup

Home, and the pleasures therein, set the tone for Carla Bley's Soup. A dish rooted in "logic and ingrained thrift," as Carla puts it, her Soup is derived from working at home, feeding those who happen to be there, and a sense of parsimony that's in tune with nature.

In the spirit of spontaneity, we depart from the traditional and let Carla herself lead us through the soup's hows and whys—and then some.

"Working at home has its advantages: Everyday I cook soup for lunch. Whoever is in my house at the time gets some. First I look in the icebox to check the leftovers from the previous night's dinner. That gives me my theme.

"Did we have chicken? Aha! Take the remaining meat off the bones, and set it aside. Boil the skin and bones with a bay leaf and a little salt or a bouillon cube for 30 minutes. Throw in any old wilted greens or celery leaves. Don't cover the pot. Strain the resulting stock through a colander into another pot. Add some diced garlic, chopped onion, and diced celery, and start boiling again while you decide what else to throw in. Did we have rice with the chicken? Is there any left over? If so, then go for a gumbo-type soup by adding okra, peppers, coriander, and as much hot sauce as you can stand. Leftover pasta? Call it minestrone and add leftover tomato sauce, basil, miscellaneous diced vegetables, or beans. Leftover potatoes? Chowder-type ingredients like potatoes, corn, parsley, carrots, onions come to mind. Or just add a handful of egg noodles if you don't have any other starch. Before you serve the soup, add the cooked chicken and some extra garlic or seasoning if it seems it needs something. Make sure it boils once more.

"Did we have fish? Or shellfish? Oh boy! Never throw away any fish heads, tails, or shrimp shells, lobster, crab, or bits of leftover bites. All these things make great soup. Throw all your shells and skeletons into a pot with a bay leaf and a little salt to extract flavor. As with the chicken stock, at this stage you can add any vegetables that have been in the refrigerator. Strain it after all the essence is boiled out. (Note: When preparing fish stock, simmer lightly for no more than 30 minutes) and proceed as with the chicken, adding leftover fish, shrimp, etc. Little bits of color, like cubed red sweet peppers, minced parsley, purple kale or squid ink pasta make a nice addition. Different textures help, too.

"If you don't have any leftover meat or fish, there are many vegetables you can use to make the stock. But if you're not a vegetarian, keep a ham hock or soup bones in the freezer for just such an occasion. If necessary, a can of chicken broth or a bouillon cube adds richness.

"I get so excited about soup! When I shop for dinner, I always think in advance about possible leftovers. And not wasting food is an extra thrill. I don't feel so cruel about eating other living things if I treat every part of them with admiration and respect."

something I'm still trying to understand," she admits. "It could take a lifetime. To me, it's the best, most beautiful form of music I've ever heard and probably one of the best the world has ever experienced. It's as mysterious as anything."

Bley's dietary habits have seen an evolution as profound as her musical shifts. "From fourteen to seventeen I became a weird food person," she remembers. "I ate only raw carrots, v-8 juice and *scorpa*—Swedish dried toast. Then I slowly began working other foods in. I went through all the stages. Macrobiotic for three years, then only Indian food for two years, then, slowly, working myself up to the greatest food in the world—French food." When she's on tour in France, Bley and companion and bassist Steve Swallow seek out the finest restaurants and chefs. Her favorites are the restaurants of master chefs Freddy Girardet, Guy Savoy, and Alain Chapel. At home she tends a large vegetable garden, a labor of love that keeps her off the festival circuit during most of July and August.

Gran' Macedonia

The unexplored path has always fascinated pianist Paul Bley. He travels not as a maverick but because he believes an entire world of valid ideas lies there waiting to be discovered. Bley has shaped a career out of making those ideas sound logical and in the process has earned himself a reputation as one of jazz's most challenging and respected freethinkers. His visionary sense moved him to collaborate with significant figures like Ornette Coleman and Don Cherry in the earliest stages of their blossoming creativity and to found a record company, Improvising Artists, that captured the often ground-breaking music of artists like Sun Ra and Ran Blake. Bley's own jazz is rarely melodic and is impossible to pigeonhole. Barbed, fragmented, and surreal are among the words that can describe it. A patient listener, though, will be rewarded with music that's not only un-expected, but deeply stirring.

Bley's upbringing and first musical experiences provided few clues that he would soon be in the van-guard of the newest, freest jazz. Born in 1932 in Montreal and adopted by Jewish parents, Bley gave his first recital on violin at seven and by his teens had estab-lished himself as one of the city's most promising young players. His first steady work came in the late 1940s when pianist Oscar Peterson left his trio. "They asked me to

"My macrobiotic diet basically con-sists of really good grains like dark rice and kasha, fresh fruits and vege-tables, and fresh fish," Bley says. "Unlike most macrobiotics, I orna-ment my food with a lot of spices, mostly Indian spices." The relation-ship between diet and energy is key to Bley's nutritional philosophy.

"I was operating on an energy depletion basis that was incredible. How can you tell what the rest of the world is like if your mind is polluted? What happens to most people, especially jazz musicians, is that they are so abusive in the first part of their lives, that they don't have a second part of their lives. In the second part of your life you'd better husband your health. Diet is the whole ball of wax. It's what you put in your body."

Bley's recipe for the breakfast/ dessert dish he's dubbed Gran' Macedonia combines homemade granola with Macedonia, a mix of fresh fruit whose name refers to ancient Macedonia, the nation that was divided into small states. The fruit, which can be varied according to what is in season and what you prefer, is cut up into small pieces and topped with fruit liqueur. To turn it into a morning meal, Bley sand-wiches the fruit between homemade granola and vanilla yogurt, and omits the liqueur.

Serves 8

GRANOLA

6 cups old-fashioned rolled oats

I cup wheat germ

I cup wheat bran

½ cup sesame seeds

½ cup sunflower seeds

½ cup shredded, unsweetened coconut

6 dried figs, cut into small pieces

I cup pecans and/or walnuts, coarsely chopped

MACEDONIA

I cored and peeled pineapple

I pound seedless grapes

3 cored pears

3 peeled and cored apples

3 bananas

16 ounces vanilla yogurt

Grand Marnier or kirsch (optional)

Preheat the oven to 250°F. In a large casserole pan or baking sheet, com-bine the oats, wheat germ, wheat bran, sesame seeds, and sunflower seeds. Bake until lightly browned, stirring once, about 10 minutes. Add the coconut, figs, and nuts and stir to combine. Allow to cool, then place the mixture in a jar. (Note: There will be some granola left over; use for another breakfast.)

Cut the fruit into bite-sized pieces. Pour ½ cup of granola into each of 8 large bowls. Add a generous helping of fresh fruit followed by vanilla yogurt to taste. To serve as a dessert, top with the liqueur.

come in for a year and try to fill his shoes," he recalls. "You have to do a lot of eating to fill Oscar's shoes. He used to have eating contests with people, especially with visiting musicians who wanted to take him on. Competitiveness was part of jazz

music's early history. Oscar would be willing to sit there and order twelve or fifteen steaks and would just keep ordering. The person who stopped eating first would have to pay the bill. I never tried it."

Bley grew up in a semi-Orthodox household where Jewish-Romanian dishes like *mamaliga* were a specialty. He moved to Manhattan in 1950 to attend the Juilliard School and relied heavily—very heavily— upon a meal he had learned to cook at home. "I wound up eating one dish for two years," he remembers, "the only thing I knew how to make: roast chicken. I just threw the chicken in the oven and hoped for the best. I started small but I was able to keep the philosophy of inventing. I don't like written music and I don't like written recipes. I believe in experimenting."

Bley soon caught Charles Mingus's ear, recorded his debut album with the bassist and drummer Art Blakey, and spent most of his free time in Fifty-second Street

clubs listening to performers like Billy Eckstine, Charlie Parker, and Max Roach. He worked constantly in clubs on Long Island and in Brooklyn and eventually moved to Los Angeles in 1957 where he worked for two years at a venue on Washington Boulevard called the Hillcrest Club. Jazz history was made there when he replaced his vibes player, Dave Pike, with saxophonist Coleman and trumpet player Cherry. Bley has often joked that the music was so intense that passersby could tell if the band was playing by whether or not a crowd was gathered in front of the club; the room emptied *during* the sets.

Bley's playing has remained consistently uncategorizable over the course of a career that has included work with his former wife Carla Bley, George Russell, Jimmy Guiffre, Barry Altschul, Sonny Rollins, Paul Motian, and Bill

Frisell. There's an underlying beauty, mystery, and wit to his spare, sometimes stark improvisations. His complex chords often arrive at conclusions that are nothing less than startling. In recent years his playing has taken on a different complexion, one he attributes to a dramatic alteration in his lifestyle.

"I chain-smoked a pipe for twenty-five years and gave it up a few years ago," he says. "When I smoked and got high almost continuously, I was famous for leaving a lot of spaces, a lot of silence. That style worked very well for me all those years. But when I gave up smoking my energy returned so my music is getting faster and faster."

Bley feels he can now apply himself fully to the tack that has made him an iconoclast in jazz circles. "My philosophy has been one of trying to make the human brain be able to be a full-fledged composer in real time," he explains. "I think that a composer is a failed improviser, somebody who takes three weeks to do what someone should be able to do in real time. We're speeding up the mental process."

The pianist, his wife Carol, and two children live a life conducive to clear thinking. While Bley maintains a studio in Manhattan's West Village, he spends most of his nontouring time at the family home in Cherry Valley in upstate New York. His diet is strictly macrobiotic. "I subscribe to the philosophy completely," he says. "Being a gluttonous person, it's been very difficult. My rationale has been that I can eat things that I can eat endless amounts of. I eat lots and lots of good food."

JoAnne Brackeen didn't have to hear Lester Young and Charlie Parker to realize that even at the tender age of six she had an affinity for music. Her parents' Andrews Sisters and Bing Crosby records did the trick. "I always knew where the songs were going to go before they got there," she says.

More than four decades and countless daring improvisational collaborations later, the pianist is composing and playing some of the world's most imaginative jazz. Brackeen herself may know where her pieces are headed, but it takes a sharp listener to anticipate her moves. Few pianists utilize the drama of the unexpected as effectively as Brackeen.

She regards her creative process as a combination of the straightforward and the unexplainable. "I breathe and the music comes out," she says. "Everything just is. You get in these waves of energy and they play music in you. Of course, you have to learn your instrument so that when they come through you, you can do something."

Since the late 1980s, Brackeen has studied the spiritual discipline known as *chi-kung* with the Toronto-based Chinese master Dr. Chu Chow. "It helps your body and your mind," she explains. "It restores what goes out of it. So, of course, it helps your playing. I have to do it every day. It's like eating. It's energy for the body."

If the vigor that laces most of her work is a guide, energy has never

been lacking in Brackeen's playing. She's an experimenter with a concentrated compositional vision who constantly employs sudden transitions and changing patterns. Many of her pieces are constructed like abstract, multicolored mosaics. Impressionism, fluid melodies, dark tonal clusters, silences, and dissonance coexist logically. She holds them together with a percussive left hand that never allows the rhythmic pulse, off-kilter though it may be at times, to stop. Brackeen's performance mix of her own arresting compositions with interpretations of standards by the likes of George Gershwin and Richard Rodgers underscores the all-encompassing nature of her approach to improvisation.

Born JoAnne Grogan in 1938, Brackeen was reared in Ventura,

California, in an environment where individuality was encouraged. Her grandfather was a member of the Los Angeles Philharmonic and her grandmother was a metaphysician, while her father worked in the office of a lumberyard and her mother stayed home to raise the three children. Brackeen's early musical interest came in fits and starts until she was eleven and heard the Frankie Carle stride piano records her parents brought home; she practiced until she sounded exactly like Carle and started performing in school assemblies. Soon she was working in clubs in Ventura and Los Angeles.

"I was tall, so people didn't know I was thirteen or fourteen years old," she says. "I just dressed up. I passed for twenty-one." A few years and many jazz-listening sessions later, she landed a gig with Teddy Edwards at the Zebra Lounge in Los Angeles, where guests like Dexter Gordon and Harold Land would sit in. It was the beginning of a high-level, real-life education that soon included associations with Don Cherry and Ornette Coleman.

During those years, Brackeen lived at home, where her mother did most of the cooking. "It was regular American food," she recalls. "When I started working when I was twelve or thirteen, I used to buy something special that we didn't usually have, mostly fruits like strawberries or watermelon." After she married saxophonist Charles Brackeen and moved to New York in 1965, her life—and diet—changed substantially. The whole family cooked. Chicken and meat were never on the menu, fish only rarely.

"When I came to New York I read a book that said you don't have to

eat meat in order to be healthy," she says. "As soon as I read that line, it brought back memories. When I was a little kid I never wanted to eat meat. My family had to entice me with desserts. I ate it because they made me eat it. But as soon as I read that, from that moment on I didn't eat any meat. After a while I added fish to the diet, and more recently chicken, because I find that during

performances I need it for my body, for the energy level."

It took a few years, but Brackeen eventually worked her way into the New York big time. Two years with Art Blakey's Jazz Messengers led to stints with Joe Henderson and Stan Getz. Since the late 1980s she has been leading her own groups and creating music that often straddles free jazz and mainstream.

Spaghetti with Peanut Sauce

"When you see what people eat it's amazing," says Brackeen. "I eat a lot of rice, chicken, vegetables, and fish, but if I didn't need fish and chicken, I probably wouldn't eat those two things. I really love vegetables."

Peanuts, pasta, herbs, vegetables, and one of those "energy producers," chicken, are all in Brackeen's recipe for Spaghetti with Peanut Sauce, an East-meets-West creation.

Serves 4

MARINADE FOR CHICKEN
- 2 tablespoons dry sherry
- 1 tablespoon soy sauce

- 1 whole chicken breast, skinned, boned, pounded thin, and cut into matchsticks

PEANUT SAUCE
- 1/4 cup peanut butter, preferably chunky
- 3 tablespoons soy sauce
- 2 tablespoons rice wine vinegar
- 1 tablespoon chicken broth
- 1 tablespoon sesame oil
- 2 teaspoons sugar
- 2 teaspoons Chinese chili oil

- 8 ounces regular or Jerusalem artichoke spaghetti, available at health food stores

- 2 tablespoons vegetable oil
- 1 teaspoon minced garlic
- 2 teaspoons minced fresh ginger
- 1/2 medium-sized red onion, thinly sliced
- 1/2 cucumber, peeled, seeded, and cut into matchsticks
- 1 medium-sized carrot, shredded
- 1/2 cup unsalted roasted peanuts, coarsely chopped

To prepare the marinade, in a large, nonreactive bowl, stir together the sherry and soy sauce. Add the chicken and stir to coat. Set aside for 30 minutes. In another bowl, combine all the ingredients for the peanut sauce. Set aside. Cook the spaghetti according to the package directions, until al dente. Drain and set aside.

In a wok or deep-sided frying pan, over high heat, warm the oil, swirling it to coat the pan. Add the garlic and ginger and cook for about 5 seconds. Add the marinated chicken and stir-fry for about 1 minute, or until the chicken just turns opaque. Add the onion and stir-fry for 1 minute, then add the cucumber, carrot, and peanut sauce. Cook, stirring, until slightly thickened, about another 1 or 2 minutes. Remove from the heat. Add the spaghetti and toss until evenly coated. Sprinkle with chopped peanuts.

Somehow it seems incongruous that a man who made the cover of *Time* magazine munches on pumpkin seeds and dried fruit whenever he gets the chance. But then, Dave Brubeck is no stranger to incongruity.

As the pianist who created a huge splash by jumping free fall into the roiling jazz waters of the 1950s, he ruffled plenty of feathers by proudly pointing to his classical influences, Beethoven, Bach, and Darius Milhaud, as well as to Ellington, Waller, Hawkins, Tatum, Beiderbeck, and Kenton. Even when his "Take Five" hovered near the top of the 1961 pop charts, the pianist was buffeted by criticism that his music didn't swing, that his solos didn't say much, and that he was a snooty classicist poaching on jazzland. A writer for the London *Sunday Times* called Brubeck's music "jazz in a grey flannel suit," a criticism that still gets leveled at the pianist in different forms even today. The bad press often didn't matter; Brubeck's groups consistently topped both critics' and readers' polls in jazz periodicals and even captured the small combo award in the first jazz poll conducted by a black newspaper.

Brubeck also had supporters like Duke Ellington, Kid Ory, Charles Mingus, and Gil Evans. Even members of the music's avant-garde profess to being influenced by the percussive underpinnings and off-beat rhythms and harmonies of the Brubeck approach. The pianist's answer to charges that he wasn't "cool," "funky," or "far out" was to simply play what he wanted to play, jazz with an often lyrical bent that was sometimes polytonal and polyrhythmic. And he made it work.

The unconventional approach

Low Cholesterol Barbecue Patties and Sauce

The pianist's health concerns plus a little ingenuity prompted him to create a barbecue sauce that was in sync with his diet.

"My wife, Iola, makes these barbecue patties in which she uses a ratio of about three parts ground turkey to one part lean ground sirloin," he explains. "We needed a barbecue sauce —we both prefer it to ketchup—but I didn't feel like going to the store. So I went through the cabinets, picked out what I thought to be the right ingredients and worked up a barbecue sauce that's perfect for the low-cholesterol burgers. When I eat these patties with some of the sauce spread on the bun, I still feel like I'm having a real old-fashioned barbecue."

Serves 4

PATTIES

1 ¼ pounds ground turkey
⅓ pound lean ground beef

Dried spices and herbs, such as
    garlic powder, oregano, and basil
Salt and pepper

SAUCE

1 ½ cups ketchup
¼ cup olive oil
3 tablespoons Dijon-style mustard
2 tablespoons Worcestershire sauce
1 teaspoon brown sugar

To prepare the patties, mix together the ground meat, herbs, spices, and salt and pepper, and form into burgers.

To prepare the sauce, in a medium saucepan, over medium heat, combine the ketchup, olive oil, mustard, Worcestershire sauce, and brown sugar. Stirring frequently, slowly bring the mixture to a boil. Reduce to a simmer and cook for about 20 more minutes, stirring occasionally. Remove from the heat and cool. Spread it on the buns as you would ketchup. Leftover sauce will keep in the refrigerator for about 2 weeks if covered tightly.

has always served Brubeck well. Born in 1920, as a young boy growing up on a ranch in the foothills of the Sierra Nevada in California he drove his piano-teaching mother crazy by improvising and refusing to accept classical piano training. He did pay close attention, however, to the great piano literature performed by both his mother and older brother, Howard. But interpreting popular songs was his thing, and at fifteen he became the pianist for a band that played Friday and Saturday night dances in towns like Angel's Camp, Grizzly Flats, Copperopolis, and Volcano. By the time he became fully entrenched in the jazz idiom at the College of the Pa-

cific, he actually was barred from the local chapter of the national music fraternity for playing jazz. He was later made an honorary member.

After only his first major club tour of the United States, in the early fifties, Brubeck acted upon a yearning that few jazz players of his day had considered seriously: finding an alternative forum for the music that was more artistically decorous—and personally healthy— than crowded, smoky bars. The college circuit was born! He crammed his four-member band into a huge Kaiser Vagabond, hit the road, and ended up making a live record, *Jazz Goes to College,* that kept him in demand for years.

Brubeck was off, and doing it his own way. Many of the steps the pianist took in those early days, then criticized as unsuitable for jazz, are now part of the accepted way in which a modern player earns his or her living. The band traveled worldwide and turned out several especially memorable albums with a quartet that included the elegant

TASTY PLATTERS

- **Dave Brubeck,** *Jazz Impressions of New York* **(Columbia Jazz Masterpieces)**
- **Dave Brubeck,** *Time Out* **(Columbia Jazz Masterpieces)**
- **Dave Brubeck,** *For Iola* **(Concord Jazz)**

alto saxophonist Paul Desmond. Brubeck's quartet even performed in Moscow during ceremonies at the Reagan-Gorbachev summit. Today, Brubeck still tours regularly with his quartet or with a group that sometimes features his sons, Darius, Chris, Dan, and Matthew, but he's just as likely to spend time in his Connecticut home composing sacred music, some of which was performed at a papal mass in San Francisco, or writing works for the orchestra, chorus, or ballet. "It's important to understand the musicology of what it is you're playing," he says, "and then strive to play the greatest music that you're capable of."

Survival in all its guises was

a lesson Brubeck learned by fending off critical darts and traveling from motel to motel in the Vagabond, but he doubts now that he would have made it as far as dinner in Moscow if he hadn't also learned several nutritional survival lessons along the way. For years now, fish and chicken have been staples of the Brubeck diet. On the road, the pianist is especially careful about what he eats. But it wasn't always that way.

"In the late fifties, I used to barbecue a lot and I got pretty good at it," he explains. "But up until '59 I was eating all the wrong things.

I used to barbecue steaks like crazy. Coming from a cattle ranch, what else? Then my doctor told me I had a high cholesterol count. I went on a low-cholesterol kick and I've been on it for close to thirty years.

"There are a lot of guys like that. Dizzy Gillespie, for example, is really aware of his health. He had his own juicer and I had mine and we'd take them on the road. We'd laugh about it. I'd get carrots by the bushel. I'd just pick up as many as I could and take them to my room and juice 'em. It's a lot of work, and cleaning that machine every day on the road when you don't have a real sink is a disaster. But the carrot juice is good for you."

Brubeck sticks to a travel and diet routine that he follows almost religiously. For at least fifteen years he has been using a health-food mix and trying various juice combinations with it. In his suitcase he also carries a plentiful supply of nuts, raisins, prunes, and other dried fruit in tins and zip-locked bags. And it's written into his contracts that bananas and sugar-free juices be provided in his dressing rooms.

"I bring all kinds of stuff with me on the road," he says. "I'm always experimenting."

Pianist Michel Camilo claims that one of the biggest adjustments he had to make when he moved to Manhattan from the Dominican Republic was learning how to function without a siesta. If the propulsive, Caribbean-hot jazz he started playing shortly after arriving Stateside in 1979 is any gauge of how well he adapted, the problem didn't last long. Judging by the fervor with which he attacks his music, a listener has to wonder how the man could slow down enough to even consider sleeping in the afternoon.

Now both a bona fide New Yorker and a budding international piano star, Camilo has moved far from the relatively leisurely pace he enjoyed in the Dominican Republic, where he was a member of the National Symphony Orchestra as well as a jazz performer. Daily routine for the pianist and his wife, Sandra, has undergone dramatic alterations, musically and culturally. The constant travel to recording dates and concerts is a far cry from hopping in the car and driving to clubs in and around Santo Domingo. And the changes in day-to-day habits like eating have affected Camilo and his wife just as much. "The system in New York doesn't

TASTY PLATTERS

• *Michel Camilo* (Portrait)
• *Michel Camilo, On Fire* (Epic)
• *Freddie Hubbard, Bolivia* (Music Masters)

allow you to have a heavy meal at noon, which is the Dominican tradition," he explains. "You have to keep on working. Believe it or not, in the beginning the concept of

eating a sandwich at noon was exciting to us."

"Exciting" describes much of Camilo's work since he arrived in the United States. His compositions and improvisations are a stew of the hot dance rhythms of Afro-Cuban jazz and his native country's merengue, bebop's harmonic complexities, structured classical discipline, and a dash of funk grooves. He has worked hard to overcome criticism that he is little more than a showboating technical whiz. His music has developed a depth, sense of nuance, and range of moods that place him among jazz's most charismatic young artists.

"I call my music full of energy, full of passion," he says. "It's me and it's also my life. Coming here meant quitting a previous life and pursuing a dream. A lot of sacrifices went along with that. That's why joyfulness is a very big ingredient in my music. It's a joyfulness at having accomplished what I set out to do. Being an international performer and playing jazz are a celebration.

"People think that jazz has to be only dark moods, but that's not true. I think there needs to be a bit more fun. The minute I stop having fun I would probably stop playing jazz. For me, the *joie de vivre* has to be there. I want to share that joy with my audience, share the excitement of being here, of being alive."

Born in 1954, Camilo has been in a celebratory mood for a long time. At four, he played "Happy Birthday" on the accordion at a family gathering. He wrote his first song, a short ballad, at five. When he was nine he took his first classical music lessons and created an ingenious method of studying at home to overcome not having a piano: he drew a keyboard on a piece of cardboard and practiced his fingering by imagining the notes. Still, despite continued years of musical promise, his family badly wanted him to become a doctor. "Musicians down there weren't viewed as professionals," he explains. "Sometimes not even today. They consider them bohemians, people who are highly fun, but not really working."

At sixteen, Camilo became the youngest member of the National Symphony Orchestra, but he soon grew restless. Hearing Art Tatum's rendition of "Tea for Two" on the radio persuaded him to pursue the jazz muse and, ultimately, to leave his island for the promise of New York. Once there, he worked in Broadway shows like "Dancin'," became a member of the studio group French Toast, and in 1983 joined the band led by the fiery Cuban saxophonist Paquito D'Rivera. The reedman encouraged Camilo to loosen up even further and provided him with the foundation for being a bandleader. He also left an impression in another respect.

"He's a big food fan," Camilo says. "That's why he's got the belly, because he eats rice and beans every

day. Every time we went anywhere in the world, he would ask, 'Where is the Cuban restaurant near this town?' At the Umbria Jazz Festival in 1989 he brought his mother-in-law to cook rice and beans every day. He brought the rice and beans and she would go into the kitchen of the hotel and cook a whole Cuban meal. Word got around and all the musicians were checking it out."

Dominican-Style Roast Pork

In true Dominican fashion, the pork in this main course is slow-cooked until the meat can be twirled with a fork and literally falls off the bone. To be faithful to the spirit of the meal, each diner's plate should be filled with a variety of side dishes.

"With our food, we don't eat just one dish," Camilo explains. "This pork should be accompanied by other things that could be meals in themselves." Camilo suggests serving white rice and kidney beans; yuca con mojo, *the starchy tuber common to the Spanish-speaking Caribbean slathered with a sauce made of garlic sautéed in plenty of olive oil; sweet plantains, called* maduros; *and bottles of cold beer, preferably Presidente, the rich, hoppy brew from the Dominican Republic.*

Serves 6

Juice of 3 *naranja agria* (sour oranges that can sometimes be found in specialty or Latin markets), or 2 grapefruits
Juice of 10 lemons
6 to 7 pound picnic shoulder, bone-in
10 cloves garlic, mashed
2 teaspoons onion powder
2 teaspoons salt

2 teaspoons oregano
Pepper

One night ahead, squeeze the juice from the *naranja agria* (or grapefruits) and lemons, removing all of the seeds. Place the pork in a nonreactive pan with a tight-fitting lid or a bowl that comfortably holds the meat. Pour the citrus juices evenly over the meat. Cover the moist meat with the garlic, onion powder, salt, oregano, and pepper. Cover the pan with its lid, or if using a bowl, cover the meat with aluminum foil. Refrigerate overnight.

When ready to cook, remove the meat from the refrigerator and preheat the oven to 350°F. Place the covered meat (either covered with the lid or the foil) in the hot oven and cook for 5 hours, basting the pork every 45 minutes or so with the drippings that form and with the juice and garlic mixture. After 5 hours, raise the oven temperature to 450°F, uncover the meat, and cook for an additional 15 minutes. Allow the meat to sit at room temperature for 15 minutes before slicing.

Note: While this recipe omits cilantro ("It can mask the flavor of the pork," says Sandra's mother), some Latin cooks would add about ¼ cup to the garlic mixture that covers the pork.

Camilo's wife, Sandra, does the majority of the cooking in their household, where the fare is much more international than the Dominican dishes like kidney beans, plantains, pork, and chicken with which they both grew up. Dominican-style roast pork, from Sandra and her mother, is a special meal that's usually prepared for Christmas or on New Year's Eve.

Pianist Tommy Flanagan could well have been the inspiration for the perceptive writer who first described jazz as the sound of surprise. Low key and dryly witty in both his personality and music, Flanagan creates rich, subtle tales that curl hither and yon before sneaking up on a listener. His conclusions can elicit the kinds of responses usually reserved for the most exquisitely crafted mystery novels. When Flanagan's surprises arrive, they're truly welcome.

The pianist, who has been perfecting his graceful, swinging, impossible-to-predict bebop for more than four decades, is characteristically modest about his accomplishments. "As long as I've been playing I've always had a pretty high goal to shoot for," he says, "that is, playing on the level of the people

TASTY PLATTERS

• Tommy Flanagan, *Jazz Poet* (Timeless)
• Tommy Flanagan/Hank Jones, *I'm All Smiles* (Verve)
• Joshua Breakstone, *Evening Star* (Contemporary)

I've admired the most. When you've got a model like an Art Tatum or a Bud Powell, it keeps you up. I've always tried to play at my highest level, keep a little creativity going."

The road to that creativity began in Detroit, where Flanagan was born in 1930. He couldn't have asked for a more fertile musical environment in which to grow. The youngest of six children, he was raised in a household where music was an important family hobby. Besides exposure to the sounds at church, his father, who delivered mail by day, sang with a quartet, his mother listened to all kinds of music, and a brother brought home the latest jazz recordings. By eleven, Flanagan was formally learning how to play the family piano. And then there was the city itself and its schools. Few places can match Detroit for the number of future greats who developed there during the 1940s and 1950s. A short list includes Hank, Elvin, and Thad Jones, Paul Cham-

bers, Lucky Thompson, Milt Jackson, Barry Harris, Sir Roland Hanna, Joe Henderson, Kenny Burrell, Betty Carter, Louis Hayes, Sheila Jordan, and Curtis Fuller. Flanagan was soon listening to or playing with many of them in clubs such as the Rouge Lounge and the Twenty Grand. Still, he believes that the encouragement he received in school was just as important.

"The school system seemed to be pretty good," he recalls. "They were interested in developing the talent they had. And there was a lot of competition in high school.

Shrimp Eclypso

Despite his dietary alterations, food and good times are not and never have been mutually exclusive for Flanagan. A preprandial creation that the pianist developed with Diana, Shrimp Eclypso takes its name from his composition "Eclypso," recorded in the late 1970s. The dish brings to life Flanagan's approach to food: low in fat and sodium, but never lacking in taste.

Serves 12, one skewer apiece

- 36 fresh jumbo shrimp
- 2 pink grapefruits
- 3 to 4 kiwis
- 2 small or 1 large avocado
- 1 to 2 bunches watercress
- 12 wooden skewers

DRESSING

- ½ cup extra-virgin olive oil
- Juice of ½ lime, or 2 tablespoons grapefruit juice, or to taste
- 1 tablespoon Dijon-style mustard

Peel and devein the shrimp. In a large pot, bring to boil enough water to cover the shrimp. Add the shrimp, return the water to boiling, and cook until the shrimp just turn pink, about 2 to 3 minutes. Do not overcook the shrimp. Drain the shrimp, cover, and refrigerate.

Slice each grapefruit in half, and with a grapefruit sectioning tool, remove the sections and set aside. (You may reserve the grapefruit juice to use instead of the lime juice in the dressing.) Peel the kiwis, slice them in half horizontally, and cut the halves into small sections similar in shape to the grapefruit sections. Peel the avocado and slice it in vertical sections radiating out from the pit. Cut each of these sections into bite-sized sections. Break the watercress into bite-sized pieces.

Each of the 12 skewers is allotted 3 shrimp and, for balance, it is best to wind up with 1 shrimp at either end of the skewer and 1 in the middle. Skewer the grapefruit, kiwi, avocado, and watercress in any order you like in between. Strive for color and balance.

To make the dressing, place the oil in a small bowl. Add the lime juice (or grapefruit juice) and the mustard. With a whisk, beat the ingredients together until the mustard has combined with the oil and juice. Lightly brush each skewer with the dressing, or place the dressing in a shallow bowl as a dip. Either way, this is meant to be finger food.

Quite a few guys were advancing at about the same pace. Plus the older musicians like Milt Jackson and Hank Jones were very helpful and inspirational, even though they weren't around that much since they went on the road very early."

After a two-year hitch in the army, Flanagan got in a car with guitarist Burrell and moved to New York. It was 1956 and the city's jazz scene was still white hot. Within a short time he found himself filling in for Bud Powell in a trio with Elvin Jones and Tommy Potter. And the Detroit connection stayed intact. "I got a little apartment, a one-room with a four-burner, that was used as a rehearsal space for a while," he remembers. "I had a piano, an old upright that I got for almost nothing, and not everybody had one in those days. There was quite a Detroit group who moved to New York about the same time."

The pianist also had a basic knowledge of cooking. "My mother was a very good cook, from small things to elaborate things," he recalls. "We always knew there would be a wonderful meal if she had the time to lay it out. She had a good imagination about cooking. From that I got interested in it myself. Everybody in the family could do a little bit of cooking. When I came to New York I was a bachelor, but I knew I could take care of myself. I cooked small stuff, survival food. I didn't want to go beyond that."

Flanagan saved his finest creations for the bandstand and recording studio. Work with J. J. Johnson, Miles Davis, and Coleman Hawkins; appearances on two of the greatest jazz recordings of all time—Sonny Rollins's *Saxophone Colossus* and John Coltrane's *Giant Steps,* a year with Tony Bennett; and a total of twelve years with Ella Fitzgerald cemented his reputation as a virtuoso whose painterly, propulsive, unexpected interpretations of songs are unparalleled. No pianist has mastered the art of melodic invention quite like Flanagan has.

In 1978, Flanagan suffered a heart attack and eventually parted ways with Fitzgerald. His career entered a new phase, one in which the pianist's own music was placed front and center. His own trios, usually with bassist George Mraz and drummers like Louis Nash, Al Foster, and Kenny Washington, have been particularly memorable.

That heart attack also changed Flanagan's diet forever. "I always did eat chicken and fish, but I started eating more of it," he says. He also started to walk more regularly. Those adjustments paid off in 1991, helping the pianist recover speedily from major heart surgery.

No jazz artist summarizes his or her music quite the way Dave Frishberg does. "I often say to the audience that my songs enter three categories: food, humiliation, and names," he explains. "Then there's overlap among those categories."

The pianist/vocalist dryly understates the breadth of his improvisational and lyrical range with that synopsis, but it is hard to argue with someone whose list of song titles includes "Brenda Starr," "Let's Eat Home," "Sweet Kentucky Ham," "Van Lingle Mungo," and "My Attorney Bernie." Frishberg, an uncategorizable original, composes some of jazz's most entertaining and clever music. He shapes lyrically quirky songs into swinging and pointed observations about life in the twentieth century. More often than not he hits the funny bone straight on.

"Each song that I write seems to turn out to be a character song," he says. "And that character is not me. It could be, and it may be, but I don't think of it that way. Some songs are crotchety, cranky; that's one character. Others sound cynical; that's another character. None of them are necessarily me—or they're all like me."

Born in St. Paul, Minnesota, in 1933, Frishberg was the youngest of four children. His Russian-born father was a salesman and clothing store owner who would sing in the temple. His mother kept the business and home life in order. Her cooking? "Middle-western, white-bread food," he recalls. "Undistinguished. I never really got into the enjoyment of eating until I was halfway dissipated, older. Now I really like to eat."

Spaghetti al Estuardo

Frishberg admits that his palate is more adventurous than his experiments in the kitchen. His contribution is borrowed from New York Newsday *jazz critic Stuart Troup, who served Frishberg his main-course pasta creation, Spaghetti al Estuardo, during one of the pianist's stopovers in New York.*

"The next day I called him and asked to be invited to dinner again, the sooner the better," Frishberg recalls. "And I insisted that he serve the same spaghetti. So the next night, I went over there and ate it again. I can easily imagine eating it every day for the rest of my life. With all that olive oil and garlic, how bad could it be?"

**Serves 4 as a main course or
6 to 8 as a first course**

- 1 cup olive oil
- 3 to 4 cloves garlic, minced
- ¾ pound ripe plum tomatoes, peeled and seeded
- 1½ pounds spaghetti
- ½ cup chopped fresh parsley
- ¾ cup chopped fresh basil

In a small skillet, over moderate heat, warm the olive oil. Add the garlic and cook until soft. Set aside. Cut the tomatoes into bite-sized pieces and set aside. Cook the spaghetti according to the package directions. Just before the spaghetti is done, return the garlic and oil mixture to a low flame. Place the cooked spaghetti in a large bowl and add the tomatoes, parsley, and basil. Mix well. Add the warmed oil and garlic. Mix from the bottom, since the oil tends to pool there. "Then call me and invite me for dinner," Frishberg says.

Frishberg had started classical piano lessons by the time he was nine, then stopped them abruptly when he was reprimanded by his instructor for adding a conga rhythm to a Mozart composition. Boogie-woogie, swing, and his parents' recordings of choice—musical soundtracks—became his inspiration. By the early 1950s, he was playing in the bands of St. Paul clubs like the Flame, where headliners included Johnny Hodges and Billie Holiday. Four years at the University of Minnesota and two in the air force led to his move to New York in 1957. He briefly held the first and last of his day jobs: writing promotional copy for a record label.

More important, Frishberg was working around New York with masters like Ben Webster, Carmen McRae, Jimmy Rushing, and, for five years, Al Cohn and Zoot Sims. "I played with everyone I ever dreamed of playing with, really," he says. He was also writing songs, which over the years have been covered by singers from Mel Tormé to Blossom Dearie. "I'm Hip," which he composed with Bob Dorough, and "Peel Me a Grape" were two of his earliest successes. During the sixties, he got involved in a dizzying array of projects, from conducting for a country-and-western singer to touring with blues and folk singer Odetta. He moved to Los Angeles in 1971 to write "The Funny Side," a weekly TV show, and later spent two years with Herb Alpert and the Tijuana Brass. In the late 1970s he took his own act on the road.

Frishberg's improvising is a unique mixed bag of all his influences—stride, bebop, boogie-woogie, the blues. A piano player first, he makes sure that a profound swing propels his music and his messages, whether it's on offbeat tunes like "Blizzard of Lies" or tributes to Billy Strayhorn or Irving Berlin. He enunciates his lyrics clearly and strongly in a voice that's as unadorned as plain yogurt. Most of all,

Frishberg is witty. Some of Frishberg's warmest and catchiest songs are on the subject of baseball, his favorite sport. "Van Lingle Mungo" is essentially a list of old-time baseball players set to a samba beat.

He's a firm believer in compact songs. "The music that I've always been interested in is the jazz that was derived from the pop song form," he says. "I still feel that jazz is the perfect three-minute art form, corresponding with the length of a seventy-eight rpm record. I think that's the ideal length for a jazz presentation to be, a form that's best presented as a short story or a vignette. It's just about right to communicate one thing to the audience. Compare it with baseball. They always talk about the perfect distance, ninety feet between the bases.

TASTY PLATTERS

- Dave Frishberg, *Let's Eat Home* (Concord Jazz)
- Dave Frishberg, *Classics* (Concord Jazz)
- Jack Sheldon, *Jack's Groove* (Fresh Sound)

The analogy doesn't really fit, but it's similar."

Frishberg has made Portland, Oregon, his home since 1986. He pays more attention to what he eats now than he has in the past. Pasta and more pasta is his favorite dish. "I've only recently begun to put on weight when I eat," he says. "I could eat anything I wanted all my life and never put on any pounds. Up until

age forty, I was buying clothes in the boys' departments because my waist was so small. I couldn't find men's slacks or suits to fit me. For a while there, in the 1960s, I followed the fads and went on a macrobiotic diet. I stayed on it for about a week and realized it was madness. But I watched certain friends of mine go into the hospital with malnutrition eating those mung beans."

For decades, the picture painted of jazz musicians in the former Communist bloc nations of Eastern Europe has been of artists who congregate clandestinely in dark places, hidden from the eyes and ears of the authorities. Variations of that scenario have doubtless been true for certain long periods in Poland, the Soviet Union, and other nations. But in countries like Yugoslavia and Hungary, artists have lived under less overtly oppressive regimes. While jazz may not have been encouraged there, in recent history it has never been officially strangled, either.

Hungarian pianist/composer Laszlo Gardony, now a resident of the United States, was born three months before the revolution took place in his country in 1956. Pre-1956, Hungarians were permitted to listen only to certain kinds of jazz, such as Glenn Miller's big band sound; Charlie Parker and bebop were outlawed. Since the 1956 uprising, however, jazz of all styles has been tolerated, if not necessarily advocated.

Gardony left Hungary in 1983, not because he was prevented from playing his music, but for a reason that sheds light on one of the side effects of a repressive society: he felt his compatriots simply wouldn't allow themselves to be moved by uplifting music. And whether he's hurtling through a heated bop-derived number or toying with the nuances of a reflective ballad, joy is at the core of Gardony's jazz.

"After '56 people had a hard time abandoning their negativism," he says. "The musicians weren't suppressed, but since the people were suppressed they wanted to hear suppressed music. If you played some-thing else which was positive, they just didn't understand how you could play this music sincerely. People had a hard time understanding that your freedom starts within you. You have to liberate yourself first. You have to try to make life better."

Gardony's sense of optimism has been inspired, in large measure, by his father. A lawyer by trade, he was forced to find other work to support his family when the Communists took over in 1945. One of those jobs was playing in a piano bar. "He's a self-taught person but he has a great sense of entertainment," his son explains. "He knows a lot of tunes and he'd be able to kind of play them, good enough so the people would have a good time."

Even though his father was the only musician in the family, Gardony recalls being drawn to the instrument at an early age.

"There was a beautiful brown piano in the living room which just came with the furniture," he

Chicken Paprikash

This famous Hungarian dish that, in English, falls under the broad name Chicken Paprikash, is known in Hungary as paprikas csirke *when it is made with sour cream, and* pörkölt *when made without it. While Gardony's more balanced diet would seem to favor the latter, there's no denying the richness that sour cream brings to the dish. For those who would rather refrain from the sour cream, the pianist suggests substituting plain yogurt.*

A strong-flavored rather than spicy dish, Chicken Paprikash's smoky taste, like so much of Hungarian cuisine, derives from the liberal use of paprika. While the ground powder from the Capsicum tetragonum *is widely used throughout the world, in Hungary it is revered.*

Serves 4

- 2 to 3 tablespoons vegetable oil
- 1 large Spanish onion, diced
- 8 chicken thighs or 4 thighs and drumsticks, separated (skin removed)
- 2 heaping tablespoons Hungarian paprika
- 1 (8-ounce) can tomato sauce
- Salt
- 8 ounces sour cream or plain yogurt

In a skillet large enough to hold all of the chicken, over medium heat, warm the oil. Add the onion and sauté until soft and translucent. Add the chicken and sear (brown) on all sides, about 3 to 4 minutes on each side. Sprinkle the paprika over the chicken, turning to make sure the chicken is evenly coated. Add the tomato sauce and salt. Bring to a boil, then lower the heat to a simmer. Cover the pan and cook for 25 minutes, checking occasionally to see if there is enough liquid and adding water if necessary. Test the chicken after 25 minutes, and if cooked through remove from the heat. Cook a few minutes longer if necessary. Add 3 tablespoons of sour cream (or yogurt) to the chicken and serve, passing the remaining sour cream (or yogurt) at the table. This can be prepared in advance and reheated; however, do not add the sour cream (or yogurt) until the chicken has been reheated, making sure that it is added only after the dish has been removed from the heat.

says. "There was a broken key, middle G. That's where I started my adventures on the piano. It was a reference point for everything else. I started when I was three. To play music for me was just like breathing or having dinner. It was a very natural thing. I spent a lot of time at the piano improvising."

Gardony eventually went on to the Béla Bartók Conservatory in Budapest. His listening and playing tastes changed while he was there, from progressive rock like Pink Floyd and Deep Purple to jazz artists like Miles Davis and Jimmy Smith. He spent many a night at friends' apartments listening to new jazz. And eating.

"We loved to stay up late and cook together," he says. "We would come back from a gig and just stay up. We would cook thousands of crêpes a night and bake some potatoes or roast pork and eat them until six in the morning."

Gardony became one of his country's best-known jazz musicians, turning out eight albums and collaborating with European stars like Polish alto saxophonist Zbigniew Namyslowski. By the time he reached the United States as a scholarship student and then as an assistant professor at Berklee College of Music in Boston, he had already honed a pianistic and compositional style that meshed jazz and classical influences with music as disparate as folk from Eastern Europe, South Africa, and Latin America. His music comes at a listener in waves, shifting between crusty prettiness and intense and rumbling pathos. His unique rhythms, bright, funky phrasing, and strong percussive bass inevitably exhibit one trait that Gardony feels the Hungarian

audience did not want to hear: exuberant passion.

The pianist's practice of Buddhism has helped him develop a philosophy of life that's consistent with his music. "What I am trying to do is help people as I help myself to realize a higher level of living," he explains. "Music is a great way to communicate emotions and subtleties in your understanding of the world. You raise questions in people. And much of music raises questions in me about my own existence. It has really helped me achieve things. That's what I try to give back.

"Jazz is the greatest thing. It's based on developing your full individuality. It shows alternative routes of self-realization. There's an incredible calm and level of happiness which is apparent. That's the reward you get from playing jazz because everything else is pretty tough. The lifestyle is tough for even the greatest jazz players."

Gardony actually enjoys one of the most difficult aspects of being a jazz musician, eating on the

road. He loves to sample the international cuisine wherever he goes. When he first started traveling in Europe he even got hooked on chain-restaurant hamburgers.

TASTY PLATTERS
- Laszlo Gardony, *The Secret* (Antilles)
- Laszlo Gardony, *The Legend of Tsumi* (Antilles)
- Wayne Shorter, *Speak No Evil* (Blue Note)

Every dish he tries, though, is guaranteed to be different from the spicy Hungarian meals his mother cooked, like goulash and Wiener schnitzel.

The pianist tries to keep a balanced diet now. He has cut back on meat and eats plenty of fish, vegetables, and chicken. Even though his wife, Edith, does most of the cooking at home for the family, the pianist does pitch in with pasta or his Hungarian chicken.

Once the art of improvisation gets into your blood, it's never again restricted to the bandstand. Pianist John Hicks, one of the music's truly versatile and multifaceted originals, learned long ago that going with the flow can be even more important offstage than on. That was driven home the night he and drummer Alvin Queen were preparing the pianist's curried oxtails dish for the first time, the same night Olympia Hicks gave birth to their daughter, Naima.

"Alvin was at our house in St. Louis," Hicks recounts. "He was playing downtown with Horace Silver at a place called the Casa and I was supposed to take him to work after dinner. We had started cooking up some food. In the meantime my wife went into labor.

"The dish was on the stove. I turned everything off and told Alvin to stay by the phone in case it was going to take longer. As it turned out my daughter was born about an hour after we got to the hospital. I was able to get them situated and I called Alvin and told him I'd be back to pick him up so he could get to work. When I did get back I just turned on the stove, heated everything up, and in about an hour's time we were eating. He got to work on time and my daughter was born. It all worked out."

Making sure things work out has become second nature to Hicks, especially when it comes to music. He has approached the disparate challenges of the worlds of swing, bebop, and the avant-garde with the same basic intent: to absorb the nuances of each style and lay down a vision that's natural, fresh, and completely his own. Woody Herman,

Betty Carter, and Pharoah Sanders are among the Hicks collaborators who have appreciated his commitment to breaking new ground.

Born in Atlanta in 1941, the oldest of five, Hicks moved with his family first to Los Angeles and when he was fourteen to St. Louis. His father was an especially busy man, between his ministry and involvement in politics. In the mid-fifties he was the first black elected to the St. Louis school board. Hicks's mother was a schoolteacher and pianist who got her son interested in playing at six years old, by which time he was

already used to hearing a potpourri of sounds at home and in church—ragtime, classical, gospel. In Atlanta he took lessons with the organist at his father's church, but in Los Angeles he almost gave up piano entirely after his instructor took him to hear Art Tatum. "I was wondering about continuing my lessons, thinking that I'd never be able to play like that," Hicks recalls.

He didn't give up, of course, but instead dug deeper into the music. From John Chapman, the St. Louis pianist hired by Charlie Parker when he passed through town,

---

Curried Oxtails with Coconut Garnish

Hicks's curried oxtails with coconut garnish is a true original. The pianist is modest about his culinary feat on the night of June 13, 1973, when both his daughter, Naima, and the recipe were born. "We just put it together from various ingredients in the kitchen," he says.

Serves 3 to 4

- 1½ cups flour
- ½ teaspoon garlic powder
- Pinch or two of salt
- 1 teaspoon pepper
- 2 pounds (about 8 medium-sized) oxtails
- ¼ cup (½ stick) butter
- 3 tablespoons curry powder
- ½ pound shelled green peas
- 1 pound carrots, peeled and cut into chunks
- 4 medium potatoes, peeled and quartered
- ⅓ cup shredded coconut

Preheat the oven to 375°F. On a large plate or piece of waxed paper, combine the flour, garlic powder, salt, and pepper. Roll the oxtails in the seasoned flour until lightly covered. In a medium-sized skillet, over low heat, melt the butter. Add 2½ tablespoons of the curry powder. Add the oxtails to the curry-butter mixture and, over medium heat, sauté for 10 minutes, turning frequently. Transfer the oxtails to a baking pan, reserving the juices in the skillet. Cover the oxtails loosely with aluminum foil and cook in preheated oven for 2½ hours.

Meanwhile, cook the peas in boiling water for 5 minutes. Cook the carrots and potatoes for 15 minutes, or until they become just slightly tender. Set the vegetables aside. Just before the 2½ hours is up, return the reserved juices to a low simmer and add the coconut and the remaining ½ tablespoon curry powder. Cook for 2 to 3 minutes, until the curry and coconut become thoroughly mixed. Add the sauce and the vegetables to the oxtails and cook, uncovered, for another 20 minutes, or until the vegetables are tender and the meat is cooked through, turning and basting frequently.

Hicks learned about stylistic flexibility and, just as important, about jazz history. Membership in Little Milton's blues band and brief stops at Lincoln University and Berklee College of Music prepared him for his move in 1963 to New York, where it didn't take him long to make a name for himself. In the fall of 1964 he joined Art Blakey's Jazz Messengers, which at the time included Curtis Fuller and Lee Morgan. His two years with the band and two separate stints with Betty Carter cemented his bebop credentials. Later came a period of teaching at Southern Illinois University and work with a stunning

variety of stylists, David Murray, Dionne Warwick, and Arthur Blythe among them.

Teaming up with a diverse array of musicians has become a Hicks trademark. It has also infused his playing with a unique characteristic: a relaxed confidence so total that at times it belies the passion he brings to a song. In his earlier years Hicks leaned more heavily than now toward the intense and often dense style favored by McCoy Tyner. Decades of mixing it up in both modal and lyrical settings have shaped him into an improviser who utilizes every option available in order to create a panoply of moods

as deep and genuine as those of any pianist working today.

"I try to bring some fire, some lyricism, some blues to it," he says. "I try to stretch the boundaries a little bit. I like to do a variety of things, to give people some kind of idea of what has been happening in the music, and possibly what will be happening."

Hicks's gastronomic tastes, broadened by travel, now have an international flavor to them, a change from the hearty midwestern dishes, for example, that his mother prepared. "My father cooked also," he says, "but there was one dish I

didn't like at all because it stunk up the house: chitterlings. I've never liked them. I'd find any excuse to get out of there."

A side benefit of travel is that the pianist can occasionally find time on the road to indulge in tennis, one of his favorite exercises. "I actually picked up the racket when Arthur Ashe won Wimbledon," Hicks says. "I was living in Queens and my daughter was really young then. We had tennis courts that were free to the residents. I would take her out in the carriage and that's how I started. I must have lost a hundred tennis balls, knocking them over the wall and into the trees."

crambling for his next meal. Giving up family and friends. Worrying about where he was going to spend the night. That's the level of struggle that jazz pianist Adam Makowicz lived through in a repressive postwar Poland in order to play the music he loved. Settled in the United States since 1978, Makowicz is one musician who takes neither the right to play jazz nor the food on his plate for granted.

The pianist didn't truly understand the extent of that stifling artistic atmosphere until a passion for jazz began to seep into his soul. "In the middle 1950s, directives came from Moscow that this music should be banned totally," explains the clas-

sically trained Makowicz, who was born in 1940. "They spread all negative, terrible propaganda that jazz musicians used drugs and drank and killed each other. All kinds of bad things. My parents read the newspa-

pers and they didn't know what was true and what was lying. Everything was upside down. They misled our society about what jazz means."

Despite the ban on jazz throughout much of the fifties, Makowicz did manage to hear future idols like Art Tatum, Miles Davis, and Charlie Parker thanks to Willis Conover's Voice of America radio show, "Music USA." His attraction to jazz eventually moved him to risk everything and forsake the classical training he was receiving at Kraków's Chopin Secondary School of Music.

"My mother didn't even want to hear that her son was trying to play

jazz," he recalls. "The same with the teachers at school. When they learned that I was playing this 'crazy and dangerous music,' they said I could not be in school anymore. I quit because they wouldn't allow me to finish. My parents didn't want me to be a jazz musician, so I was on my own. I knew that it would take a lot of years to be a professional jazz musician. I wanted desperately to play jazz music. So I was a street boy, homeless for a while. I didn't have money. I wasn't ready to play publicly to earn money. Nobody paid me for practicing."

As the fifties progressed, the authorities began relaxing their restrictions on jazz, even sponsoring occasional international festivals. When the Helicon jazz club opened in Kraków, Makowicz literally moved in, many nights sleeping under the club's piano.

"I was cleaning floors there," he says. "They gave me some food. I was so hungry it didn't matter what the food was. It was valuable for me to survive. They had a piano which I could practice on, and during the evening hours I could play with some of the people who were around. It was the most difficult period of my life, but I survived somehow."

In 1956, at sixteen, Makowicz

moved to Warsaw and began working steadily both in and out of Poland. He also started sitting in with touring Americans like Lucky Thompson, Ben Webster, and Sonny Rollins outside of his country. "I started to learn what jazz really means," he says.

From 1956 to 1978, when he moved to New York, Makowicz earned respect as one of Europe's preeminent jazz pianists. In New York, he quickly gained acclaim for the qualities of his style, but he has not been without critics in the States. Some have found his squeaky-clean playing technically adept, yet too cold and Tatum-esquely flashy. His playing in recent years, though, has silenced most detractors, as he exhibits a greater emotional depth that enriches his often airy style and concise approach to improvisa-tion. And he has proven time and again that he can swing with the best of them, turning standards like "Summer in Central Park" and Artie Shaw's "Moonray" into romping powerhouses. Makowicz prefers to keep his performance settings eclectic, playing solo, with symphony orchestras, or with the likes of drummer Al Foster and bassists Buster Williams and Dave Holland.

Polish-Style Zrazy—Stuffed Beef Rolls with Buckwheat Kasha

Although his wife Irene is a fine cook, the pianist handles most of the meals. "From traveling so much and living in West Germany, where they use so many spices and have a lot of fatty foods, I have developed some problems with my stomach," Makowicz says. "Right now, I try to be careful with what I eat."

The Makowiczes enjoy Chinese and Italian fare when they dine out and, for home-cooked meals, purchase a wide variety of fruits and vegetables from the many markets in their New York Lower East Side neighborhood. Their recipe here, however, is zrazy, *a traditional dish from northeastern Poland that has been passed down in Irene's family.*

"This is a special dish," says Mako-wicz. "It takes a long time to prepare. It's the type of dish you might make when friends are coming or for a Sunday meal for family members. It's delicious and worth all the time it takes to make."

Serves 4

ZRAZY

1½ pounds sirloin, top of the round, or good-quality chuck
3 ounces smoked bacon, sliced
⅓ cup dill-marinated cucumber or dill gherkin pickles
Freshly ground pepper
Mustard
10 pitted prunes, halved
¼ cup plus 1 tablespoon flour
3 tablespoons oil
½ cup water
1 bay leaf
3 whole allspice
1 onion, sliced
1 cup sour cream
Salt

KASHA

3½ cups water
1 tablespoon oil
Salt
1½ cups buckwheat kasha
1 tablespoon dried mushrooms, finely chopped (optional)

To prepare the *zrazy*, cut the meat against the grain, into 4 slices. Beat lightly with a wooden hammer to flatten. Cut the bacon and cucumber (or gherkins) into strips about 3 inches long and ¼ inch wide and sprinkle with the pepper. Lightly and evenly spread the mustard on both sides of each slice of meat. In the center of each slice of meat, place 2 to 3 slices of bacon, 2 to 3 slices of cucumber (or gherkins), and 4 prune halves. Roll up tightly and secure the rolls with very thin thread. Dust with some of the flour.

In a heavy skillet, over high heat, warm the oil. Brown the *zrazy* very quickly and evenly, being careful not to burn them. Transfer the *zrazy* and the oil from the skillet to a big pot. Add ½ cup water, the bay leaf, allspice, the remaining prune halves and onion slices, and braise over low heat, until tender, about 1½ hours. Remove the mixture from the pot to a platter and cover to keep warm. Add the remaining flour to the pot, stir well, and cook over medium-high heat until the flour is dissolved and cooked through. Add the sour cream, salt, and more water if necessary. Remove thread from the *zrazy* and spoon sauce over them. Serve with the buckwheat kasha and a vegetable or lettuce salad.

To prepare the kasha, about an hour before the *zrazy* are cooked, in a pan with a tight-fitting lid, bring 3½ cups water to a boil. Add the oil and a few pinches of salt. Add the kasha and mushrooms (if using), and stir once. Cover and reduce the heat to low; the liquid should be barely simmering. Cook the kasha until all of the water evaporates, about 45 minutes. Let sit for a few extra minutes with cover on pan. The kasha should be fluffy and the grains should be easy to separate.

Les McCann just might be the funkiest Renaissance man alive.

Whether he's painting, cooking, creating music, or shooting photographs, McCann makes sure that

"My philosophy is very simple," he says. "Love yourself. By doing that everything is possible. You can do whatever you want to do: sing, cook, dance, write, draw. Whatever

an electrifying hit in 1969 with saxophonist Eddie Harris, "Compared to What," a million-seller that decades later still resonates with hard-driving passion. In the early 1980s he took up watercolor painting; he now exhibits his impressionist works in a gallery in Scottsdale, Arizona. His photographs have been hung in museums, and his

TASTY PLATTERS

- Les McCann, *Swiss Movement* (Atlantic)
- Les McCann, *Les McCann LTD* (Pacific Jazz)
- Richard "Groove" Holmes/ Ben Webster, *Groove* (Pacific Jazz)

he lives up to his twin goals of making people feel good and feeling good himself.

your heart desires. Enjoy life, love, and be free."

McCann discovered the power of his own talents when he recorded

cooking skills have won him consistent rave reviews from peers and friends. Nowadays he visits the kitchens of the finest restaurants worldwide and videotapes chefs preparing their dishes. And engage McCann in a foul-shooting contest on the basketball court and you may find that you're in over your head. He actually decided to move into his apartment in Van Nuys, California, because there was a hoop next to the building.

McCann was born in Lexington, Kentucky, in 1935, one of six children. "My father was a good cook but he rarely had time to do it," he recalls. "My mother, well, we wish she had taken up sports-car driving. I grew up in a poor family. My average meal every day in the evening was a bowl of corn bread or biscuits with molasses on them. Everything we ate in those days was ten pounds per bite. My father went hunting and fishing all the time. We had rabbits and squirrels for our meat."

The family radio picked up a show from Gallatin, Tennessee, called "Randy's Record Shop" that played the latest hits by the likes of Nat "King" Cole, Stan Kenton, and Louis Jordan. Those sounds, combined with piano lessons that started at age six, impromptu performances with his brothers and sisters, and a spot in the church choir, left their mark on McCann. Especially church. "That was my true baby food, gospel music," he asserts. He played sousaphone in high school, yet it wasn't until he was in the navy that he immersed himself in jazz.

"One day I was marching in formation and as I was passing the PX I heard this music," he remembers. "So I went in this direction and they all went in that direction and I got in a whole lot of trouble. But I found out it was Erroll Garner playing 'Lullaby of Birdland.' From then on I wanted to play the piano for real."

McCann heard plenty of jazz greats during his three years of travel in the navy. Billy Eckstine, Count Basie, and Louis Armstrong in Oklahoma. Tommy Dorsey in Chicago. And everyone from Miles Davis to Stan Getz at the Blackhawk Club in San Francisco, where he worked part-time as ticket taker —in his navy uniform. He settled on the West Coast after the service, began playing with a trio in the early sixties, and by the late sixties and early seventies was experimenting with synthesizers. More than forty albums, hundreds of original songs, and one discovery—Roberta Flack—later, McCann is still keeping it funky.

Saddie's Love Cake

McCann loves the moistness of this pudding-enriched cake that was given to him years ago by Saddie Rowser, wife of his then bassist Jimmy Rowser. "We called it Saddie's Love Cake," he says, "because after you had a slice, you felt like making love."

Serves 8 to 10

- 2½ cups flour
- 1 cup (2 sticks) butter, melted
- 1 cup cooking oil
- ½ cup warm water
- 7 large eggs
- 2½ cups sugar
- 2 (3½-ounce) packages Jell-O brand vanilla pudding
- 1½ teaspoons vanilla
- 1½ teaspoons lemon extract

Preheat the oven to 350°F. Lightly grease a 13-by-9-inch rectangular cake pan. In a very large mixing bowl, combine the flour, butter, oil, warm water, eggs, and sugar, stirring until the eggs are incorporated. Add the pudding and the vanilla and lemon extracts and stir well. Pour the batter into the pan and bake for 40 to 60 minutes, or until a toothpick inserted into the center of the cake comes out clean. It's good warm, right from the oven or at room temperature.

His voice is darker and even gruffer now, and he's more likely to play acoustic piano than electric these days, but the trademark McCann fire still heats much of his music. His improvisations tend to adhere closely to the melody lines, more often than not drenching his uptempo material with wave after wave of tension-and-release gospel celebration. While fans of his older hits are not always enamored of his current propensity for playing a variety of styles, especially his message-thick ballads, McCann isn't concerned.

"A lot of people who come to hear us would rather we play 'Compared to What' and leave," he says. "But I'm not limited to a type of music. I used to question why I was even put in the 'jazz' category, because people always say, 'You make those commercial records.' Well, hopefully they are commercial. I hope people buy my records."

A vegetarian for nine years, McCann started eating meat again in the 1980s. He loves to eat—he's not exactly slight of build—but more than that he seeks out the best food whenever he can. "If I'm in France and they say the finest restaurant is 150 miles up the road, I'm the kind of guy who's going to get a bunch of people to go there and check it out." He used to belong to a group in New York that tried a different restaurant in the city each week. Japanese food is his current favorite. Living by himself, he doesn't cook at home as often as he did when he was raising a family, but his skills are still plenty sharp on specialties like layered crêpes and Saddie's Love Cake.

Tom Pendergast, Kansas City's corrupt Depression-era mayor, may not have had much to do with building the city's reputation for memorable barbecue, but the jazz world owes him a tip of the hat anyway. Many of the country's finest jazz musicians converged on "Tom's Town" during Pendergast's laissez-faire rule. Jay McShann, a native of Muskegee, Oklahoma, was among them.

"Kansas City was a hotbed of jazz during that time," the piano player/vocalist recalls. "It was a wide-open town. When a town's wide open that makes it move because all the chicks and pimps and gamblers descend upon a town like that. Because it's action twenty-four hours a day. I

TASTY PLATTERS

- Jay McShann, *Airmail Special* (Sackville)
- Jay McShann, *Going to Kansas City* (New World)
- Pete Johnson, *Boogie Woogie Mood* (MCA)

heard Joe Turner singin' the blues, Pete Johnson rollin' 'em over on the piano. Oh man, it was really exciting to me. The different musicians with their horns, they'd be sittin' in and blowin' too. And you got a chance to hear the guys from north, south, east, and west. Kansas City was more or less like a melting pot of jazz. Basie had just left and went east with his big band. Andy Kirk and his Clouds of Joy had left just before Basie. They had a lot of big bands around Kansas City at that time."

McShann, a young man when he arrived there in 1937, wasted little time establishing a reputation of his own. He put together one of the hottest—and last—big bands in town, a powerhouse of an orchestra that relied on seething riffs, crack arrangements, and a bluesy underbelly to generate raw excitement. It also featured a local alto saxophone player named Charlie Parker.

When McShann arrived in Kansas City, he was bursting with pent-up musical frustration. Born in 1909, raised in a devoutly religious household, he feigned being sick on Sundays in order to avoid church. Left alone, he snuck in a couple of hours of practicing the blues. His parents called it "the devil's music." They would have hated Kansas City.

But if the blues came into sharper focus for McShann when he settled there, the importance of eating lost its edge. "When I came to Kansas City, my mind didn't have time to think about food," he said. "I was listening to the sounds."

One meal, in fact, took on a completely new meaning for McShann. "They used to have what they called 'spook breakfasts,'" he explains. "You went right through breakfast time without really eating breakfast. It was an early-morning thing where the nightclub people would gather at one particular club when all the other clubs closed. It would usually be a different club each night. It started around five or six in the morning because most of the guys played till then. And it'd last until ten, eleven, twelve o'clock.

"Bartenders, waitresses, waiters, musicians —the night people—this was their time. People were relaxing, unwinding. There would be singing and dancing. There was always a group playing. It wasn't really a breakfast. Everybody was drinkin' and gettin' high. Everybody was gettin' full of that mess. Then I'd rush home and take a quick nap because I hated to go to sleep. I was afraid I'd miss something."

McShann indeed made up for lost time, turning out hits with his big band like "Confessin' the Blues" and becoming the first bandleader to include Charlie Parker in a recording session. But his orchestra stayed together only until World

Pot Roast Meatloaf

"Jay's a very good cook," says Mary Ann. "He told me that when he was growing up, if they were eating something he didn't like, he'd just go into the kitchen and fix something else. Sometimes I'll cook, but Jay does most of the cooking at home. When he's out on the road, I find that I go out to eat a lot."

The McShanns give meatloaf a pot-roast twist by surrounding the loaf with potatoes, onions, and carrots.

Serves 4

1 pound ground beef
⅔ cup evaporated milk
⅓ cup finely ground bread crumbs
¼ cup ketchup or chili sauce
2 teaspoons Worcestershire sauce
1 teaspoon salt
¼ teaspoon pepper
3 medium potatoes, thinly sliced
3 medium onions, thinly sliced
3 carrots, peeled and cut into chunks
2 teaspoons dried parsley flakes, or 2 tablespoons finely chopped fresh parsley, mixed with 1 teaspoon salt and a few grains of black pepper

Preheat the oven to 375°F. In a mixing bowl, combine the beef, evaporated milk, bread crumbs, ketchup (or chili sauce), Worcestershire sauce, salt, and pepper. Shape the meat mixture into a loaf and place it in the center of a large loaf pan or rectangular baking pan, making sure that there is room for the vegetables to sit around the meatloaf. Place the vegetables in layers around the meat and sprinkle each layer with the parsley-salt-pepper mixture. Cover tightly with foil and bake for 1 hour, or until the vegetables are tender. Uncover and bake for an additional 10 minutes to brown the meat.

improviser slyly utilizing all the possibilities of melody and tempo. McShann's tenor voice, pleasant, often high-pitched, and always without frills, is the perfect complement to his rocking piano.

He sees his music, and Kansas City's place in musical history, in larger terms. "Music is like a river that has a lot of tributaries running into it," he says. "When that river gets down to the gulf, then it goes into the ocean. It's all water. Some of 'em start small, little tributaries getting into the river. The river gets bigger and bigger. Music is the same way."

In spite of his early Kansas City days, when food was a low priority, McShann eventually took such a liking to the kitchen that for years now he has been the primary cook at home. "He puts a lot of weird things together that I'd never think about," says his wife, Mary Ann. "When he decides he wants to cook something he just goes in there and does it. When he comes in off the road, he cooks what he can't get on the road."

War II; band members were drafted, including the leader himself. When he tried to start another big band after the war it quickly became clear that the economics of the music business had changed. Big bands had become too costly to maintain and take on the road. They gave way to small groups. For the next twenty-five years McShann contented himself with raising his three daughters with his wife and honing his rollicking blues and boogie-woogie piano in midwest clubs and, occasionally, on the West Coast. And then during the 1970s the itch hit again. This time a much larger public was ready for him.

Concerts in Europe led to recordings, tours of the United States, and the release of a film, *The Last of the Blue Devils,* that captured the joyful musical essence of the Kansas City days and of players like Basie, Turner, and McShann. His career has been going full tilt ever since.

Blues or not, McShann's playing is about good times. His rich fusion of stride and rhythm-and-blues influences, along with sweet swing and furious boogie-woogie, is a party person's delight. But McShann is by no means a heavy-handed stylist. Under his infectious, percussive rhythms lie the graceful inventions of a subtle

When you listen to the music Amina Claudine Myers makes today, it's easy to imagine her organ-playing four decades ago rattling the walls of Texas and Arkansas churches. While only some of her jazz has overtly gospel overtones, just about all of it resounds with an underlying intensity and release that's found most often in houses

TASTY PLATTERS

• *Amina* **(Novus)**
• **Amina Claudine Myers,** *Country Girl* **(Minor Music)**
• **Various Artists,** *Greatest Gospel Gems* **(Specialty)**

of worship. The keyboard player/ vocalist/composer has spent a lifetime absorbing other vivid lessons as well: the deep country blues she heard on the radio as a young girl; the rhythm-and-blues tunes she pumped out in a Lexington, Kentucky, club; the friendships she made with the free jazz thinkers of the Association for the Advancement of Creative Musicians (AACM) in Chicago. Her willingness to soak up these disparate experiences has made her one of jazz's most exciting and eclectic stylists.

Myers was raised primarily by her uncle and great-aunt in Blackwell, Arkansas. Little Rock was fifty miles away, the nearest grocery store and school seven. Her uncle, a carpenter and practicing Baptist, loved to sing. Young Claudine sang right along with him and was rewarded for her musical sense with classical piano lessons at seven. After the

family moved to Dallas, Myers formed a gospel group, later became choir director and pianist for several area churches, and spent summers with her mother in Louisville, Kentucky, where she kept up her church playing and directing. She went on to major in music education at Philander Smith College, a

Methodist school in Little Rock. While she continued singing in gospel choirs and handling the church organ on Sundays, she also began playing an occasional jazz gig in Little Rock. Summer vacations found her onstage at a rhythm-and-blues club in Lexington, Kentucky.

"I had read in *Jet* magazine when

I was in Louisville that Earl Bostic played jazz," she recalls. "That's when I decided I liked jazz. I didn't even know who Earl Bostic was. Something about the word 'jazz' I liked."

In 1963, after graduating from college, Myers moved to Chicago and taught music in the public schools. She eventually gravitated toward some of the city's West Side clubs, where she played organ. Up until that point in her life, and indeed, until she came into contact with the AACM members and their families, Myers had not paid attention to her diet. "I never had to cook," she explains. "I never liked any of it. When I started living on my own in Chicago, I had to learn how to cook. I was twenty-three or twenty-four. I got inspired by friends who were into eating healthy. I didn't know how to cook anything really. I stopped eating pork in 1969, chicken and beef in 1972. At the same time I stopped smoking cigarettes."

Her AACM connections were invaluable to her career. Through them, she hooked up with saxophonists Sonny Stitt and Gene Ammons. She played with the latter for 3½ years. More important, the AACM was a liberating experience for her musically. Artists like Muhal Richard Abrams, Joseph Jarman, Roscoe Mitchell, and Lester Bowie influenced her deeply. "I came alive during the AACM period," she attests. "There was so much creativity, it was wonderful. Art, painting, theater, music, acting. Everything was happening. It was one of the best periods of my life."

Myers's music certainly owes a debt to all of her experiences, from the grit of her rhythm-and-blues days and the soulful jazz of "Jugs" Ammons to her gospel roots and the passionate freedom of the AACM. In the end, though, it's all Myers. As a composer she thrives on complexity, yet makes spare harmonies and languorous patterns sound simple and funky. Her keyboard playing, on acoustic piano, organ, or synthesizer, has a rolling feel to it that's driven by percussive urgency. Her singing is unadorned and straightforward. She leans toward lyrics that are elliptical, almost as if she's letting her audience in on a subtle joke that demands extra thought to be appreciated. Myers's individuality comes through whether she's covering songs by Bessie Smith, leading an eight-member choir in operatic, gospel, or Broadway material, or utilizing talking drums and congas in an ensemble. "I'm thankful that the Creator blessed me with the ability to make music," she says. "To me it's the greatest way to communicate. I am merely an instrument through which the music speaks. Hopefully my music brings joy to people and reinforces positiveness in their lives."

Myers spends much of her non-performing time teaching theory, composition, piano, and voice. When she's home, she eats fairly simply: raw salads, fish, rice, cheese sandwiches. She also enjoys eating out, especially Chinese food. Still, she finds a special pleasure in preparing a well-thought-out meal. "Cooking is such a personal thing," she says. "Musicians like to make people feel good, and food is one way to do that. People show their appreciation by the way they eat your food. That's inspiring!"

Fish Fry

When Myers stopped smoking in 1972, she also planned to begin a diet consisting only of raw vegetables. "But I gave it up," she says. "I wasn't ready to give up fish, bread, ice cream, stuff like that."

Part of her simple kitchen repertoire is her Fish Fry, a crunchy preparation that can be prepared with any salt- or freshwater fillet. "It's just something I made up," says Myers.

Serves 4

4 large or 8 medium-sized whiting fillets
1½ cups yellow cornmeal
Cayenne pepper
Garlic powder
Salt and pepper
Corn or safflower oil
1 medium onion, thinly sliced

Wash and dry the fillets. In a plastic bag, mix together the cornmeal, cayenne pepper, garlic powder, salt, and pepper. One at a time, place the fillets in the bag and shake to coat. (**Note:** You may find it easier to coat the fillets by first dipping them in beaten egg before shaking in the bag.) Heat the oil in a skillet (preferably cast-iron) large enough to hold the fillets without crowding. Add the onion to flavor the oil. When the onion begins to brown, add the fillets and fry until golden on both sides, turning once. Remove to a platter and drain on paper towels.

When Japanese-born pianist Makoto Ozone joined Gary Burton's band in 1983, he was appalled at the fast-food life that seemed to go hand-in-hand with Stateside touring. "In Japan you can get all kinds of nutritional stuff with quick service," Ozone says.

"I was unhappy about eating in the States because the quick joints are McDonald's and Burger King."

After a few years on the road with the vibraphonist, though, Ozone succumbed. And he never heard the end of it. "Gary used to tease me," he recalls. "He'd laugh and say, 'I guess you finally got used to eating hamburgers here.'"

Burgers on the road are no longer part of the Ozone nutritional repertoire. In 1990, after nearly a decade in America, he returned to Japan. It's a move that did more than just change his eating habits. His music changed as well, away from the relatively straight-ahead improvisation that was his calling card for many years and into a more contemporary, electrified direction. "I was looking for something else," he explains about his stylistic shift.

Born in 1961 and raised in Kobe, Japan, the pianist has been "looking for something else" since he was four years old and doodling on a Hammond B-3 organ. His father, Minoru, a pianist and TV and radio personality in Japan, ran a club in Kobe where young Makoto would play the house organ. He discovered jazz piano a few years later when Minoru brought him backstage at Festival Hall in Osaka, where Jimmy Smith, Illinois Jacquet, and Kenny Burrell were holding court around a piano in the dressing room. Encouraged by his father, Makoto sat down and played the blues. He soon found himself joined by the trio of masters, with Smith accompanying him on the keyboards.

At twelve, Ozone came under the spell of Oscar Peterson after seeing the legendary pianist in a solo concert. He was so taken with his style that he bought and transcribed nearly four dozen of Peterson's recordings. At fifteen, he joined the Arrow Jazz Orchestra, one of Japan's finest big bands, and at nineteen enrolled at Berklee College of Music in Boston. Shortly thereafter, descriptions like "wunderkind" and "phenom" started to accompany his name in reviews around the United States. Peterson's stately, bluesy bebop was still his main inspiration, but other, more impressionistic influences came in after he joined Gary Burton's band. Ozone soon developed a style of his own. Its hallmark was power and lyricism, surprising colors and rhythms, and brightness contrasted with an elegant classicism. In the *Los Angeles Times* in March, 1985, noted jazz critic Leonard Feather called Ozone "the most important new artist to have entered the jazz piano world in the 1980s."

And then Ozone changed direction, looking for yet something else. The turning point was his *Starlight* recording in 1990, a much more commercial release that featured synthesizers, electric guitar,

TASTY PLATTERS

- Gary Burton, *Real Life Hits* (ECM)
- Gary Burton, *Whiz Kids* (ECM)
- Marc Johnson, *Two by Four* (EmArcy)

and lots of frisky funk. "I was struggling with the music I had been playing," he says. "I was feeling uncomfortable. I reached a lot of jazz fans, but I would like to reach even further than that. I'd like to reach the average Joe. Then they can shake their bodies and say, 'Yeah, this is nice!' That's the kind of response I want to get from someone who doesn't know about music at all. I want something to go straight to their souls, into their hearts. To me, the most important thing is to put someone in tears or make someone happy or make them dance."

Ozone likens improvisation to cooking, a task that he handles

Chinese-Style Chicken Gizzards

"I'm a kitchen improviser," says Ozone. "When I make something, it comes out different every time. I love to make Japanese-style dry curry. Sometimes I'll grate an apple into it to change its taste. But my curry secret is that I add cider vinegar and cook it long and slow enough so that the sour vinegar actually turns sweet-tasting."

Ozone's recipe for Chinese-Style Chicken Gizzards is inspired by the yakitori, *Japanese-style grill restaurants that abound in Japan. "The* yakitori *restaurants use every part of the animal when they cook," he explains. "I tasted grilled chicken gizzards many times and began to think, 'Why can't I do something else with chicken gizzards?'"*

Blending some Chinese flavors and cooking techniques with traditional Japanese tastes, Ozone has created a dish that's both strong-tasting and rather crunchy. "I like the feel of the gizzards," he says. "They're not chewy like tripe. Your teeth can easily break them down."

Serves 2 as a main course or
4 as a side dish

Approximately 1 pound chicken gizzards ("The secret is to get them as fresh as possible," the pianist says.)
Salt and pepper

2 tablespoons vegetable oil
2 cloves garlic, minced
3 tablespoons soy sauce
¼ cup sake
¼ cup mirin (Japanese rice wine vinegar), or ½ cup sake, mixed with ⅓ cup sugar, cooked gently until the sugar dissolves and the liquid reduces to ¼ cup)
1 to 2 tablespoons miso (a Japanese soy paste) or cornstarch
1 tablespoon sesame oil
Few flakes of hot red pepper
3 scallions, minced

Wash and dry the gizzards, then cut them into quarters and season with salt and pepper. In a deep-sided pan or wok, heat the oil. Add the garlic and cook for 30 seconds. Stir in the gizzards and cook for 1 minute. Add the soy sauce. Toss the gizzards in the soy sauce, then add the sake. Taste the sauce and if it is too salty or not sweet enough, add the mirin (or sake-sugar mixture). Remove about ½ cup of the liquid from the pan, place it in a small bowl, and mix in the miso (or cornstarch). Stir until smooth, then add this paste to the pan. Cook over medium-high heat until the liquid is nearly evaporated, but no longer than 15 minutes. Remove from the heat and stir in the sesame oil, red pepper flakes, and scallions. "It can be served over rice, but I prefer it as a separate course," Ozone says.

most of the time in the Tokyo home he shares with his wife, Himako. "When you talk about colors of harmonies, when you hear a chord and want to add certain notes, it's like that when you cook," he says. "I try to go with what's needed. I use my tongue to find out what's needed and I use my ears to hear what note is needed. Improvisation is like composing a tune to me. As you get more experienced, your instincts tell you what's needed and not needed. There have to be certain rules to improvisation because it's like a conversation. It's similar to cooking because I could read a recipe and make one thing, and the next time I'll try to change it."

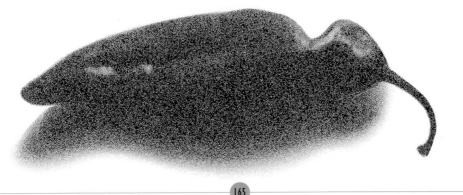

Danilo Perez remembers December 20, 1989, as if it were yesterday. At midnight on that date the United States invaded his native Panama. When the bombs began to fall, he was sleeping at his parents' home near the airport, and though the pianist and his family rode out the night unharmed, the attack did serve to strengthen Perez's resolve on at least one very important count: "I felt that everybody was fighting with guns," he says. "I was going to fight with music."

Perez had returned to Panama City from the United States two days before the invasion to perform with his trio. Delayed though it was, the show did go on. "I decided that people were going off mad and scared and we should have a concert," he recalls. "People for and against Noriega were there. It was incredible."

The pianist doesn't restrict himself to bringing together disparate political camps. His jazz manages to unite the musics of different cultures in a way that brings out the finest elements in each, which puts him in the vanguard of the youthful improvisers who use their roots as a means of pioneering uncharted courses. Perez's particular vision starts with the *tamborito,* the traditional music of Panama, which is a combination of the sounds of Colombia and of the Panamanian Indians. From there he angles off into the Cuban and Puerto Rican traditions, with heavy doses of bebop and even classical music included.

At an early age Perez absorbed the percussive edge that's in his playing. Born in 1966, he was playing bongos in his father's salsa band by the early seventies. A few years later he was arranging for that ensemble. By the time he reached college, first as an electronics major at the University of Panama and then as a music student at the city's conservatory, he had mastered the routine of evenings onstage and days in the classroom. Parental approval wasn't unanimous, however.

"My mother saw that I was killing myself," he recounts. "I told her that if they took me out of my father's group I wasn't going to get good grades, I was going to drop out of school."

In a family where both parents were professors, Perez's threat was close to heresy. Not only did he stay in school, he traveled north to study classical music at Indiana University; he later transferred to Berklee College of Music and graduated *summa cum laude.* The company he kept during school and after graduation was fast: Clark Terry, Terence Blanchard, Jon

Tamales Panamenos—Panamanian Tamales

As given here by Perez and his mother, Elizabeth, tamales, both healthy and rich in tradition, are a Perez favorite. "Every Latin American country makes tamales," says Perez. "But Panamanian tamales are different because we stuff them with prunes and raisins. We eat these in Panama on special occasions like Christmas Eve or Christmas Day, times when all of the family and friends gather."

Makes about 5 tamales and serves 5 to 6 as a first course

  2 small onions, finely chopped
  2 large green bell peppers, chopped
  2 tomatoes, finely chopped
  3 cloves garlic, minced
  6 sprigs cilantro
  1 small (3-pound) chicken, cut into
    serving pieces
  Olive oil
  1 small (6-ounce) can tomato paste
  1 teaspoon saffron
  $\frac{1}{2}$ pound *masa hariz* or cornmeal
  Salt
  6 plantain or banana leaves, or 6
    10-inch pieces of aluminum foil

32 pitted green olives ("I like to use *aceitunas* and *al capras*, but any mix of green olives will do," Perez says.)
  1 cup pitted prunes, chopped
  1 cup seedless raisins

In a large bowl, combine the onions, bell peppers, tomatoes, garlic, and cilantro. Add the chicken and marinate for at least 2 hours, preferably overnight. Coat the bottom of a large skillet or frying pan with olive oil. Warm over medium heat, then add the chicken with its marinade. Brown the chicken well, then reduce the heat and add the tomato paste and saffron. Cover and simmer until the chicken is cooked through, about 45 to 50 minutes. Remove the chicken from the skillet and set aside, reserving 6 tablespoons of the sauce and as much of the onions, peppers, and tomatoes as possible.

Pour the remaining sauce from the skillet into a large bowl. Slowly add the *masa hariz* (or cornmeal) and salt, mixing and kneading until the sauce is thick enough to form and hold a consistent shape. (You may need to add a few tablespoons of water.) Remove and discard the skin from the chicken, then slice all of the meat away from the bone. Coat one side of a banana leaf or piece of aluminum foil with oil and place, oiled-side up, on a flat surface. Spread a handful of the *masa hariz* (or cornmeal) mixture and about one-fifth of the reserved sauce and vegetables on the leaf (or foil). Add some of the cooked and boned chicken, 6 or 7 olives and some prunes and raisins. Fold the *masa hariz* (or cornmeal) mixture around the filling. Crimp the edges like a package and make sure the *masa hariz* (or cornmeal) is secure. Secure the package by folding the leaf (or foil) around the filling. Repeat until all of the filling is used.

Submerge the tamales in a large pot of boiling, salted water and cook for 25 minutes, until the cornmeal easily peels away from the leaves (or foil). Remove with a slotted spoon and place on a wire rack to drain. Peel away the leaf or foil. "*Dios veniga la comida!*" the pianist proclaims. "*Sabor*—God bless this food! Enjoy!"

Hendricks, Tom Harrell, Paquito D'Rivera. But no lessons in the classroom or on the bandstand were as valuable as the one Dizzy Gillespie gave Perez when he hired him for the piano seat in his United Nations Big Band.

"When we are young, we think that more is more," Perez says. "Dizzy taught me how to make more of less. And he gave me a lot of confidence in myself. He said to forget your problems because no matter what, when you go onstage you have to make people happy."

Perez learned well. His bebop education prompts him to groove as hard as he has to, and he loves to venture into the incendiary. Thanks to Gillespie, he now prefers the lean to the jam-packed phrase. Both his writing and improvising tend to be almost hummable, a trait no doubt honed with Hendricks and grounded in his Latin roots. Perez rarely forces his passion. Instead, it percolates beneath everything he plays, ready to surface at precisely the right moment.

"I've learned that the music is not just intellectual. There's an energy, a spiritual part, that takes over when you're onstage. Every time I play I'm trying to bring that spiritual thing onstage. That's what it's all about."

On the physical plane, Perez notes that what he eats can actually enhance his performances. And rice and beans is the dish that gives the pianist, raised in a household where Latin fare was dominant, a special boost.

"I try to eat healthy. When I'm well, I eat very well and feel very strong. My music comes out really strong, too. When somebody plays hungry, you can hear it."

"**M**arcus was cooking when he was in high school," remembers Eugene Roberts about his younger brother, one of today's most original pianists. Roberts could as easily be discussing Marcus's early musical talents as his prowess with the pots, but in this case he's referring to his brother's culinary experiences when he was in the Florida School for the Deaf and Blind in St. Augustine.

Born in 1963 and raised in Jacksonville, Florida, Roberts, who lost his sight to cataracts at age four, acquired a sophisticated

palate from his years of travel with Wynton Marsalis and with his own bands. He's relatively modest about his kitchen skills, preferring instead to give credit to his parents and his girlfriend, Patricia McGriff, for the abilities he has. The pianist doesn't stray far from the foods he grew up with. "At home, especially at my mom's house, I eat the same stuff I ate as a little boy," he says. "Get me some greens, some vegetables, a cake

or two, black-eyed peas, okra, and tomatoes. I never get tired of it."

Few players respect the power of roots more than Roberts. After having the jazz past put into especially sharp focus for him by Marsalis, the pianist is extending the vision of keyboard masters like Tatum, Monk, Ellington, Tyner, and Jelly Roll Morton. It began in the churches he attended with his mother, a gospel singer, and his father, a longshoreman.

"I remember Marcus was at our grandmother's church trying to play the piano," says Eugene, now his brother's manager. "He was about six or seven. My aunt ran him away from it, thought he was making noise. But he was playing a tune. He wasn't just banging on the keys."

Shortly thereafter Roberts started taking classical lessons, studies that lasted nearly a decade. By twelve, after hearing Ellington, he expanded his interests to include jazz, honing his skills at school in St. Augustine. A college career as a mu-

sic major at Florida State University led to his dream gig: the piano chair in Marsalis's band. Legend has it that he stunned the trumpeter when he first joined him: he had already

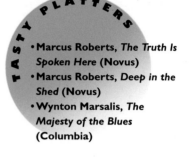

TASTY PLATTERS

- Marcus Roberts, *The Truth Is Spoken Here* (Novus)
- Marcus Roberts, *Deep in the Shed* (Novus)
- Wynton Marsalis, *The Majesty of the Blues* (Columbia)

learned the band's entire repertoire from tapes sent to him by the leader.

Roberts has grown into an artist whose composing, arranging, and improvising skills connect the past to the future as seamlessly and powerfully as do those of any musician on the scene. His rich writing, which utilizes bluesy, rhythmic grooves and variations of color and tempo, has a snap to it that's vivid and constant. His light touch on the piano helps keep the music, especially the melodies, clean-lined and purposeful. Roberts's tools vary from gritty swing and dissonance to impetuous bebop, but his goal remains constant: to achieve depth of emotion. It's no surprise that he considers John Coltrane a primary influence.

"You have to know where you've been to know where you're going," he says. "Ultimately that's true with life. Music basically is about life, about living. It's just an abstract, esoteric communication about living. That's why people of all walks of life like music, because it always touches a part of their soul that has something to do with their life

Black-Eyed Peas, Okra, and Ham Hock Stew

One of the pianist's favorite recipes is a stew-like dish of black-eyed peas with okra, tomatoes, and ham hocks. "It's my mom's recipe," he explains. "She showed it to both me and my brother, Eugene. It's pretty much like a Sunday dinner. But it's the type of dish that's not hard to do. It's a real strong Southern meal, real soul food."

Serves 6

3 large ham hocks

3 (16-ounce) cans black-eyed peas

2 large (29-ounce) cans whole
   tomatoes

1 pound fresh okra, thickly
   sliced crosswise

3 teaspoons sugar

Salt and pepper

Put the ham hocks into a large kettle and add enough water to reach the same level as the meat. Bring to a boil, reduce to a simmer, then add the black-eyed peas. Cook for 15 minutes. Add the tomatoes and cook for 15 more minutes. Add the okra along with the sugar, salt, and pepper, and cook about 30 to 35 more minutes, until the okra is soft and can be pierced easily with a fork. Stir it up and season with more salt and pepper, if needed. Serve in soup bowls.

circumstances. Only through the technique of really studying other great artists who have come before you do you have any real chance to present something that will have depth to it.

"I try to just communicate something of substance. It's equally important to express something of emotional clarity, something that has some type of spirituality to it that will uplift someone. I try to play music with a different range of emotions that are stated in a very organized, coherent fashion.

Intellect, emotion and technique are all necessary components of playing jazz.

"I want to continue to very meticulously document the fact that I have great love for the tradition of the music. Wherever that takes me, that's where I'll go."

When Roberts is home in Tallahassee, Florida, he settles down quickly into the comfortable soul food dietary habits of his youth, although Italian food now runs a close second. "I love real wholesome types of things," he says.

Never underestimate the power of a record store. Pianist/composer Michele Rosewoman, whose parents ran a small record shop near her hometown of Oakland, California, learned early on that there's an entire world of fascinating sounds being made both on and beyond America's cultural shores. Folkloric music from around the globe—South America, Africa, Indonesia—was played both in the Rosewoman household and in the record store, along with jazz and, later, the soul music that she and her older brother grew to love. The often-startling jazz she creates today is a joyful celebration of those discoveries made years ago.

At a young age, Rosewoman also appreciated another international —and wholesome—phenomenon in her household: her mother's cooking. The nutritious Indian, Chinese, and Italian dishes she prepared rubbed off on the pianist's own style of cooking. "Before they called it health food, my parents were into that way of eating," she says. "I really learned from my mother, and then I've done my own thing with it over the years."

Rosewoman has been following her own muse for years on a number

TASTY PLATTERS

- Michele Rosewoman, *Contrast High* (Enja)
- Greg Osby, *Greg Osby and Sound Theatre* (JMT)
- Gary Thomas, *While the Gate Is Open* (JMT)

of fronts, a trait that runs in the family. Her mother is a painter, her brother a musician. When he was forty, her father got out of the record-selling business and went back to school to earn a master's degree. He's been a teacher ever since.

Born in 1953, Rosewoman started playing piano at six. "My folks brought home an old upright," she says. "I'll never forget it coming in through the garage door and seeing how huge it was." Later, she'd occasionally sit in with her brother's funk and rhythm-and-blues bands before she shifted her attention to African and Afro-Cuban music. At seventeen she took up conga drumming. After that the jazz and Afro-Cuban rivers in her creative process flowed together continuously. Her associations with future-leaning conceptualists like Oliver Lake and Baikida Carroll led her to New York in 1978, where she soon found herself also working with Latin performers such as Daniel Ponce and Celia Cruz. In 1983 she founded New Yor-Uba, a large ensemble that interprets the evolution of the music of Nigeria's Yoruba people by way of Cuba to modern-day New York.

"New Yor-Uba allows me to put

Turbo Salmon

"When—and if—I cook depends totally on what's going on with my schedule," says Rosewoman. *"If I'm out on the street, I'll go to restaurants, but I might cook four nights a week. My schedule's pretty crazy."*

Enter Turbo Salmon.

"Turbo, like turbo jets," the pianist explains. *"You know, fast, speedy. It's just a thing I've always cooked, and I've perfected it. It's my own recipe. It's a recipe for a fast gourmet meal —fifteen minutes max. You can't be interrupted while cooking this because you might overcook the salmon or cook away the sauce. So turn on your answering machine."*

Serves 2

1 tablespoon sesame oil

1 big onion, cut into 8 chunks

1 tablespoon margarine (or butter)

Oregano

Salt and pepper

2 salmon steaks or fillets, washed and dried

1 big tomato, cut in 8 chunks

1 to 2 tablespoons (or more) orange juice or orange-pineapple juice

Juice of 1 to 2 lemons

3 cloves garlic, crushed

About 5 sprigs cilantro

4 tablespoons dry white wine or dry sherry

2 to 3 tablespoons soy sauce, or 1 to 2 tablespoons tamari

Basil

In a cast-iron frying pan, warm the sesame oil. Add the onion and sauté, until browned. Add the margarine (or butter). Sprinkle in the oregano, salt, and pepper. Place the salmon in the pan and turn over after 1 minute. (Note: While the dish is cooking, the salmon should be turned several times.) Add more of the seasonings followed by the tomato. Keep the pan from getting too dry by adding the orange (or orange-pineapple) juice and/or some of the lemon juice. Add the garlic and cilantro. ("Cilantro is a key ingredient," the pianist says, "so use as much as you want. I use a lot.") Add the rest of the lemon juice, the wine (or sherry), and soy sauce (or tamari). Season with the basil. "The amount of sauce can be controlled by adding more fruit juice, soy sauce, or wine—but don't add water. The thickness can also be controlled by the heat. A high heat will make a thicker sauce, lower heat a thinner sauce."

Continue to turn the fish every 1 or 2 minutes, cooking for a total of about 8 minutes, or until the salmon shows a thin strip of pink in the center. Turn off the heat when the salmon is at this stage. Cover, and serve in 5 minutes with couscous and a salad.

together everything I hear," she explains, "because I hear everything as one. Cuban and American music are extremely connected through gospel, blues, rhythm and blues, jazz, ethnic influences, and the roots in Africa. I would never do something in one idiom stripped of all the other influences."

Indeed, Rosewoman's writing consistently sounds as if any number of disparate influences have been integrated into a seamless whole. The pianist's tight, uncluttered compositions for her jazz groups make use of dissonance as powerfully as they do swinging bebop grooves, a reflection on a passion for the schools of both Cecil Taylor and Art Blakey. Given her

Afro-Cuban bent, Rosewoman's improvising tends toward the rhythmic and percussive, with a loose-limbed blues feel saturating many of her probing works. In both her writing and playing, she has found a way to make the somewhat familiar sound distinct, dynamic, and at times downright danceable. And she's constantly extending her reach, now utilizing electronic keyboards more often and composing rhythm and blues–based songs that showcase her vocal talents.

Rosewoman's recording and touring schedule becomes fuller with each passing year, yet she still makes time to lead a contemporary youth choir and fulfill her duties as musical director for a New York City Parks Department program called "New York Kids on Stage." She also gets plenty of exercise for herself simply by coming home and going out; she lives on the eighth floor of a building near the Manhattan Bridge and finds herself taking the stairs fairly regularly. "I really stay in shape and I attribute it to my stairs," she laughs.

Diet is extremely important to the pianist. "I spent some years exploring my health and physical well-being through my eating by experimenting, researching, and studying it in a way that's similar to approaching the music and trying to learn more and more about it," she says. "I haven't eaten red meat in many years. I eat strictly poultry and fish and I like a lot of fresh fruit and salads. When I moved to New York I started eating more dairy and meat products because I found I needed more energy for the city's lifestyle—and for those eight flights of stairs."

A quick recap of pianist Renee Rosnes's career reads a bit like the outline of a Hollywood script. Born in Saskatchewan, Canada, 1962. Adopted and raised in Vancouver. Drops out of college, eschewing classical training for jazz. Wins grant; sets out to absorb New York City jazz world. Hooks up with music's biggest names. Earns accolades as young, rising star. Sky deemed limit.

Her path hasn't been quite as smooth as that,

TASTY PLATTERS

• *Renee Rosnes* (Blue Note)
• Renee Rosnes, *For the Moment* (Blue Note)
• Walt Weiskopf, *Mindwalking* (Iris)

of course, or as completely glamorous, but Rosnes has carved out for herself a reputation as one of jazz's new bright lights. She has impressed veterans of the bebop and free jazz wars with a crisp, uncluttered approach to improvisation that respects, but doesn't genuflect to, the music of the past.

Her route was both unlikely and uncharted. Neither of her parents was a jazz fan. Her father, a fisherman by trade in his native Norway before he moved to Canada in the 1950s, was a devotee primarily of Norwegian folk songs. Her mother listened to classical music and

made sure that Rosnes and her two older sisters learned piano and a stringed instrument at an early age.

One passion their father did pass along was a love for fish. "It was always in his heart," Rosnes says.

"He went fishing almost every week. Lots of times he would bring home salmon and it would be great. When I first had salmon in a restaurant it just didn't taste right. I was so used to having it fresh."

Her mother cooked meals like shepherd's pie and, for breakfast, porridge and eggs. "She made a seven-grain porridge with wheat grain and all sorts of things in it,"

the pianist recalls. "When I was growing up that's what we'd eat almost every morning before school. Now it's gotten to the point where she puts seaweed in it and I can't stand it. Saturdays we'd have pancakes and Sundays we'd have waffles."

There was always plenty of fresh fruit and vegetables. Her parents' garden produced everything from corn, potatoes, and rhubarb to onions and zucchini. Along with blueberry bushes and apple, pear, and peach trees, the garden ensured the family was able to stay well-supplied even when growing season was over.

Musically, Rosnes had to look outside the family circle to expand her tastes. High school is where she started. "I had a really hip music teacher who kind of recruited me for the jazz band," she says. "I didn't know what jazz was at all. I didn't really like it at first, and then it became a challenge to learn how to play. Right away he gave me records by Oscar Peterson and Horace Silver and Herbie Hancock."

Rosnes moved to Toronto after high school to study classical piano, but she would sneak into clubs to hear Canadian jazz stars like Don Thompson and Ed Bickert. She quit school after two years. "I realized how seemingly impossible it was to become a successful classical performance artist," she says. "There were so many good classical pianists even at the school. I couldn't imagine how to make a living at it unless you were going to be Rubinstein or Horowitz. And I didn't want to play for ballet classes the rest of my life. Besides, I felt more at home with jazz. I wasn't as nervous when I was performing jazz. I felt like I could relax more and that I didn't have to play something perfectly. I was creating it. I was in charge versus the notes on the page being in charge."

Rosnes began meeting players like Steve Turre, Woody Shaw, and Wynton and Branford Marsalis at a Vancouver after-hours club, Basin Street, that she ran with a friend on weekends. When she got to New York in 1985, courtesy of a Canada Arts Council grant, she was already acquainted with a fair number of the city's best players. She studied with heavyweights like Mulgrew Miller, Cedar Walton, and Barry Harris and soon found herself in groups with Wayne Shorter, Jon Faddis, J. J. Johnson, and Sonny Fortune; then stints with Joe Henderson, Frank Morgan, and James Moody; and eventually a recording contract with the Blue Note label.

Rosnes's adaptability is one of her strongest suits. Her exposure to a variety of artists has prodded her to develop a clear voice all her own. Her classical training has left a disciplined foundation that frees her to create without fear of losing her center, either on modal material or straight bop. She finds logical spots for pretty colorations, brittle darts, and tumbling orchestral cascades. Rosnes knows how and when to leave space, a talent that's most evident in the melodies she writes for her own groups. Horn players in particular thrive on the never-overbearing direction that her light

touch provides. And she has two attributes fellow jazz artists crave: she listens well and she swings.

"I attempt to play for the moment every time I sit down," she says. "I don't want to have any preconceived notions about what's going to happen. I advocate taking chances. I may not sound like that, but that's my goal.

"My stint with Wayne Shorter really opened my mind as well as my ears. He's just so free. He's the

classic example of somebody who just plays for the moment."

The pianist met drummer Billy Drummond, a veteran of Bobby Hutcherson's and Joe Henderson's bands, when they were both in the group Out of the Blue. They married in 1990 and have settled in Brooklyn. Rosnes maintains that her husband is the better chef. She calls herself a "moderate" eater who primarily sticks to fish, chicken, rice, and fresh vegetables.

Nanaimo Bars

In addition to her memories of the salmon that's so abundant in the Pacific waters adjacent to Vancouver, Rosnes also recalls an even more indigenous specialty of western Canada—Nanaimo Bars. Named for a small town on Vancouver Island, the pianist explains that there are numerous versions of this recipe.

"I obtained this one from my aunt, Marion Loud, who lived on Vancouver Island, not far from Nanaimo," she says. *"Most, if not all western Canadians are familiar with this popular treat, but the further east one travels in Canada, the less likely one is to run into Nanaimo Bars."*

Makes 16 bars

CRUST
½ cup (1 stick) butter
¼ cup sugar
4 tablespoons cocoa
1 large egg, beaten
1 teaspoon vanilla
2 cups graham cracker crumbs
1 cup finely grated coconut
½ cup chopped walnuts

FILLING
¼ cup (½ stick) butter, softened
2 cups confectioners' sugar

2 tablespoons instant vanilla pudding mix
3 tablespoons milk

TOPPING
2 (2-ounce) squares semisweet chocolate
2 (2-ounce) squares unsweetened chocolate
1 tablespoon butter

To prepare the crust, grease a 9-inch-square baking pan. In the top of a double boiler, over hot water, melt the butter. Add the sugar, cocoa, egg, and vanilla and stir to combine thoroughly. Remove from the heat and stir In the graham cracker crumbs, coconut, and walnuts. Spread the mixture over the bottom of the prepared pan. Chill.

To prepare the filling, cream the butter. Add the confectioners' sugar and vanilla pudding mix. Beat well. Add the milk and beat until the mixture has a smooth consistency. Spread over the graham cracker crust. Chill.

To prepare the topping, in the top of a double boiler, over hot but not simmering water, melt the chocolates with the butter. Remove from the heat and spread over the filling. Chill for several hours, then cut into bars.

was probably Mozart's guide dog in a previous life," pianist George Shearing exclaims with a laugh. "I really don't know how I got into music. I do know that when I was a little tiny tot I would pick up any bottle I could and hurl it out of

That good sense—and good humor—has never left George Shearing. Born in London in 1919, he has matured into one of jazz's most elegant and complete stylists, a pianist, composer, and occasional

locked-hand chordal technique, is marked by an airy sensitivity that can be romantic, bittersweet, or joyous. Stride, bebop, Dixieland. Ravel, Beethoven, Charlie Parker. They're all in Shearing's head, heart, and fingers, whether he's weaving one of his lush ballads or sprinting through the changes on "If I Had You."

In England, as a member of an all-blind jazz band that played Jim-

mie Lunceford and Duke Ellington arrangements, Shearing developed a crisp style that reflected his idols Teddy Wilson, Fats Waller, and Art Tatum. His first job after moving to New York in 1947 was playing between sets for Sarah Vaughan at the Onyx Club on Fifty-second Street, his second was as intermission pianist for Ella Fitzgerald at the Three Deuces right down the street. Shearing wasn't shy. "When I got up to play with Charlie Parker," he recalls, "instead of saying 'What would you like to play, Mr. Parker?' the cocky, twenty-eight-year-old Englishman lost all his inhibitions and proper upbringing and said, 'What do you want to blow, Bird?' When I said that, I guess he figured he'd better take the kid in hand and show him a few things."

The pianist learned quickly, forming his quintet of drums, bass,

a second-story window so I could hear it clank on the cobblestones downstairs. I had the good sense to use the milk bottles for classical and the beer bottles for jazz."

vocalist who has straddled the classical and jazz worlds with witty, endearing panache. Whether with his quintet of nearly three decades or in his later duet and solo work, Shearing's style, which employs a unique

Irish Stew

Using his thumb as his measuring guide, Shearing is able to uniformly cut the slightly larger than half-inch vegetable slices for his Irish Stew. "It might take me two hours to cut all the vegetables and all the while I'm driving Ellie crazy," he laughs. "But I've never cut myself."

"I don't eat 'jazz food.' At home, we love to make bread—French country rounds, corn bread, sourdough. But I don't use the oven."

His recipe for Irish Stew—definitely not jazz food—comes from the braille cookbook used in his cooking class. "I slow-braise the meat so it becomes very tender," Shearing says. "For this stew, you want a deep-tasting broth. I add Bisto. It's a wonderful-tasting gravy mix that we'd use all the time when I was growing up. You can find it in most specialty food shops. If you can't find Bisto, use bouillon cubes and water." Shearing suggests serving this dish with a salad, crusty bread, and beer.

Serves 6 to 8

3 pounds beef rump, trimmed and
   cut into 1-inch cubes
Salt and pepper
Paprika
Flour
3 tablespoons cooking oil
1 cup sliced onions

2 tablespoons Bisto gravy mix, or
   3 bouillon cubes dissolved in
   1½ cups boiling water
3 cups diced potatoes
1 cup diced carrots
1 cup diced turnips

"We make the meat portion of this stew the day before we're going to serve it," Shearing points out. Wipe off the meat with a damp cloth and season with salt, pepper, and paprika. Dredge the pieces of meat in the flour (best done by shaking the meat in a bag partially filled with flour). Heat the oil in a heavy skillet and brown the meat. When browned, remove the meat, set aside, and add the onions to the skillet. Stir the onions and cook until browned. Return the meat to the skillet with the onions. Cover the meat with the Bisto gravy mix, following the directions on the package, or use the beef bouillon. Reduce the heat and simmer, uncovered, for 1½ hours or more. Refrigerate until the next day.

On the day it will be served, parboil the potatoes for 5 minutes, drain, and set aside. Place the meat and gravy in a deep pot, heat, and add the carrots and turnips. Simmer for 10 minutes and then add the drained potatoes. Simmer an additional 20 minutes or until all the vegetables reach desired tenderness.

guitar, vibes, and piano only two years after he arrived in the States. He recorded "September in the Rain" with the group, sold nine-hundred-thousand copies, and kept the band recording and performing steadily for an amazing twenty-nine years. His composition "Lulla-by of Birdland," written in that period, is a jazz classic. Since then, Shearing has been occupied with a wide variety of projects, from playing with Mel Tormé to bass/piano duets, symphony engagements, and solo work. "I am eclectic within the confines of good taste and some-thing relating to either jazz or classical music," he maintains. "And I don't consider myself a jazz pianist. I'm a pianist. I happen to play jazz. I don't consider myself a blind pianist. I'm a pianist who happens to be blind."

Before the quintet made its mark, Shearing and his family lived close to the vest. "We had an apartment in Elmhurst, Long Island," he says. "French fries were cheaper than steak. I ate approximately three plates of French fries a day and followed it up with ice cream."

Shearing vividly recalls one routine he had during his early years in New York. "The same cab driver—I remember it as if it was yesterday—a guy named Frank Baker, would pick me up every night at the Five Deuces. We would stop at the White Tower on the way home for a fresh orange juice—they would squeeze it right in front of you—and maybe a hamburger."

The youngest of nine, Shearing has always been "a meat and potatoes Charlie," as he puts it. His marriage to his wife, Ellie, broadened his tastes considerably, however. She owns more than two hundred cookbooks as well as bound volumes of *Gourmet* magazine dating back to 1965, sources she uses regularly for inspiration for the dinner parties she and her husband often host. The pianist pitches in with the meal preparation in their Manhattan apartment whenever he can, an interest which stems from a cooking course he took several years ago sponsored by the Jewish Guild for the Blind.

"My favorite part was learning how to cut vegetables," he says. "It's something I love to do at home."

It takes a special vision to become both a major innovator respected by your peers and the quintessential jazz eccentric. Welcome to the world of Sun Ra.

"You got to listen to the rhythms and the music of what the cosmos feels," the keyboard player/bandleader/composer says. "That's where we're headed. This planet can no longer remain isolated. We've got millions and zillions of planets out there. We shouldn't stay on one planet and not see the beautiful creations out there. They say travel broadens the mind. I'm trying to get folks to go somewhere else."

For nearly four decades, the vehicle Sun Ra has used to transport his listeners is a big band with nearly as many names as there are stars, among them the Solar Myth Arkestra, the Omniverse Jet Set Arkestra, and the Out-of-Bounds 21st Century Arkestra. Despite their attire —a theatrical array of glittery ancient Egyptian– and science fiction–influenced costumes which sometimes even include hats that light up—and despite the fact that they even go so far as to employ a tailor for some tours, the band, playing Sun Ra's engaging, well-executed blend of hard swing and

avant-garde, makes the music far more than a whimsical intergalactic joke. It has enough of a serious and substantive edge to support the philosophy.

"It's about purity," Sun Ra explains. "I'm sincere and the music is sincere and pure. People can tell the difference between music that's dangerous and bad for them and music that's pure. Once they get on the level of purity, amazing things can happen. That's what I'm dealing with, the impossible, the amazing."

Born Herman "Sonny" Blount at some point between 1910 and 1918, Sun Ra was raised in Birmingham, Alabama, although he says now that he arrived from Saturn. After leading bands in high school and attending Alabama A and M University, he eventually moved to Chicago. By the mid-forties he was holding down the piano seat and arranging the house band at the Club DeLisa, a dual role that led to similar positions with Fletcher Henderson.

In the mid-fifties he formed his first Arkestra. That group's slightly off-kilter hard bop sound evolved into a pioneering precursor to the avant-garde movement that combined collective free improvisations with African rhythms and multiple percussions. Sun Ra was among the first to use electronics, specifically keyboards and bass, and during the sixties his concerts became mystical extravaganzas that featured multimedia shows, dancers, and even fire-eaters. Over the past twenty years the bandleader has toned down the outrageousness of those days somewhat, placing more emphasis on the music itself and especially on his rollicking

Sun Ra's Moon Stew

"I'd say Moon Stew is a lot like his music," says Spencer Weston, a friend and associate of the bandleader, who is also the Arkestra's manager. "The taste can vary. Just like the music, the final outcome comes from Sun Ra's mood and what's happening around us."

While specific flavors may be hard to pinpoint, Sun Ra notes that there are universals in every batch of Moon Stew. "It makes you sweat and it's invigorating," he says.

Serves 6

(In providing the recipe, Sun Ra fittingly only listed ingredients. He made no mention of amounts or how many servings a pot of Moon Stew will make. The authors have supplied this information.)

3 tablespoons cooking oil
2 green bell peppers, cut into bite-sized pieces ("You can't cook one pepper too many," Sun Ra says.)
1 medium onion, chopped
2 cloves garlic, minced

9 cups of water, or more if desired
Salt and pepper (optional)
3 medium potatoes, cut into bite-sized pieces
3 small okra, cut into small ovals
1 small (12-ounce) can tomato sauce (optional)
4 tomatoes, seeded and diced
3 ears fresh corn, broken in half

In a large stainless steel pot, over medium-high heat, warm the oil. Add the peppers and sauté for 3 minutes. Add the onions and cook, stirring continuously, for 2 more minutes. Add the garlic and stir for 2 more minutes. Add the water, more depending on how thick or thin you prefer your stew. Season with salt and pepper if you wish. Add the potatoes and bring the mixture to a boil. Reduce the heat to a simmer and cook for 8 more minutes. Add the okra and the tomato sauce (if using). Cook for 10 minutes, then add the tomatoes and corn and cook for 5 minutes. Check to see if the potatoes, corn, and okra are done. Ladle into deep soup bowls.

interpretations of swing works by Henderson, Ellington, and Jelly Roll Morton. At live shows those works are now interspersed generously with "greatest hits" drawn from the leader's more than one hundred albums, songs like "Rocket Number Nine," "Space Is the Place," and "We Travel the Spaceways."

Campy, happily chaotic, ragged and disjointed—Sun Ra's music can fit all of those descriptions. Yet with the sterling reedmen John Gilmore, Marshall Allen, and Pat Patrick still forming the core of the Arkestra, and with the leader's crisp, elegant compositions and arrangements as its conceptual backbone, Sun Ra's music convincingly covers a wide spectrum of emotions and moods. At its most exhilarating, with Sun Ra himself pumping up the heat on organ, the band becomes a bluesy, swinging, finely tuned powerhouse with just enough skewed ideas thrown in to remind an audience that, yes, the leader does claim to be from Saturn. It's a rare visitor to a Sun Ra performance who leaves without grinning.

"My whole thing is telling people they have to change," he says. "I can tell by the response of people that they feel what I'm talking about. One of the songs I'm singing now is 'You Got to Face the Music.'"

In the late sixties Sun Ra re-located to Philadelphia, which remains home base for the band-leader and a number of members of the Arkestra who live with him. It's where he perfected Moon Stew, a dish quite different from the meals he grew up with in Alabama.

"On the earth plane, I ate what my grandmother cooked, and that wasn't good for me," he recalls. "I had stomachaches all the time.

She used a lot of poke. I didn't know what was wrong. I found out later and I stopped eating it. My mother ran a restaurant and I'd eat there, but she didn't do any cooking at the house. My grandmother was in charge."

Sun Ra warns that cooking Moon Stew correctly is extremely difficult. "A lot of people have tried it, but it comes out another way," he points out. "They couldn't duplicate it. This is psychic cooking. They couldn't get the fire to burn like it burns for me, that's why it never tastes the same. The fire burns swifter for me. You can know the ingredients, but it does not come out right if you don't have these other ingredients: sincerity and love. You can't say, 'One teaspoon of this, or one teaspoon of that.' Like a musician, you improvise. It's like being on a spirit plane; you put the proper things in without knowing why. It comes out wonderful when it's done like that. If you plan it, it doesn't work."

"It's a challenging job, and if you don't maintain your health it's very difficult to function," McCoy Tyner says about the life of a jazz musician. "Diet and consequently your psychological state are very important."

If anyone is an authority on what it takes to succeed in the jazz world, it's the Philadelphia-born Tyner. John Coltrane's pianist for five years during the early 1960s prior to embarking on a stunning career of his own, Tyner is assured a prominent niche in the music's history. And while it's arguable whether eating poorly would have diminished his accomplishments much, the fact that Tyner makes a serious point of linking diet, state of mind, and creative output should persuade more than one aspiring jazz player to rethink his or her habits.

TASTY PLATTERS

- McCoy Tyner, *Inception/Nights of Ballads and Blues* (MCA/Impulse!)
- McCoy Tyner, *Revelations* (Blue Note)
- John Coltrane, *Coltrane Live at Birdland* (MCA/Impulse!)

The pianist no longer takes a juicer on his road trips these days, but he still carries with him the same stirring, deeply spiritual musical style that he first developed in the Coltrane quartet with bassist Jimmy Garrison and drummer Elvin Jones. Tyner created something new that has influenced an army of followers: an extension of bebop with a liberating structure replete with meandering modal melodies, relentlessly percussive rhythms, and dense, resounding chord clusters. The pianist has also made great use of texture in his post-Coltrane

years, utilizing vocal choirs, strings, woodwind ensembles, and powerful reed and rhythm sections with the likes of Wayne Shorter, Gary Bartz, Jack DeJohnette, and Ron Carter. Whether he's performing solo or leading a big band or small group, the orchestral atmosphere produced by his improvising is rich in warmth, intensity, and meditative, tender beauty. Few jazz players can soothe the soul like Tyner does.

Born in 1938, the pianist was around music from a young age. His mother, a beautician by profession, also played piano. By thirteen Tyner was practicing on the instrument in the beauty parlor, which was in the same building in which the family lived. He soon found himself playing for various dance groups, and he put together his first band in high school. At seventeen he met Coltrane at a Philadelphia club called the Red Rooster. Four years later, much of which he spent as a shipping clerk by day and a musician by night, he cut short a stint with the Benny Golson/Art Farmer Jazztet to join the saxophone giant.

Tyner was aware of the merits of good nutrition even then. "Ever since I was a teenager I've been into health foods," he recalls. "I was never a vegetarian, but I can live with a vegetarian diet." Casseroles and macaroni and cheese were the types of dishes his mother put together for the pianist and his brother and sister, squeezing the time to do so from her busy schedule. "In between doing heads she'd prepare meals," Tyner remembers. And even though his parents' roots were in North Carolina, soul food was

Western Omelette

"Omelettes aren't just for breakfast," says the pianist, echoing what the French have known for years. *"With a salad and some French bread, they can make a nice lunch or dinner when you're not looking to fill up. Of all the omelettes I make, the Western is my favorite and the one I make most often. I really have it down."*

This American classic was most likely originated by the Chinese chefs who cooked for the gangs building the Union Pacific Railroad. Tyner's version, unlike the original, uses chopped ham instead of crisp bacon.

Serves 1

- 2 to 3 large eggs
- Salt and pepper
- Splash of milk or water
- 1 tablespoon butter
- 1 teaspoon vegetable oil
- 1 tablespoon chopped green pepper
- 1 tablespoon chopped onion
- 2 tablespoons diced ham

In a small bowl, beat the eggs with the salt and pepper, then add a dash of milk (or water). In a shallow-sided skillet, heat the butter with the oil. Add the green pepper, cook for 30 to 40 seconds, then add the onion and cook until both are slightly limp. Stir in the ham. Make sure the pan is hot, then add the beaten eggs, shaking the pan to move the eggs around. As the edge of the omelette cooks, carefully lift it with a spatula to allow the remaining uncooked egg to run underneath. When the eggs are set, but still moist, tilt the pan away from you, and, using the spatula or a fork, begin to roll the omelette from the top down. Set the pan on the heat for a second or two and then slide the omelette onto a plate.

rarely on the menu. "I didn't really get into the ham hocks and all that," he laughs.

The pianist found both a kindred musical and nutritional spirit in Coltrane. "John went through a health food period," he says. "I made a lot of carrot juice and he really got into it." Tyner stuck to his diet after leaving the reedman in 1965 and continues it today, searching out natural foods stores wherever he performs. "I've always liked health food products," he says. "They're a very, very important part of my diet. Juice helps as a supplement because artists have to take care of themselves. They're traveling, eating different foods, drinking different water."

When he's home in Manhattan, Tyner makes it a point to work out at the YMCA when he has the time. He also finds cooking an excellent way to slow down. "It's like a hobby with me," he says. "It's nice and I don't do it too badly. At times it can be relaxing."

When your father owns a restaurant that's frequented by, among others, Sonny Rollins, Max Roach, Elmo Hope, Thelonious Monk, and Miles Davis during the heyday of bebop, the question isn't whether you absorb the musical flavor, but how much of it you absorb. Pianist Randy Weston, whose father, Frank Edward Weston, operated a small restaurant on Sumner and Putnam avenues in Brooklyn during the forties and fifties, soaked up plenty. Not only that, his parents exposed him to a wide range of culture, from Count Basie and the comedian Pigmeat Markham in venues like the Brooklyn Paramount and Apollo Theater to spirituals in the AME church. All in all, they laid the groundwork for a career that's recognized as among the most illustrious and original in jazz.

Weston, who was born in 1926, grew up in a neighborhood in Brooklyn that was chock-full of great jazz musicians. Pianist Eddie Heywood lived across the street. Drummer Roach was around the corner; Weston first met Charlie Parker there. In fact, Weston spent nearly as much time talking about music and life with players in their houses as he did talking with them in the restaurant he managed for his father. His own apartment became a meeting spot as well. Weston's musical education, especially in the years after his hitch in the army, consisted of inspiration as well as practice.

"In my frustration of not playing like I wanted to, I had a kind of gallery in the back of the restaurant," he remembers. "I had photos of Monk and Duke, and I also had the most fantastic jukebox in the

world. You could hear Monk or Sarah Vaughan or Tadd Dameron or Louis Armstrong or Stravinsky or Prokofiev or Mahalia Jackson."

The restaurant, one of two his father owned, featured southern and West Indian cuisine. His mother's family was from Virginia. His father was born in Panama of Jamaican ancestry.

"My dad was a great cook," Weston says. "He used to cook for all the musicians. They'd come to Dad's house and he'd bake bread,

make pies, cakes, West Indian dishes. He was so fantastic. All we would do was eat and listen to his stories or he'd listen to our stories. He loved music so much. All the musicians knew my dad. They were always welcome."

His father's philosophies made as deep an impression on his son as did the bebop of the day. A follower of Marcus Garvey and a student of African history, he steered the pianist toward that continent's rich heritage. Weston then took it

Couscous

When Weston travels to Africa he goes out of his way to enjoy certain local dishes: Moroccan couscous, groundnuts stew in Ghana, and jollof *rice, a lamb and rice dish popular in West Africa.*

"Since my music more and more emphasizes the contributions of Afrikan traditional music to the classical art form of jazz," says Weston, "it is appropriate that my recipe should also be Afrikan."

The pianist's recipe for couscous, culled from myriad Moroccan kitchens, is indeed in sync with his African influences. "This reflects where my strongest influences have come from," he explains. "I've visited, lived, and learned in Afrika."

Serves 4

- 1 whole (3½- to 4-pound) chicken, cut into serving pieces
- ¼ cup olive oil
- 2 tablespoons butter
- 1 medium onion, sliced into rounds
- 1 large tomato, chopped
- ½ teaspoon salt
- ½ teaspoon freshly ground pepper

- 1 cinnamon stick
- ¼ cup chick-peas, soaked overnight in plenty of water
- 1½ cups instant couscous

In a large pot, over medium heat, combine the chicken, oil, butter, onion, tomato, salt, pepper, and cinnamon stick, stirring to coat the chicken. Cook for 5 to 7 minutes, or until the chicken is browned, then add 1½ cups water to the pot and bring to a boil. Toss in the chick-peas, cover the pot, and simmer for 30 to 45 minutes, or until the chicken is tender. Remove the chicken and refrigerate. Continue to cook the mixture until the chick-peas become tender, about 1 to 1½ hours, adding water when necessary to keep the level constant. When the chick-peas are tender, return the chicken to the pot and heat through. To serve in the traditional North African manner, spread the couscous into a large bowl (or a platter with curved edges) and ladle on as much liquid from the stew as the couscous will absorb, stirring the couscous to incorporate the liquid. When the couscous expands, pile the chicken in the center and ladle the chick-peas and remaining sauce over everything.

several steps further; he traveled extensively there and eventually relocated in Morocco for a time, all the while absorbing the cultural and artistic nuances of the people and music. Even though he divides his time now between Brooklyn, France, and Africa, his commitment to the last is stronger today

TASTY PLATTERS

- Randy Weston, *Carnival* (Freedom)
- Randy Weston, *Jazz à la Bohemia* (Fantasy/OJC)
- Randy Weston, *Self Portraits* (Verve)

than ever. "Afrika gave me the spirituality in my music," he asserts.

Weston makes music that meshes the jazz and African traditions seamlessly. The spirit and moods of his five acknowledged pianistic influences—Monk, Ellington, Tatum, Basie, and Nat "King" Cole—show up unabashedly, yet Weston takes an overall orchestral approach that's intensely rhythmic and percussive, his nod to Africa. His writing can be stunningly melodic, in waltzes like "Little Niles" and boppers like "Hi-Fly." A weighty-sounding player with a lean, uncluttered style, Weston revels in the unexpected twist, be it in stride pieces or sambas, impressionism or the blues. A feeling of mystery and simmering passion, propelled by an almost drumlike potency, permeates much of Weston's work.

"I think music should be truth," he says. "It's a healing force. Music comes from the Creator.

Man doesn't control music; we are just messengers."

Weston lived in Africa from 1967 to 1973 and spent three of those years in Tangier, Morocco, where he ran the African Rhythms Club. Besides leading a trio—including his son, Azzedin, on percussion and a dancer—he kept a jukebox stocked with Marvin Gaye and James Brown and brought in live shows that ranged from Congolese singers to American blues and jazz bands. The pianist still collaborates regularly with African musicians, especially percussionists, and spends much of the year on that continent.

"People are beginning to understand, to listen more, to Afrikan music," he says. "It's very good because our history was just completely taken away from us here. It's slowly coming around now that this music didn't just come out of the air and didn't just happen because of oppression. It came out of the very, very high musical culture of Afrika. When you go there you see the knowledge that they have of music. Their relationship to God and music is very, very deep."

Few hometowns have influenced a player as profoundly as Memphis, Tennessee, has influenced James Williams. The pianist was raised on classic southern fare like barbecue and greens and thoroughly understands the difference between dry- and wet-rub Memphis ribs, yet he considers himself more a basic cook than a five-star chef. It wasn't the food in Memphis that left the strongest imprint on Williams's soul. It was the music. The sounds he heard have helped shape him into a truly compelling jazz inventor.

Williams speaks with reverence about his city's heritage. "Memphis is one of the great cities of jazz," he asserts. "It's where pianists Phineas Newborn, Jr., and Harold Mabern are from, and saxophonists Frank Strozier and George Coleman. There's this romantic notion about New Orleans, but you'll find that cities like Memphis, St. Louis, Chicago, Kansas City, and New

TASTY PLATTERS
- **James Williams,** *Magical Trio 2* **(EmArcy)**
- **Art Blakey,** *Album of the Year* **(MCA/Impulse!)**
- **Phineas Newborn, Jr.,** *A World of Piano* **(Fantasy/OJC)**

York played roles just as important as New Orleans."

Born in 1951, Williams was in his teens when the Memphis soul scene was happening. Stax/Volt, the record label based in the city, drew artists like the Bar-Kays, Booker T. and MGs, Rufus and Carla Thomas, King Curtis, Otis Redding, and Isaac Hayes, and their music could be found up and down the local radio dial. "Growing up in Memphis, you were really in contact with rhythm and blues," Williams says. "Most of us who came out of Memphis have a respect and feel for the blues. Music was accessible when I was growing up. I think a lot of kids stayed out of trouble by just singing on the corner."

Williams recalls being a "jock" during his early years. Basketball and baseball were his games. At thirteen, his mother convinced him to take up the piano. "It wasn't fashionable," he

Elizabeth Williams's Apple Cobbler

While cooking is a sporadic affair in his current kitchen, it was anything but that in the Memphis home of Williams's youth. "My mother has some great recipes," says the pianist. "For dinner, one of my favorites was something she called oven-chicken supreme, where she'd coat the chicken pieces with Worcestershire sauce, fresh lemon juice, and garlic. Two of my favorite desserts were her lemon chess pie and her apple cobbler. My mom's a great cook."

Serves 6

½ cup (1 stick) margarine, melted
1 large (29-ounce) can of apples,
   or 6 apples, peeled, cored,
   and sliced
½ cup sugar
1 teaspoon nutmeg
Few pinches of cinnamon
Few pinches of ground cloves

COBBLER TOPPING
1¾ cups flour
1 tablespoon baking powder
½ teaspoon salt
Few pinches of nutmeg
Few pinches of cinnamon
Few pinches of allspice

6 tablespoons margarine, cut into
   chunks (at room temperature)
2 tablespoons sugar
⅔ cup milk

Preheat the oven to 350°F and coat a baking dish with some of the melted margarine. Combine the apples, sugar, nutmeg, cinnamon, and cloves, and place in the baking dish. Pour the rest of the melted margarine over the apples. Set aside.

To prepare the topping, into a large bowl, sift the flour, baking powder, salt, nutmeg, cinnamon, and allspice. Cut in the margarine. Mix well with your fingers, until the mix resembles coarse meal. Add the sugar followed by the milk, stirring just until everything is combined. Turn the dough out onto a floured surface, knead a few times, and spread it out to a ½- to 1-inch thickness. With a biscuit cutter or round object, cut out circles. Place these circles of dough on top of the apples in the baking dish, overlapping the dough, if necessary. Sprinkle the sugar over the biscuits, if desired. Place the cobbler in the oven and cook for 45 to 50 minutes, or until the topping turns golden and the apples begin to bubble and become tender. Serve warm.

remembers. "My friends said things like, 'I'm sure glad you don't take me to those lessons.'" Williams eventually went on to study music at Memphis State University, where he befriended two other hometown pianists, Mulgrew Miller and Donald Brown. He moved to New York in 1984 and soon landed a gig that would affect him almost as powerfully as his Memphis up-

bringing: he took over the piano chair with Art Blakey's Jazz Messengers, a seat he held from 1977 to 1981. Stints followed with veteran masters like Milt Jackson, Benny Carter, Art Farmer, and Dizzy Gillespie. All the while Williams was developing a mature style of his own. In recent years, he has also taken to producing, handling recordings by young lions such as

Brown, pianist Geoff Keezer, and saxophonist Bill Pierce.

Williams has an affinity for grooves, an approach that can be traced back directly to the boiling Memphis soul he grew up with and, later, to drummer Blakey's relentless hard bop. There's an underlying blues and gospel feel to much of Williams's playing that reveals itself especially on his mid- and uptempo originals. The pianist digs into a melody, fearlessly keeping the romance in ballads, yet improvising by freely bending the harmonies and melodies. His jazz has soul.

"I want to communicate with people, try to enlighten and hopefully uplift them so they feel better," he says. "I don't believe in playing down. I believe in challenging the listeners. The audience is very much a part of my performance. I use audiences like I use the rhythm section: to be inspired and draw energy from."

Given that he's single and on the road often, Williams rarely has time to put together an extensive menu. "Economically speaking, it's more practical to prepare your own meals if you're in one place for a while," he says. "That's one of my problems. Even when I'm home, it's only for a few days, and I might just buy enough to cook every day."

VOCALS

Modesty can be a casualty when you've had a rise to fame as meteoric as Harry Connick, Jr.'s. The New Orleans–born vocalist/pianist, though, remains fairly humble about his musical accomplishments and is often as quick to credit his influences—Monk, Sinatra, Art Tatum, and others—as he is to engage in snappy onstage repartee with his audiences. His opinion regarding his abilities in the kitchen isn't quite so reserved: "I cook my butt off, I surely do," he says.

Culinary swagger isn't exactly foreign to those raised in the Crescent City. Connick doesn't claim to be another Paul Prudhomme, yet he does feel he was taught by a master. "My dad can cook anything," he says. "He's a terrific cook. I started as a kid, probably eight or nine years old. I used to bake cakes and then I got into more complicated things like boiling eggs. My dad still helps me out."

Harry Connick, Sr., the district attorney of the Orleans Parish, and his wife got their son interested in music years before he perfected soft-boiled eggs. A large stock of albums, culled from the record store they owned during the fifties, sat ready for him to hear. "They seemed to have a sense of what the greatest music was," says Connick, who was born in 1967. "I always remember Nat 'King' Cole, Erroll Garner, Duke Ellington, all the greats, plus a lot of classical and Dixieland music. It was always the best of a particular genre of music."

Connick started toying with the piano at three and took his first classical lessons a few years later. At six he played the national anthem

at his father's swearing-in ceremony as district attorney. He joined the musicians' union at nine, and by thirteen he was sitting in at Bourbon Street clubs, where he played just about every style imaginable, from funk to Dixieland to rap. Even though high school found him absorbed in the likes of Led Zeppelin, the Bee Gees, and Stevie Wonder, his ongoing studies with James Booker and Ellis Marsalis, two of New Orleans's most revered pianists, cemented the direction he was to take.

A relatively brief period of scuffling around New York after he

arrived in 1985 ended with the 1987 release of his debut album. Soon afterward began the stunning succession of events that have since catapulted Connick not only to the top of the jazz world, but to star status in the entertainment business at large.

They came with staccato rapidity: thirty-six sold-out shows at Manhattan's fabled Oak Room at the Algonquin Hotel in the winter of 1989; three albums on the pop charts, including the megasellers *When Harry Met Sally . . . Music from the Motion Picture,* and *We Are in Love,* which won a

Red Beans and Rice

"If you want to eat good food and there's nobody around, you got to do it yourself," says Connick. One of his favorite dishes, as is the case with so many from New Orleans, is Red Beans and Rice. "Most of us in New Orleans use Camellia brand red kidneys, and the recipe for this delicious dish appears on each package," he explains. "I use the basic recipe, with a few variations, depending on my ability to get to the market or what's in the refrigerator."

Serves 4 to 6

  1 pound red kidney beans,
    preferably Camellia brand
½ pound ham
1 onion, chopped
1 clove garlic, chopped
2 tablespoons chopped celery
2 tablespoons chopped parsley
8 to 10 cups water
1 large bay leaf
Salt and pepper

Soak the beans overnight in enough water to completely cover them. In the morning, drain, rinse the beans, and discard any debris. Render the ham in a skillet by cooking until the fat becomes liquid, and remove the meat and place to the side. In the fat that remains, sauté the onion, garlic, celery, and parsley. In a large pot, combine the beans, water, meat, bay leaf, salt, and pepper. Bring to a slow boil, lower the heat to a simmer, and cook for about 1½ hours, stirring occasionally, until the beans are tender. (If necessary, add more water.) Remove the bay leaf and serve hot over rice. A few suggestions: Make a stock using ham bones. Soak the beans in the cooled stock overnight. "This gives the beans a really great flavor," Connick says. "Also, I grate my onions—usually two —and don't usually sauté any of the ingredients. Instead, I just put them into the pot uncooked with the beans. I also allow my beans to cook until they begin to get creamy."

Grammy Award in 1991; appearances on "Saturday Night Live," the "Tonight Show," "Good Morning America"; profile articles in just about every major periodical in the country, including fashion spreads in the likes of *GQ ;* acting roles in the movies *Memphis Belle* and *Little Man Tate;* and sold-out concerts with both his big band and trio at festival arenas and clubs like the Village Vanguard.

All of this has generated nearly as much controversy in the jazz world as it has congratulations in Hollywood. Connick has been criticized by some as a talent quick to trade in on comparisons with idol Sinatra and a player intent on working as many sides of the street as possible. The charges don't faze him. "I do more than one thing," he declares. "I'm not going to not do one because some stuck-up jazz purist thinks I'm a sellout. I'm having a great time."

A charismatic performer, Connick is an anachronism, a throwback to earlier jazzmen like Louis Armstrong and Fats Waller. He wants people to value his music, but he also gets a kick out of moving them to laugh and have fun.

Much of Connick's appeal to non-hardcore jazz aficionados is that he offers an uncomplicated,

unintimidating introduction to the music. It's a tack that leaves him wide open to criticism when his improvising in particular is tested for originality. Broken down into pieces, his stop-start melodies and stride excursions can sound like watered-down versions of Monk and Tatum, his funky, rolling New Orleans boogie-woogie very much like the music of the legends before

him. His romantic croon on swing tunes does suggest early Sinatra, although his voice has a full-bodied raspiness to it that Sinatra's never did. Yet when the pieces are combined, when the clothes-loving stylist does what he does best— entertain—it's difficult to deny that Connick has created something that's closer to the spirit of bebop and swing than it is to Mantovani. He is now concentrating on his composing and arranging, for big bands in particular. While in the process of developing his own art, he not only likes to show his audience a good time, but he also respects the jazz tradition. His fame has reached the point where the opportunity is always there to "cross over" to prime time and the middle-of-the-road approach it demands. So far,

at least, Connick continues to pay homage to his roots.

"I'm really fortunate," he says. "I just try to keep my head on straight. I have more responsibility

TASTY PLATTERS
- *Harry Connick, Jr.* (Columbia)
- *Harry Connick, Jr., Lofty's Roach Souffle* (Columbia)
- Dave McKenna, *Shadows 'n' Dreams* (Concord Jazz)

now because I represent jazz music to a lot of people. A lot of jazz musicians would be kind of hurt if they saw that I was bastardizing it or prostituting it in any way, which I would never do. My main objective is to broadcast jazz music to as many people as I can, no matter how long that takes."

Being on the road as much as he is, Connick doesn't get a chance to prepare the big pots of red beans and rice or Creole gumbo that he likes to put together when he's home. He's careful about his diet and maintains a regular exercise regimen. "I try to keep away from fried foods and caffeine," he says. "I exercise pretty religiously on the road; I hit the weights pretty hard."

indeed able to maintain just the sort of existence she prefers.

Born in 1927, Connor was raised in a Kansas City wracked by the Depression. "We really had to pinch pennies, the whole scene," she recalls. "I never went hungry. My dad always had a job. But we were poor."

TASTY PLATTERS

- Chris Connor, *Classic* (Contemporary)
- Chris Connor *Sings the George Gershwin Almanac of Song* (Atlantic)
- Chris Connor, *New Again* (Contemporary)

Connor was the only musically inclined member of her family of four. "I don't know where I got it," she laughs. "It's really weird. I'm a black sheep, I guess. My grandmother's name was Ramona, and I could hum the old song 'Ramona' before I could talk." When her mother died, Connor, aged nineteen, moved to Jefferson City, Missouri, to live with her sister. From there, where she worked as a secretary, she traveled to the University of Missouri at Columbia to sing with the college band on weekends.

"They had all Stan Kenton arrangements," she remembers. "I really started getting into it, buying records. That was my passion. I'd lock myself into a room and listen to Anita O'Day, Kenton, June Christy, Ella, everybody. I wanted to sing with Kenton. That was my goal during those years."

Connor eventually realized her dream, but not before she paid some steep dues shortly after mov-

"I live a quiet life," says Chris Connor. "It's too hectic on the road."

When you've traveled for as long as the veteran vocalist has, built a base of fans as large and loyal as hers, and established yourself among the top-ranking artists in the business, having your choice of pace is a just reward.

In her New Jersey home just two miles from the ocean, with the Pine Barrens in her backyard, five thousand books in her personal library, and a huge collection of recorded music at her fingertips, the singer is

ing to New York from Jefferson City in 1947.

"I starved for a couple of months," she says. "My father worked for Western Union and would send me ten dollars a week so I could eat. Can you imagine living on ten dollars a week in New York? One day I came back from an audition and I was locked out of my hotel room with all my clothes, all my brand-new luggage, everything, in it. I spent a couple of nights sleeping in Forty-second Street movies."

Her break came after a year of trying to make ends meet: she landed a job with Claude Thornhill's big band. "I'll never forget this," she says. "The night before, I went into St. Patrick's Cathedral—I'm not Catholic—and I prayed like I've never prayed before. The next morning I got the job."

Five years as Thornhill's lead vocalist led, finally, to an invitation in 1952 to join Kenton's band. June Christy herself recommended Connor. Despite quickly garnering national attention with her recording "All About Ronnie," she called it quits after ten months of a grueling tour schedule. Six years of one-nighters was enough. "I was riding the white line and eating a lot of White Castle hamburgers," she says. "As anyone can tell you who's ever traveled with a band, it's not very healthy. I needed a rest."

By that time, the vocalist's reputation as a wondrous interpreter of the American popular song was cemented. With the exception of some slack periods during the sixties and seventies, Connor and her sensuous, graceful style have been in demand on the recording and club scene ever since. Utilizing a

Spoonbread

Typical of her "rib-sticking" fare is Connor's recipe for spoonbread. A versatile starch with a strong Southern heritage, this version was given to Connor by Lee Hall, a writer and friend from North Carolina. "I've made the spoonbread for Thanksgiving," says Connor. "It's quite simple and good. It would go well with Southern-type dishes and those old Missouri dishes like pork-butt-and-beans that I was brought up on."

Serves 4 to 6

- 4 large eggs, separated
- 1 cup water or milk, or a combination
- Salt
- ½ cup yellow cornmeal
- ½ cup (1 stick) unsalted butter, cut into small pieces, at room temperature

Preheat the oven to 400°F. Thoroughly grease a large soufflé dish. In a large bowl, beat the egg whites until quite stiff, being careful not to beat them until they are dry. Set aside. In another bowl, beat the yolks well and set aside. In a heavy saucepan, over high heat, bring 1 cup of water (or milk, or a combination) to a boil. Salt to taste. Slowly add the cornmeal, stirring continuously, until the mixture thickens. Add the butter and stir to combine. This all takes about 5 minutes. Remove the pan from the heat and allow the cornmeal mixture to cool slightly, about another 5 minutes. Stir in the egg yolks. Add the cornmeal–egg-yolk mixture to the egg whites. Pour into the soufflé dish. Bake for 10 minutes, then reduce the heat to 350°F and bake for an additional 30 minutes, or until the spoonbread is slightly brown and crispy on the top. Serve with a spoon as it shouldn't be too firm.

rich, elegant alto voice that has become huskier-toned and plusher with age, Connor consistently takes rhythmic and melodic risks that charge her songs with added layers of drama. She wrings the deepest emotions imaginable out of lyrics by Gershwin, Berlin, Coward, Porter, Kern, or Wilder, emotions that never sound less than genuine. The music's most moving ballads seem like they were written expressly for Connor.

"I want to do nothing but good music," she explains. "That's why I stick with mostly standards. I've done research into the contemporary music, but I haven't found much that would suit me at this point in my career and at my age. I find that the lyrics of, say, Cole Porter, mean something, have substance to them. I can put some of my emotions into it. It isn't drivel."

Until she moved to New Jersey in 1990, Connor had lived nearly thirty years in Plainview, on Long Island. Besides her reading and listening habits, she developed an affinity for cooking, especially barbecuing, which she brought with her to her New Jersey home. Connor and her companion, Lori Muscarelle, share the culinary tasks. "When Chris cooks, it's enough for the week," Muscarelle says. "I eat basically the same things now that I've eaten all my life," Connor points out. "I like rib-sticking food with taste."

Recording dates with Miles Davis, Wynton Marsalis, and Carmen McRae. Lengthy overseas tours. Recognition by peers and fans alike as one of the *crème de la crème* of the vocal and piano worlds. While these may sound like the fruits of labor of a performer driven to achieve success regardless of personal cost, they're actually the credentials of Shirley Horn, homebody and family person, who's also one of the most graceful and compelling singers and pianists in jazz.

"I love home," the Washington, D.C., native declares. "I don't like the road. I love the music. I hate the distance. I'm only happy when I'm at the piano."

During the course of a four-decade career, Horn has had to choose more than once between family and potential fame. Family has usually won. Only in recent years, with her daughter grown and her popularity enjoying a major resurgence, has Horn seen clear to take her music far and wide.

Back in the early seventies, the singer/pianist pulled herself off the road in order to raise her daughter, Rainy, who was eleven at the time. While she continued to play in her hometown and in nearby Baltimore and to record periodically in New York and Los Angeles, for nearly a decade Horn put her career on the back burner.

"I needed my daughter as much as she needed me, so I said, 'I'm going to go home now and see about her,'" she explains. "I don't regret it."

The oldest of three children, Horn was raised in an environment that was nothing if not supportive. Her mother and father weren't musicians, but there was plenty of Ellington, Billie Holiday, and Dinah Washington played in the house. "My parents were poor," she says. "I had an uncle who was well-to-do, a doctor, and he took care of my piano lessons. My grandmother

had a parlor that was always very pretty and very cold, but there was a piano there. I remember having a coat on and plunking on the piano. My grandmother, who played piano and pipe organ, said to my mother, 'Give her lessons now!' This was before I was four. When I took my first piano lessons I couldn't read a note.

"It seemed like my life was charted. It just happened. Music just came right along with living. I have to play music or I'll explode."

When she was twelve, Horn sang and played her way to first prize at an amateur show in Washington. Her professional singing debut was unplanned, however. It happened in the club where she played piano occasionally during the period when she was attending a Howard University–associated school for gifted students.

"An elderly gentleman came in every evening, tipped his hat, had dinner, and left," she recalls. "When it was getting close to Christmas, he came in with this teddy bear. Somehow I knew it was for me. It was as tall as I was. He wrote a note that said, 'If you sing "Melancholy Baby," the teddy bear is yours.' So I sang 'Melancholy Baby.' I kept the teddy bear until 1959. Then he just demised on me. He was so pretty."

"Melancholy Baby" would be one of hundreds of songs that Horn would sing in the busy next decade. She also became a club owner twice during that time. Her second venue, Pepe's, served as both a musical and culinary outlet for her; preparing fifty pounds of chitterlings for the crowd wasn't an unheard-of occurrence. When she wasn't running her clubs, she toured. Miles Davis had heard her first album and convinced Village Vanguard owner Max Gordon that Horn had to work opposite him at the club. She even made a commercial during the period for a Colgate-Palmolive product called Groom and Clean. "All I had to sing was 'do's,'" she remembers. Besides a case of Groom and Clean, Horn received residuals the size of which she'd never even imagined. "It was so much money it scared me to death," she laughs. "I'll never forget, I got the first check, called my manager, John Levy, and said, 'John, I've got a check here from Colgate-Palmolive. What do I do with it?' 'Spend it!' he said."

With an audience that continues to grow steadily larger, Horn's paydays come more often now. Her pliable piano style captures rollicking joy and bittersweet regret with equal élan, and always with a swinging core. She's the perfect accompanist—Carmen McRae used her in that role in a tribute to Sarah Vaughan—a gift that comes in handiest when she's center-stage herself. She can lead or follow with either her voice or her hands. Horn's breathy, delicate vocals belie the intensity of her messages. On ballads especially, her dry, no-frills voice conveys unmistakable passion; the drama and clarity of her delivery pulls an audience along even when she practically suspends her lyrics in mid-phrase. Horn's tone extends from dark and robust to soft and fragile, a range that provides her with an endless palette of shadings. Few musicians capture the breadth of human emotion with the understated power that Horn does.

Immersing herself in home repair projects and cooking helps Horn unwind. "Give me a hammer and nail, that's the best therapy," she says. The meals she fixes for her husband, her daughter, and her daughter's family are much the same as her own mother prepared, with the exception of the seafood she has added to her repertoire. "Growing up we lived next door to an Italian family," she recalls. "You can imagine the mixture of odors in the summertime. Between whatever they were cooking and my mother's turnip greens or chitterlings, it smelled like the League of Nations."

Beef and Beer

One dish from Horn's childhood that is in her current repertoire is a creation her grandmother dubbed Beef and Beer. "But I don't think she used as much beer as I do," the singer laughs.

"It's hard to overcook this as long as there's liquid in the pot," Horn says. "It's done when the meat just falls to pieces. I like to serve it with boiled red-skin potatoes, carrots, and mustard greens that I make with smoked pork jowl."

Serves 6 to 8

- 5 to 6 pounds chuck roast, bone in
- Coarsely ground black pepper
- 3 tablespoons vegetable oil
- 4 cloves garlic, minced
- 2 packages Lipton's French onion soup mix, dissolved in 5 cups boiling water
- Approximately 3 cups beer

Wash and dry the meat. Coat it liberally with the pepper. Place the meat in a deep-sided black, cast-iron pot with a tight-fitting lid. Over medium-high heat, and uncovered, add the oil and brown the meat on all sides. Remove the meat from the pot and add the garlic. Cook for 2 minutes, lower the heat, and return the meat to the pot. Add the soup and enough beer just to cover the meat. Cover the pot and, over medium-low heat, cook for 2½ to 3 hours, or until the meat falls to pieces. Check to see that there's liquid in the pot at all times; if the pot begins to run dry, add more beer and/or water.

Listening to the unbounded pleasure with which Sheila Jordan bends and embraces a song can feel like eavesdropping on a very private conversation. Every phrase she shapes seems to reveal another layer of the joy and pain in her past.

Born Sheila Dawson in Detroit in 1928, she was raised in Pennsylvania coal country, in the small town of Summerhill, by her maternal grandparents. "We had to hunt for our food because we were extremely poor," she recalls. "We didn't have lights or an inside toilet, only kerosene lamps and an outhouse with the Sears Roebuck catalog for toilet paper. We'd have fried or baked rabbit, squirrels as a base for soup, groundhogs, and porcupines even. Can you imagine skinning porcupines? Deer was the big thing, naturally. That would carry you for the whole winter."

Her grandmother, who cooked, and grandfather, who hunted and cooked occasionally, had plenty of mouths to feed. The singer had eight young aunts and uncles whom she regarded as brothers and sisters. "We were on welfare, so they gave you potatoes, oleo, flour, coffee," she says. "We never got whole milk. We had evaporated milk in cereal and oatmeal. I hated it. It was horrible. But if you're raised like that, you learn how to cook that way."

"My family was not immune to alcohol, so that didn't make it easier," she acknowledges. "It was a very, very hard life."

Music helped lighten the load. "My grandmother was a piano player and singer," Jordan says. "She had a beautiful voice as did my great aunt, who was a piano teacher. My grandfather also had a beauti-

Endive, Walnut, and Apple Salad

This salad that combines Belgian endive and watercress with walnuts and apples is one of Jordan's favorites. "I learned it from some guy's wife who was French," she says. "I love the different textures in this dish and the fact that it's in step with my diet. If you don't break up the endive leaves and leave them whole, it's also a pretty dish because the other ingredients seem to curl up on the endive."

For dessert, she's fond of puréeing fresh raspberries with a little honey and a bit of lemon juice and serving the purée over sorbet, yogurt, fruit, or angel food cake.

Serves 6

- ¼ cup extra-virgin olive oil
- 2 tablespoons balsamic vinegar
- 2 pounds endive (about 6 heads), separated into leaves and thoroughly washed and dried
- 1 small bunch watercress, cleaned, dried, and coarsely chopped
- 1 small red onion, cut into very thin slices
- 1 Granny Smith apple, cored and cut into thin, fan-shaped slices
- 1 cup walnut pieces, coarsely chopped

In a small bowl, combine the olive oil and vinegar. Place the endive leaves in a large bowl. Mix together the watercress, onion, apple, and walnuts. Reblend the dressing, pour over the endive mixture, and toss well until the endive leaves are well coated.

ful voice. We didn't have a radio because we didn't have electricity, although we got one later. I grew up in a time when a lot of the tunes that I sing today, like 'My Ideal,'

were popular. I used to hitchhike two miles to South Fork to see all the Fred Astaire and Ginger Rogers movies on Saturdays. I loved those and learned a lot of songs from them. I'd work for this lady and scrub her floors just so I could get money to go to the movies."

When Jordan was a sophomore in high school, her mother took her to Detroit to live. The environment was far from stable. Her mother, who was married a total of seven times, had a drinking problem. "Sometimes she cooked, sometimes I cooked for myself," the vocalist remembers. "When she wasn't in a condition to cook, I ate a lot of hamburgers. I stayed with her until my last year of high school and then I moved out because I couldn't take it anymore. I didn't like the fact that my stepfather was beating her all the time."

Despite the travails, Jordan considers her relocation to Detroit a blessing in disguise. In high school she befriended future jazz stars Tommy Flanagan, Barry Harris, and Kenny Burrell, who were bitten by the same bebop bug as the singer. Jordan got it so bad that she eventually moved to New York to hear Charlie Parker as often as she could, to "chase Bird," as she puts it. She studied with pianist Lennie Tristano, settled into a loft on Twenty-sixth Street between Seventh and Eighth avenues, married Parker's piano player, Duke Jordan, and started a family. Her loft became a hangout for everyone from Allen Ginsberg and Sonny Rollins to Paul Bley and Bird. Especially Bird.

"He'd come at all hours," Jordan says about Parker. "He'd say, 'Oh, I saw fire trucks,' and it would be five o'clock in the morning. Or he'd knock on the door and ask, 'Do you have a match?' And he'd go rest on the couch or somewhere. He was in bad shape toward the end. He was lonely and unhappy. Drugs and alcohol can do weird things to you. I know about drugs and alcohol. I've been there."

Jordan recorded her first album, the moving *Portrait of Sheila*, in 1962. She didn't record again under her own name until 1982. Even so, her collaborators have always been among jazz's finest players, from George Russell to Steve Kuhn to Harvie Swartz. In 1987, she left the job she'd held for twenty-one years as a clerical typist to devote herself full-time to music.

"I never wanted to starve again," she says about keeping a day job. "Once in a life is enough. I didn't want my kid to have to suffer. I wanted to sing the music the way I heard it and keep it pure. In order for me to do that, I had to wait until it was my turn."

When she stepped onstage or into a recording studio during those years, Jordan sounded like anything but a part-time vocalist. She's a truly unusual stylist—not a belter, but a vocal gambler who dares to conceive melodies with a voice that's nor-

mally associated with romantic crooners: smooth and optimistically sweet. She respects the words of a song as deeply as she respects her inspirations Parker and Billie Holiday. Yet she's an improviser who can combine humor and pathos, the mundane and the profound in a single song, spontaneously inventing lyrics about how wonderful her hotel room is and then honoring the power of Miles Davis's horn only a few phrases later. Whether she's in the middle of a slow reshaping of a solitary note or a careening scat break—she's one of jazz's most natural-sounding and riveting scat singers—Jordan always maintains a rhythm. Her style puts new vitality into workhorses like "How Deep Is the Ocean?" or "Falling in Love with Love." She sounds like she's simply happy to be singing.

"I sing what I feel," she says. "I'm not waylaid by what somebody else tells me might sell, and I don't look at it as something that I'm going to be a star with. I don't even care about that. My philosophy with this music is to dedicate my life to it and do it honestly."

Jordan has arterial sclerosis, so she's no longer able to eat favorites like steak and eggs or drink cream in her coffee. She keeps an apartment in Manhattan but spends most of her time in a thirteen-room farmhouse on five acres in Hunterland, New York, where she grows her own vegetables, flowers, and herbs.

TASTY PLATTERS

- Sheila Jordan, *Lost and Found* (Muse)
- Sheila Jordan, *Portrait of Sheila* (Blue Note)
- Sheila Jordan/Harvie Swartz, *Old Time Feeling* (Muse)

"I see myself as an actor and a singer," Abbey Lincoln says. "I bring characters to the stage."

And what characters she brings. Powerful. Passionate. Uncompromising. In fact, the characters Lincoln chooses are oftentimes mirror images of her own personality. More than any other vocalist in jazz, she unflinchingly conveys the essence of her feelings and beliefs to an audience. It's a no-holds-barred approach that can be breathtaking in its impact.

"My philosophy of life is reflected in my music," she explains. "Lester Young said that the musician is a scientist and a philosopher who uses the science of music to put forth his philosophy. Duke Ellington was like that. For me it's experimental. It expands as my personality expands.

"I'm different from a lot of women singers. I write a lot of my own songs and I'm social, which can bother some people. I observe what's going on and can't help but comment. I believe that we can't always go for self-aggrandizement.

We have so many opportunities to say something that sometimes I feel like we're ministers and priests. We can't misuse our talents or our stage."

Making the most of her artistic gifts and being social—acting with a social conscience—are longtime Lincoln trademarks that have grown more pronounced over the years. Born Anna Marie Wooldridge in 1930, she was raised in rural Michigan, the third youngest of twelve children. Her clearest musical memories are of the lullabies her father sang to her as a child and the hours of contentment she spent at the piano.

"I was the only one who played the piano," she recalls. "I began to play when I was five, and I really think I started so I could be alone. We didn't have separate rooms. When I would go to the piano I was alone. Nobody ever told me to stop. It never got on their nerves, I think, because of the approach I took. I didn't just sit there and bang on the keys. There was peace when I sat there."

When her family and friends brought home recordings by the likes of Billie Holiday and Coleman Hawkins, the hand-cranked Victrola in the house became Lincoln's link to the outside world. After trying out her vocal talents on her family and schoolmates, she earned her first income—five dollars—performing in the basement of a church.

From age nineteen, when she struck out on her own in California, it's possible to follow the singer's professional and personal evolution by tracing her name changes. During her early supper club years, she was Gaby Wooldridge, then Gaby Lee, and later in that period she took on Abbey Lincoln, a moniker which was given to her by her then-manager, Bob Russell. By the late 1950s, when she met Max Roach, the drummer to whom she was married for much of the 1960s, Lincoln's musical transformation from entertainer to jazz artist had taken hold. She associated with a wide range of black actors, writers,

Abbey Lincoln's Fried Porgy

"When I came to New York from Los Angeles, I discovered porgy," says Lincoln, adding with a laugh that she always thought of porgy in terms of a man. *"I recorded 'I Loves You, Porgy,' so it was funny to see a fish called porgy. Now it's one of my favorite fish."*

Porgy, the fish, not the character from Gershwin's Porgy and Bess, *generally weigh less than a pound each. These sweet-tasting fish also go by the name scup.*

"I like to serve it with linguini cooked in butter and oil that's

finished with lemon and parsley," says Lincoln, *"and cold beer."*

Serves 2

  1 whole porgy per person, cleaned
    and scaled, head and tail intact
    (see Note)
  1 large egg, beaten
  2/3 cup cornmeal
  Salt and pepper
  Approximately 3/4 cup vegetable oil

Using a sharp knife, make two 45° angle slashes on each side of the fish. Coat the fish with the beaten egg. Combine

the cornmeal, salt, and pepper on a plate or a piece of waxed paper. Roll the fish in the cornmeal mixture until it is totally coated. Loosely cover the fish with the waxed paper and place in the refrigerator for about half an hour, which will help the cornmeal adhere to the fish. In a skillet large enough to hold the fish without crowding, add enough oil to fill about 3/4 inches of the pan. Heat the oil until very hot. Fry both sides of the fish until crisp.

Note: Red snapper, small sea bass, and redfish are acceptable substitutes for the porgy.

and poets and with seminal bebop figures like Sonny Rollins, Wynton Kelley, and Kenny Dorham. In 1961 came her inclusion in the recording *We Insist: Freedom Now Suite,* a testament against racism written by Roach and Oscar Brown, Jr. Several film roles fol-

lowed, including that of Sidney Poitier's co-star in *For Love of Ivy.*

In the early seventies, Lincoln moved to Los Angeles to look after her ill mother. Soon after, during a visit to Africa, she took the name Aminata Moseka. "Moseka has a lot to do with my growth and this shilly-shally life that I've been living, trying to find myself, looking for myself in the void," she says. "It's in honor of my African ancestors so that they know that I know in whose image and likeness I'm living. They're the reason I have my talents."

Lincoln, who now uses both her stage and African names, essentially dropped out of the public scene for almost a decade, composing music, teaching, writing, and painting instead of performing publicly. When she returned to New York in 1981, it was with newfound vigor and commitment. She has again been making the most of her stage, collaborating with old friends Clark Terry and Jackie McLean, and new

ones like Steve Coleman, acting in the film *Mo' Better Blues,* and running Moseka House, her shelter for young artists and musicians.

It's with her dark, rough-hewn voice, however, that Lincoln has the broadest impact, addressing the world's oppressed—and the world in general—with messages of hope through her lyrics. A master of drama, lyrical nuance, and bluesy phrasing, Lincoln tells her melodic tales at an unhurried pace to drive home the potency of her words.

"To me," she says, "a song is a prayer."

The vocalist has always kept her eating habits simple. "I didn't care that much for food as a child," she explains. "I ate for sustenance. Even today I'm not a big eater, although I love wonderful food, with taste, that's beautifully presented. I try to get by on one meal a day. Maybe it's because I'm not sensuous in that way. I'm motivated in my head and in my heart. Food doesn't rule me."

Years before the globalization of music took hold as a commercial and artistic force, Helen Merrill, one of the finest vocalists in jazz, was living a life that was the embodiment of internationalism.

During a career that began in the mid-1950s, Merrill has called Italy, Japan, and France home. She still spends a lot of time touring overseas. "I feel as close to Europe as I do to America," she admits. "I felt pretty comfortable in Japan, too."

The naturalness with which she has taken to life outside her native United States has its roots in her background. Born in the Chelsea section of Manhattan to parents of Yugoslavian descent, Merrill—originally Yellena Milcetic—was raised in the melting pots of the Bronx and Queens. Both her mother and her father, a tugboat captain, were born on the small island of Krk, off the coast of Yugoslavia. Her father prepared dishes like roast lamb and *bacala* with polenta, influenced by the cooking of Italy, the Slavic countries, and the Arabic region. "He cooked in a real gourmet fashion," she recalls, "but we didn't appreciate it. We hardly ate what he cooked because we thought it was awful."

But Merrill did appreciate her mother's singing, which she heard only around the house. It had a lasting impact on her own music. "My mother sang very fine standard songs, folk-flavored songs like 'I'll Take You Home Again, Kathleen.' My mother was also an expert in a twelve-tone music peculiar to Krk, called *klapa*. It is true folk music and very, very difficult. It's a form of storytelling—songs about the news of the day.

Chicken or Veal Parmesan

"I'm a seat-of-the-pants cook," says Merrill. "I use recipes as guidelines. For company or dinner parties, I like to make either chicken or veal Parmesan because in addition to ease and taste, either one can be prepared ahead."

Serves 2 hungry diners or
4 weight-watchers

1 egg
2/3 cup Italian-style fine bread crumbs
4 thinly sliced chicken or veal cutlets
3 tablespoons olive oil
2 tablespoons butter
1/2 cup homemade or high-quality store-bought tomato sauce
4 slices mozzarella cheese
1/3 cup freshly grated Italian Parmesan cheese

Preheat the oven to 375°F. Beat the egg in a pie plate and place the bread crumbs on waxed paper or a plate. Dip the chicken or veal in the egg, then coat with the crumbs. Place the chicken or veal on a plate and refrigerate to set the crumbs. In a frying pan, heat up half of the oil and butter and sauté two of the cutlets until cooked through. Drain on paper towels. Clean the pan, then add the remaining oil and butter to the pan and sauté the remaining two cutlets. Lightly grease the bottom of an ovenproof shallow dish. Spread a very thin layer of tomato sauce on the bottom of the pan. Place the cutlets in the dish in a single layer. Spread the remaining sauce over the meat and cover each cutlet with a slice of mozzarella. Sprinkle with the Parmesan cheese. At this point you can cover the dish and set it in the refrigerator until ready to place in the oven. Bake for 10 minutes or until the cheese begins to melt.

"So when I started to listen to Thelonious Monk, for example, it was quite natural. Nothing sounded strange to my ears because I had heard this music. Close harmonies sound perfectly natural to me."

Merrill caught the jazz bug early. By fifteen she was frequenting, and soon performing in, the 845 Club in the Bronx and, later, Manhattan venues such as Basin Street East and Birdland. "Part of what was great was getting into the clubs," she says. "I was brought up a Seventh-Day Adventist, so you can imagine what I felt like. I still feel twinges of guilt around alcohol. When I first worked at Birdland, I felt I shouldn't wear perfume and too much makeup, as was the rule of the church. So I made a little compromise. I didn't wear any perfume and I didn't wear too much makeup, so I thought it was OK for me to be singing at Birdland. Oh, God, it was funny."

In 1954 Merrill made her first recording, an album produced by Quincy Jones that featured trumpeter Clifford Brown. It should have served as a springboard for a career in the States, but Merrill instead moved overseas, first to London and then to Italy for four years. She even had her own TV show there. She returned to New York briefly during the 1960s but by 1967 she had married and moved to Japan, where she settled down for five years with her husband, who worked for a wire service. Always one to adapt to her environment, Merrill actually recorded several albums in which she sang in Japanese accompanied by the traditional bamboo flute. She became known to Japanese fans as "The Sigh of New York."

Merrill has sung in an amazingly wide range of settings, always with the best musicians available. George Russell, Stan Getz, Stephane Grappelli, Steve Lacy, and Bill Evans make up a short list of her collaborators.

"I'm very lucky that I didn't fall into a success syndrome where I would be copying myself," she says. "I never became so popular that I had to keep singing the same song. So I experimented a lot. I work with different people all the time. My conception of music changes. I come from the purist school. I don't believe that you can just hop about, cross over. I come from the era where everybody was an artist and that's where you stayed, come hell or high water."

Merrill interprets the full spectrum of jazz standards and material

TASTY PLATTERS

- Helen Merrill, *Just Friends* (EmArcy)
- Helen Merrill/Gil Evans, *Collaboration* (EmArcy)
- *The Complete Helen Merrill on Mercury* (Mercury)

from the American popular songbook with equal ease, but she's at her most convincing on ballads and midtempo material. In her precise renditions she creates a drama that's never overblown, always in control. Utilizing a dry, smoky delivery that's both soft-toned and tightly emotional, she conjures up moods that lean toward the wistful and bittersweet. Few singers do justice to the nuances of lyrics and melody as well as Merrill.

An appreciation of food has always been an important part of her life as a jazz musician, and the same holds true, she feels, for many of her peers. "I love *good* food, not just food," she says. "Whether it's peasant-type or very elegant, I like it. It's our pastime. Eating definitely becomes the reward."

One of the singer's most memorable meals, in fact, was a Thanksgiving dinner spent at the farm of Miles Davis's parents outside of St. Louis. "I was really very flattered," she says. "Cannonball Adderley was there as was Miles's

dad, who was a very sweet gentleman. At that time he was raising prime hogs. I was a city girl. Miles took me out to the field and a horse came toward us and I ran away. I was not one to adapt to rural life."

Living in Manhattan, Merrill is able to indulge her catholic tastes in food. She takes advantage of the fact that Indian, Italian, and Japanese restaurants are all within only a few blocks of her house. When she does cook, it tends to be a dish like veal ragout, various stews, or chicken Parmesan.

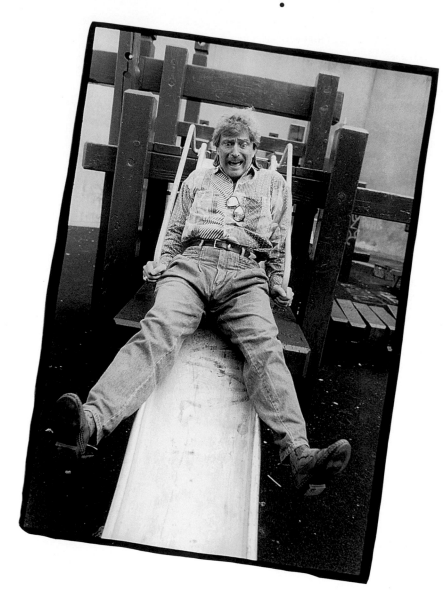

For nearly four decades, Mark Murphy has been one of the music's most consistently uncompromising singers, an improviser who explores the vocal possibilities of swing, bebop, Brazilian rhythms, and modality with exuberance. His desire to push the limits rather than simply croon his way onto the pop or easy listening charts goes to the heart of his outlook on life and music.

"Philosophically and soulwise I come to jazz because I am kind of a free spirit," he explains. "It has something to do with that sense of freedom, of being able to keep being relevant rather than a museum piece. I prefer staying musically fluid rather than static."

That dedication hasn't come without a cost. Even with more than thirty recordings to his credit,

TASTY PLATTERS

• Mark Murphy, *Stolen Moments* (Muse)
• Mark Murphy, *The Complete Nat Cole Songbook, Volumes 1 and 2* (Muse)
• Mark Murphy, *What a Way to Go* (Muse)

acclaim from critics, and praise from legends like Ella Fitzgerald, Murphy still remains a treasure held dear primarily by jazz vocals aficionados. But he sees very real advantages that make it easy to accept a non-Hollywood fate. "As artists, we can go places beyond entertainers emotionally and harmonically," he says. "Taking people places others can't is sort of what this life is like."

Based in San Francisco since the seventies, Murphy was born in 1932 in Fulton, New York, a small town outside of Syracuse. "We were all musical," he says about his family. "My mother and father met in the Methodist church choir. He had come down from Syracuse to Fulton to conduct it. My grandmother was playing the organ. On Sundays, as soon as we were old enough, we had breakfast, went to church, sang, came back home, and had Sunday dinner. In the afternoon we usually went to my grandmother's house and my grandfather played opera. Then one day my uncle gave me an

Art Tatum record. And that was it. I was thirteen."

Murphy soon joined his brother's dance band and also started singing along with the records of vocalists like Sarah Vaughan, Nat "King" Cole, June Christy, and Billy Eckstine. He studied music and acting at Syracuse University and moved to New York after graduating in 1953. "I found a little apartment for $11.50 a month," he recalls. "I worked as a night clerk at the Gotham Hotel for nine months, managed a doughnut shop, did some summer-stock shows. It was fun. I was a small-town kid; I didn't know nothin'. But you learn. You get knocked around a bit and you survive."

The singer learned quickly enough to win several talent contests at the Apollo Theater that eventually led to club work and a record contract with Decca. His first real break came when comedian Steve Allen, host of the "Tonight Show" during TV's infancy, invited Murphy to appear. This was followed by a semi-hit in 1963, "Fly Me to the Moon," which made the charts just before he moved to London, where acting occupied him for the better part of a decade. Upon his return to the United States in 1973, he began recording and performing again.

Murphy is a risk-taking vocalist. Many of his most harmonically and melodically challenging songs, like John Coltrane's "Naima," Oliver Nelson's "Stolen Moments," and Herbie Hancock's "Maiden Voyage," were originally recorded as instrumentals. He not only navigates the changes handily, he delivers lyrics with a poignancy that captures the essence of the song. Like the best improvisers, he can skip behind or in front of a note as effortlessly as he can nail it. His diction is as clean as the tone on a perfectly tuned piano, and his scat singing is especially inventive. With a smooth, understated power, Murphy works wonders with a wide range of vehicles, from the blues to the Nat "King" Cole songbook to "Body and Soul" to his ode to Beat Generation novelist Jack Kerouac.

Murphy's nutritional habits have been prone to a fair amount of

Sage-Rubbed Free-Range Chicken

Ease, nutrition, and life on the road all take a bow in Murphy's Sage-Rubbed Free-Range Chicken. More than twenty years ago Murphy was taken aback by a tasty chicken dish on a United Airlines flight.

"I asked, 'What kind of spice you got in here?'" he recalls. When the flight attendant told him it was sage, he decided that it was something that he could duplicate at home. In a nod to today's more health-minded times, Murphy prepares this roast chicken dish with hormone-free, organically fed free-range chicken. However, for those who can't find free-range chickens, a standard roaster is an acceptable substitute.

Serves 4

1 (4- to 5-pound) free-range chicken
Olive oil
4 or more tablespoons dried sage
Freshly ground pepper
2 stalks celery, cut in half horizontally

Preheat the oven to 350°F. Remove the innards from the chicken and wash the bird. With your fingers, rub the olive oil into the skin of the chicken, then sprinkle on the sage. (Murphy says, "Don't be afraid to use a lot. It gives the chicken almost an outdoor, mesquite flavor.") Add a few twists of pepper. Sprinkle more sage on the split celery sticks and stuff them into the cavity. Place the chicken on a rack and set it in a roasting pan. Bake for 1¾ to 2 hours, basting every 20 minutes with the pan drippings, until the juice runs clear, or a meat thermometer inserted in the inner portion of the thigh registers 180°F. Let the chicken "rest" for 15 minutes or so before serving.

change in the course of his career. Raised on "plain American food," he gravitated toward cafeterias when he moved to Manhattan and then got used to heavier British fare like kidney pie and beef Wellington during his years in London. "I love very heavy food," he admits. "I have to really watch it and some days just not eat. My metabolism is very bad now, slowed way down, so I have to be careful. It's a continuing battle."

Murphy has a plan that would ensure a settled stomach: he'll retire at sixty-five. "I love northern California," he says. "To me it's heaven on earth. My dream is to have a little bed-and-breakfast up there on Highway 1 near the coast. Change the beds, cook 'em breakfast, and get them out. I think I will have had this singing lark by then."

For now, Murphy "cooks for ease," although he finds it difficult to maintain a strict nutritional regimen with so much of his time spent on the road. To help offset the stress and the water and food fluctuations of travel, he fortifies himself daily with a hefty handful of vitamin pills that contain the likes of wheatgrass, chlorella, and zinc.

An appreciation for thrills came early for Annie Ross, who was born after her vaudevillian mother's matinee performance at the Metropolitan Music Hall in London and a stage actor herself by three. Blessed with a matchless voice, generous dollops of pluck, and a personality willing to roll with the punches, Ross has shaped a career that has been the antithesis of boring: she was a member of the greatest jazz scat singing group of all time, Lambert, Hendricks and Ross; she tried her hand at the supper club business; and she took up acting a second time after the vocal trio ran its course.

Even as young as four, when she was moved from Scotland to America to live with her aunt Ella Logan, Ross proved she was both adaptable and a quick study.

"On the first day my aunt asked, 'What do you want for lunch?'" Ross remembers. "In my very thick Scottish accent I answered, 'Cake and bananas.' And she said, 'Well, you're not getting that,' and gave me a plate of stew. I said, 'I'm not eating it,' and she told me, 'You don't have to.' She took it away. Breakfast came and it was stew and I wouldn't eat it, and lunch came and it was stew and I wouldn't eat it. And dinner came and I ate it. I've never looked back."

Not only did the singer not look back, she eventually developed her own cooking skills to the point where they were almost as notable as her stage talents. For two years during the late sixties, Annie's Room in London featured fine food and international jazz performers. She wrote a cookbook called *Come On In*. And during the more than two

Simple Salmon à la Ross

In those hectic halcyon days when she was overseeing Annie's Room, one of the club's most requested dishes was Simple Salmon à la Ross. "I thought it would be a good idea to team the two—garlic and teriyaki," says Ross. "We'd serve it with small, steamed red-skin potatoes with either dill or parsley. It goes nicely with a chilled dry, white wine. I think it's delicious, and judging by the empty plates, my friends do, too."

Serves 4

   2 tablespoons olive or corn oil
   6 to 8 cloves garlic, thinly sliced
   4 salmon fillets, approximately
      ½ pound each
   2½ cups teriyaki sauce ("The best
      comes from health food stores,"
      Ross says.)

In a small skillet, heat the oil. Add the garlic and fry until the garlic is a touch darker than golden brown. Place the salmon fillets in a shallow noncorrosive baking dish large enough to hold all of the fish without crowding. Pour the teriyaki sauce over the fish. Place the fried garlic on top of the fish and let the fish marinate for 30 to 45 minutes ("So that the flavors can get to know one another," says Ross). Position a rack in the center of the oven and preheat to 350°F. Bake for 12 to 14 minutes, until the salmon is cooked through, or to your preference. Serve immediately. "And be prepared for sheer bliss," Ross advises.

decades she lived in England, beginning in the mid-sixties, she opened up her home, and her kitchen, to friends, many of whom were fellow musicians. She does the same now that she's living in New York.

"They'd all come over to the house, Billy Eckstine, Sarah Vaughan," Ross recounts about her years in England. "They wanted a home-cooked meal. Sarah would always make chili. It took some beating! She was a great cook."

For Ross the connection between the worlds of food and music is a basic one. "I think that music is sensuous, eating is sensuous, and taste is sensuous," she says. "It all goes together. You get the ingredients and then you put your seasonings in. That's the way it is in music."

Ross couldn't have asked for a smoother entrée into the jazz world than the one provided in the Los Angeles home of her aunt, a singer, and her uncle, a screenwriter and record collector. Roy Eldridge, Duke Ellington, and Lena Horne were among the house guests who shared their experiences with the young vocalist. "They were all modern, and that's where my ear went," she points out.

At sixteen she went off on her own, first to the American Academy of Dramatic Arts in New York, then to Scotland, London, and Paris. Each experience, especially her five years in France, prepared her for the challenges she would take on with Lambert, Hendricks and Ross. She immersed herself in the entertainment world, developing deep relationships with some of its most charismatic individualists: drummer Kenny Clarke—who was the father of her son—Tony Bennett, and Lenny Bruce.

Still, Lambert, Hendricks and Ross remains a highlight. "It's like eating a fabulous meal," she explains. "When you've known the best, why have dreck? Jon and Dave and I always had a moment in the evening when it was magic, when we were all on the same wavelength. Sometimes it would last all night. Sometimes it was just five or ten minutes. It was such a flowing, wonderful thing. Knowing that sensation and how wonderful it is, that's what I strive to get."

The trio's bop vocalese—witty, intricate lyrics set to classic jazz instrumental solos and ensemble passages in which each singer duplicated an instrument—was absolutely breathtaking, especially when it clicked into break-neck high gear. Led by Hendricks's vocalizing and sophisticated songwriting, they were even dubbed "the James Joyces of jazz" by one American periodical. The repertoire included "Cloudburst," "Goin' to Chicago," and "One O'Clock Jump," with Ross's most famous contribution being "Twisted," the odd-ball song she wrote about neurosis that was set to a Wardell Gray tenor sax solo.

The voice with which Ross then played her piercing, high-end trumpet part has taken on a huskier tone over the years. With her diminished octave range necessitating that she ply the middle register more, Ross finds herself concentrating on show tunes and ballads in her fairly rare solo showcases these days. But she still swings. "As I get older I find that simplicity is the most difficult thing. I just want to be as pure in my music as I can be."

She also finds that her acting,

which has included roles in plays and operettas like *The Pirates of Penzance* and movies like *Pump Up the Volume,* is a natural extension of her singing. "Words are very important to me," she explains. "If you can tell a good story, that applies to an actor as well."

Ross's willingness to adapt remains one of her strongest assets, onstage and off. "I'm very at home

TASTY PLATTERS

- Annie Ross/Gerry Mulligan, *Annie Ross Sings a Song with Mulligan* (Pacific Jazz)
- Lambert, Hendricks and Ross, *Everybody's Boppin'* (Columbia Jazz Masterpieces)
- *The Best of Lambert, Hendricks and Ross* (Columbia)

in the country," she says. "I think it's my Scottish genes. I love walking. I can chop wood. I can do a garden. Once, during the eighties, I was snowed in up north in Scotland for New Year's. I was staying with friends and we were running out of food. We'd already run out of coal. A ranger came by and said, 'I'll get you a beast,' which was venison. I went to the dairy to get milk and when I got back, there on the porch was half a stag, still steaming. It had just been killed. Two guys from the house came out and said, 'Ugh, what are you going to do with that?' 'You're going to take it to the kitchen for me,' I said. 'It's got to be skinned.' So they did, and I skinned it, butchered it, and we had a fabulous venison meal. I'm very practical."

It would be less than accurate to credit Carol Sloane's parents with either launching her rich vocal career or supplying her with the hands-on skills necessary to become as comfortable in a kitchen as she is today. What they did provide was an intangible that may have been even more important: warmth. It's an ingredient that's now apparent in every aspect of Sloane's own music and cooking.

Born in 1937 and raised in Georgiaville, a town near Providence, Rhode Island, Sloane has memories of large family barbecues on weekends in the summer, a mother who was "a great can opener," and World War II–era roast chicken Sunday dinners. Her parents worked in a nearby textile mill, and during the war her father landed a seven-day-a-week job in the shipyards near Narragansett Bay. More than once he would drive to the USO in Providence and transport a carful of soldiers to Georgiaville for a home-cooked meal.

Music was an important part of most of those gatherings. Much of the family sang together in church, while the radio and her father's big band swing records brought home the popular sounds of the day. When Sloane decided to dig deeper, she discovered gold. "As a young person," she recalls, "I listened to pop music on the radio, which was usually white singers. Teresa Brewer. Rosemary Clooney. Tony Bennett. And then suddenly I realized there was another whole world of music and, although I didn't think about it at the time, they were black people: Carmen McRae, Sarah Vaughan,

Ella Fitzgerald, Billie Holiday, Joe Williams. Somehow there was another dimension to their singing. For me, listening to Sarah or Carmen sing was much more

important than listening to the other women who were being played constantly who had lots of hit records."

Fed by two Providence radio jazz shows and, on late nights when skies were clear, by Al "Jazzbo" Collins's program from New York, Sloane's knowledge of and love for the music mushroomed. In her early teens she'd get together with a few friends from school and put

jazz records on the turntable. "We wanted to sit and listen and see if we could decipher, find the key to, this code that was being transmitted," she says. "The more we listened, the more we began to understand, the more we began to love it. Many of us realized it was a life of dedication."

Sloane took on the challenge. She toured with Larry Elgart's orchestra for two years before she set out on her own, occasionally filling in for Annie Ross in Lambert, Hendricks and Ross, recording two albums for Columbia, and hitting the nightclub circuit, where she shared bills with comedians like Woody Allen, Richard Pryor, and Lenny Bruce. In the late sixties she moved to Raleigh, North Carolina, where for seven years she worked in a law office by day and held a regular gig at a jazz club by night. The mid-seventies found her back in New York living with pianist Jimmy Rowles before she returned again to North Carolina for five years. In 1986 she settled outside of Boston, her home now.

Throughout all of those moves, Sloane stayed true to the philosophy that first attracted her to jazz. "When I sing, the thing that's foremost in my mind is to do precisely what I know the two women I admire most—Carmen and Shirley Horn—do: move an audience. I also work to be unswervingly faithful to the accolade 'jazz singer,' which is an honorary title. What it means is that you improvise, you never sing the

TASTY PLATTERS

- Carol Sloane, *Love You Madly* (Contemporary)
- Carmen McRae, *Sarah: Dedicated to You* (Novus)
- Mozart, *Famous Arias* (Eurodisc)

Welcome Home Roast Chicken

Her Welcome Home Roast Chicken is the ideal antidote to travel and jet lag. "It's very satisfying, very comforting," she says about the dish. "To me it feels very much like home. When I return from a road tour, this is my favorite dish to prepare because its aroma is so comforting. It's also easy to make." Sloane likes to serve her chicken with carrots or green beans. "Crunchy bread and a really splendid Chardonnay make it complete," she adds.

Serves 3 to 4

- 4 tablespoons (½ stick) butter
- 4 sprigs fresh rosemary
- 1 large (4- to 5-pound) roasting chicken, giblets and liver discarded
- 1½ pounds (about 6 medium-sized) potatoes, sliced thick
- 1 pound (about 3 to 4 large) onions, cut into thick slices
- Salt and pepper
- 1½ to 2 cups chicken stock

Preheat the oven to 350°F. Spread 2 tablespoons of the butter and 2 sprigs of the rosemary inside the chicken cavity. Spread 1 tablespoon of the butter on the bottom of a roasting pan. (Alternatively, spray the pan with nonstick cooking spray.) Place the chicken in the center of the pan and surround it with the potatoes and onions. Add the remaining rosemary and season with salt and pepper. Pour 1½ cups of the stock over the chicken and vegetables and dot with the remaining 1 tablespoon of butter. Roast for about 2 hours, occasionally basting the chicken and vegetables with the stock. If desired, add some or all of the remaining ½ cup chicken stock as you cook. If the chicken is browning too quickly, cover it with foil.

song the same way twice. If you do, you are not a jazz singer."

Sloane's talents go far beyond never duplicating a song. Few vocalists caress a phrase in quite the elegant, softly musical way she does. Her contralto voice, husky, clearly enunciated, and dramatic, is the perfect vehicle to explore the nuances of the great American songbook. Whether she's scatting or simply bending a song subtly and effortlessly, Sloane exhibits a respect for the power of swing and melody that harks back to the hours she spent absorbing the music of Ben Webster and Zoot Sims. "I hear tenor saxophone in my head sometimes when I'm singing, particularly Ben and Zoot," she says. "I try to hear the warmth of the improvisations and be as inventive."

The singer travels extensively now, especially overseas, and more and more finds that she appreciates the familiarities and comforts of home. "I always look forward to coming home," she says, "because one of the first things I want to do after I've gotten settled and unpacked the bag and hugged and kissed my husband to death is to go to the grocery store. I know he had corned beef sandwiches and two microwave dinners while I was gone. The cupboard is usually bare by the time 'Mother Sloane' gets home."

A cook who learned well from Julia Child's television series and from years of exploring different tastes, Sloane likes to prepare the same types of meals that her husband, Buck, enjoys. Opera or Mozart on the stereo makes the preparation even more pleasurable. "I don't do a lot of trendy cooking," she points out. "I do hardy, simple food because my husband is also of the generation I am, so he prefers meals like roast chicken and in the wintertime beef stew, a lovely one made with red wine and mushrooms and good stuff."

challenge singer Joe Williams to recall his most memorable meals and you're liable to get an answer that could be an abridged profile of a career as illustrious and star-studded as any in jazz. Clam chowder and cod in Boston with Lionel Hampton in 1943. Chicken pot pie in Milwaukee with Albert Ammons and Pete Johnson in 1945. Johnny Hartman's chili in their Detroit motel in 1963. *Shabu shabu* in Japan with his own band in 1990.

Millions of "Cosby Show" fans know him as Grandpa Al, Cliff Huxtable's father-in-law, but prime-time television is only a sideline for Williams. That is as it should be, given that he's one of the most versatile and expressive vocalists jazz and blues have ever known. His originality as a stylist renders the debate about which camp he falls into irrelevant; no one has been able to make blues as stately and jazz balladry as strong and sweet quite like Joe Williams has.

Jazz and the blues were but two of the sounds he heard growing up. Born an only child in 1918 in the small town of Cordele, Georgia, he was brought to Chicago at three by his grandmother to be reunited with his mother, who had found work there earlier as a cook. His mother not only kept delicious food on the table ("I remember eating mounds of spinach cooked in butter and oil with a sliced boiled egg on top," Williams recalls about one of those dishes), she inspired him musically by playing piano, taking him to hear the symphony in Grant Park, and singing, along with his aunt, in church. Between sports and making a few dollars carrying ice or selling newspapers,

Pressure-Cooked Lima Beans with Smoked Turkey

"Jillean is a good cook," says Williams. "She makes a great beef Stroganoff. Me, when I cook, I try to keep it simple, not a lot of preparation."

Simple indeed is his recipe for Pressure-Cooked Lima Beans with Smoked Turkey. "It's a good recipe," says Jillean. "Mind you, on the fourth day it's kind of tiring. One of those pots does last us quite a while." Serve with rice, sliced tomatoes, and a vegetable, such as peas.

Serves 4 to 6

- 4 tablespoons oil
- 1 large onion, coarsely chopped
- 8 cups chicken stock or water
- 2 cups lima beans, washed and sorted through to remove any debris
- ½ pound smoked turkey, cut into chunks
- ¾ teaspoon oregano
- Pepper
- "And as much hot sauce as you can take," the singer says.
- Salt

In a small skillet, sauté the onion in 2 tablespoons of the oil, until lightly browned. Drain and set aside. In a pressure cooker, heat the remaining oil. Add the browned onion, the chicken stock (or water), lima beans, turkey, oregano, pepper, and hot sauce. Lock the lid into place and, over high heat, bring the cooker to high pressure. Adjust the heat to maintain the pressure and cook for 15 minutes. Allow the pressure to drop naturally. Season the beans with salt.

Williams made time to absorb the Chicago blues that was all around him. He got a taste of performing at fourteen as a member of a quar-

tet called the Jubilee Boys which soon led to his sitting in with orchestras on the city's South Side, yet he didn't find his true direction until several years later. It happened at one of Chicago's early-morning breakfast dances when he heard Big Joe Turner. What he brought away from listening to the blues singer was a respect for the power of precise diction. From that point on, Williams aimed for a clear style that always did justice to the lyrics.

The vocalist joined Coleman Hawkins's big band in 1941 and then Lionel Hampton's two years later, but much of his time during World War II was spent searching for steady employment. He worked as a theater doorman and even sang before boxing matches. Things got worse before they got better. In 1947 he was hospitalized for a nervous breakdown. When he was released a year later, he sold cosmetics door-to-door and slowly got back into singing. His perseverance eventually paid off: just before he turned thirty-six, he joined the Count Basie Band. Within a year his voice was known around the world. *Count Basie Swings, Joe Williams Sings,* his debut recording with the band, included hits like "Alright, OK, You Win," "Roll 'Em, Pete," and the tune that was to become his trademark, "Every Day (I Have the Blues)."

He also soon discovered that the bandleader, who called him his "number one son," didn't leave his distinct personality on stage. "Basie loved desserts," Williams laughs. "He'd go to a dinner party and everybody would be sitting around eating greens and corn bread. Mr. Basie would start with the pie. He made sure he got his dessert so he didn't have to leave room for it. It was beautiful to watch."

Six high-profile years with the pianist's orchestra established Williams as a driving, bluesy swinger. His subsequent thirty years as leader of his own groups honed not only his blues but also his mastery of lush, intimate ballads.

With a burnished, mellifluous bass-baritone voice as foundation,

Williams climbs comfortably through the tenor range and up into the falsetto, although the years have stripped away a bit of his upper-register command. Variously elegant, gutty, and robust, he tackles material as diverse as "Green Dolphin Street," "Ol' Man River," and "Goin' to Chicago" with a style that's nuanced, quietly passionate, and always warm and genuine. His suave stage presence and good humor only add to his appeal. It's a combination that has made him a jazz festival and television staple; he has appeared several hundred times on the "Tonight Show."

"The things that we do have been known to be called 'metaphysical,'" he says. "That's what it's all about, which is one reason why people all over the world enjoy good, honest jazz music. People feel better when they hear it."

Age and experience have deepened Williams's own appreciation of the art of creating. "I'm enjoying it more because I listen more," he explains. "I hear more. The more you listen, the more you learn. You're part of a play. You're a vignette. It's wonderful to be part of that. I've sung with Basie, Ellington, Coleman Hawkins, Lionel Hampton, Woody Shaw, the greatest musicians in the world, and if you don't listen, you don't have any business there."

Since 1968, the singer and his wife, Jillean, have lived in Las Vegas, where Williams belongs to two golf clubs and generally relaxes

when he's off the road. Except for concocting an occasional red beans and rice dish and his pressure-cooked lima beans with smoked turkey, Williams now leaves most of the cooking to his English-born wife. Just as when he was growing up, "meat and potatoes and two veg" remain the basis of his diet, with chicken and fish taking precedence over red meat. His love of vegetables goes back to his earliest days. "I remember sitting with my grandmother, she and I shelling the peas," he says. "It never felt like work doing it with kid's hands."

Stardom can serve to heighten appreciation for life's domestic comforts, especially, as in Nancy Wilson's case, when they involve the kitchen and family. The vocalist, whose penchant for the intimate, romantic sides of jazz and pop has won her fame worldwide, prefers the unglamorous life when she's off-stage, particularly when it comes to food. "I'd rather eat my mother's cooking than eat in the finest restaurants," she says.

And if her natural mother and her stepmother, both excellent cooks, are unavailable to prepare a meal, there's no dearth of capable chefs to handle the chores for her husband and their three children. Wilson, her son, and her two teenage daughters are all willing and able.

Even though more than two thousand miles and five decades separate her current residence near Palm Springs, California, from her childhood home on the outskirts of Columbus, Ohio, the rural Midwest of her youth is where the singer developed her culinary self-sufficiency. Everybody, including her parents, their six children, and her grandparents, took turns preparing meals, a combination of southern and midwestern fare. "When you got old enough to reach the stove, you cooked," she recalls. And then there were those occasions when her father brought home a little something special.

"Where I grew up, you hunted," Wilson explains. "That was the way of living. Rabbit. Raccoon. And my father would get possum, but we didn't eat it."

What Wilson really loved to see her father bring home were records. Lionel Hampton, Jimmy Rushing, Nat "King" Cole, Louis Jordan, Billy Eckstine, she heard them all. She soon sought out the music of the female vocalists who would end up influencing her own style: Dinah Washington, Ruth Brown, La Vern Baker. Little Jimmy Scott, vocalist with the Hampton band, became a particular favorite. Wilson was singing in choirs in grade school and in Columbus venues like the Club Regal at fifteen. She even had her own television show, "Skyline Melody," on a local station before she graduated from high school.

In 1959, having spent three years on the road with Rusty Bryant's band, she moved to New York, where her career shifted into high gear. Between April 1960 and July 1962, Capitol records released five Nancy Wilson albums. A year later she had her first big hit with "Tell Me the Truth." She also had the good fortune to befriend—and record with—alto saxophonist Cannonball Adderley.

"Cannon was a wonderful musician," she remembers. "He was so knowledgeable about many, many things. And he was just wonderful to be around, a lot of fun, just nice people." Wilson also got a chance to witness the vaunted Adderley

TASTY PLATTERS

- Nancy Wilson, *But Beautiful* (Capitol)
- Nancy Wilson, *Forbidden Lover* (Columbia)
- Julian "Cannonball" Adderley/ Nancy Wilson (Capitol)

Smothered Rabbit

Wilson still makes the Smothered Rabbit she loved in her youth. "My father would hunt the rabbits and my mother would cook them," she says. When the singer prepares her mother's recipe today, she adds some fresh garlic to the onion and green pepper.

Serves 4

½ cup flour
1 teaspoon salt
1 teaspoon pepper
1 teaspoon paprika
6 to 8 tablespoons vegetable oil
1 (2- to 3-pound) rabbit, cleaned and
   cut into 6 to 8 pieces
1 bell pepper, sliced vertically into
   thin slices
1 onion, thinly sliced
4 tablespoons drippings from the pan
4 tablespoons flour
2 cups water
Salt and pepper

Mix flour, salt, pepper, and paprika in a paper bag or Baggie. Shake well. Place rabbit one piece at a time in bag and shake, coating each piece well. In a 12-inch skillet, measure oil until it reaches ¼ inch. Turn to medium heat, and when hot, brown the rabbit pieces well, making sure not to crowd the rabbit in the pan. You may have to do this in two batches. As pieces brown, remove from pan. When all the rabbit is browned, remove all but 4 tablespoons of oil from the skillet. In the remaining pan drippings, sauté the pepper and onion until tender. Lower heat and, a little at a time, stir in flour, mashing to blend it in. When it is all added and smooth, slowly add the water, stirring constantly. Allow it to come to a boil, then reduce to a simmer. Add the rabbit and cover the pan. Allow to cook over a low simmer until the rabbit is tender, about 20 minutes. Salt and pepper to taste, and serve over rice.

appetite firsthand. "I don't think I've ever known anybody who could eat more than he could," she says. "He was a very good cook. You could always trust yourself to have wonderful food at the Adderley house."

With her increased celebrity Wilson was soon tasting cuisine from around the globe with regularity. She was placed center-stage under scores of different spotlights and in many settings other than jazz: her own Los Angeles–based, Emmy-winning television program, "The Nancy Wilson Show"; appearances with everyone from Flip Wilson and Carol Burnett to Johnny Carson; acting roles in "I Spy," "Hawaii Five-O," and the "Cosby Show," where she played Denise's mother-in-law; involvement in countless charitable organizations like the National Urban Coalition; and the job of hosting a nationally syndicated TV program on music, "Red, Hot and Cool." She's even got her own star on Hollywood Boulevard's Walk of Fame.

And still she finds time to record—she has more than fifty albums—and perform constantly. Is she a jazz singer? Wilson prefers to be described as a song stylist.

"It allows me to be all those other things that people say I am," she says. "There's a kind of music that people want to hear from me that's the same kind of music I want to hear. It just so happens that what the public likes is what I like. I don't feel the need to be challenged and climb higher mountains and do things for the sake of doing them. When a great song comes up, I want to do it. I like simplicity. The object of the game is, Is this a good song or not?"

Wilson's early love for rhythm-and-blues crooners permeates much of her own style, which can be gritty and passionately moving. Her exacting ballad singing has influenced whole generations of vocalists, including stars like Anita Baker. As a versatile performer who's not shy about dipping into contemporary sounds and surrounding herself with lush orchestration, Wilson has at times come off as a bit too cool or slick for some tastes. But the success of her eclecticism is impossible to deny. Songs like "How Glad I Am" and "Guess Who I Saw Today" sound as fresh now as they did when she first recorded them years ago. While she doesn't choose to scat or spontaneously alter the feel of her material as some jazz singers do, she has always managed to achieve that most important of accomplishments for any jazz singer: deep respect for the lyrics and essence of a song.

"I'm not interested in how high my range is, or in how many octaves I have," she says. "It's really about telling a story, getting a good lyric and singing it."

During the six months or so of each year that she spends at home in Pioneertown, Wilson makes it a point to eat well. "I eat what I like," she says. "I haven't had any problems thus far. I like food that's seasoned nicely, with excellent taste. I don't want bland food."

RECIPE INDEX

NAME INDEX

Designed by Jim Wageman

*Composed with QuarkXpress 3.0 on a Macintosh IIsi
in Adobe Garamond and Gill Sans by Barbara Sturman
at Stewart, Tabori & Chang, New York.
Output on a Linotronic L300 at The Sarabande Press,
New York, New York.*

*Printed and bound by
Dai Nippon Printing Co., Ltd.,
Tokyo, Japan.*